CAR

WARS

Also by John Fialka

Sisters: Catholic Nuns and the Making of America

War by Other Means: Economic Espionage in America

Hotel Warriors: Covering the Gulf War

CAR WARS

The Rise, the Fall, and the Resurgence of the Electric Car

JOHN J. FIALKA

THOMAS DUNNE BOOKS
ST. MARTIN'S PRESS • NEW YORK

THOMAS DUNNE BOOKS.
An imprint of St. Martin's Press.

www.thomasdunnebooks.com
www.stmartins.com

The Library of Congress Cataloging-in-Publication Data is available upon request.

ISBN 978-1-250-04870-7 (hardcover)
ISBN 978-1-4668-4960-0 (e-book)

Our books may be purchased in bulk for promotional, educational, or business use. Please contact your local bookseller or the Macmillan Corporate and Premium Sales Department at (800) 221-7945, extension 5442, or by e-mail at MacmillanSpecialMarkets@macmillan.com.

First Edition: September 2015

10 9 8 7 6 5 4 3 2 1

To Ron Goldfarb:

There is nothing better for a writer of books on off-beat subjects than an agent who *loves* to go fishing.

CONTENTS

PREFACE

There are few technological adventure stories that are as rich, quirky, and peculiarly American as the early rise, the precipitous fall, and the modern resurgence of the electric car. If you are one of the millions of buyers who are now considering an electric vehicle, you should know that this car, like the lead character in a movie, has an intriguing backstory.

Peering out at you from the showroom window is a creature that is a product of enormous risks, long, frustrating struggles, dismal failure leading almost to its extinction, an unlikely resurrection, and finally a list of improbable victories. They include little wins that are happening daily as hundreds of thousands of car buyers begin to break buying habits that have dominated the economy for almost a century.

You have probably never been in love with your toaster or your refrigerator, but here is an electric appliance that might seduce you. Many Americans have fallen in love with their cars. Our country's varicose network of highways was built for them. They have created millions of jobs, helped erect a robust manufacturing base, and generated a freedom of travel that is unparalleled in the world.

And they have also caused traffic congestion, pollution, noise, and a costly, sometimes dangerous reliance on imported oil. Then there are the carbon dioxide emissions that have convinced most scientists that our planet will become dangerously overheated unless we do something to minimize the emissions.

The electric vehicle that you're looking at may be your way of trying to help solve some of these problems. It may just be a quest for a reliable, fuel-saving set of wheels. Or it may scratch that itch for performance that you've had for years. When you have to move, this car will give you a burst of silent power that you have probably never experienced.

The current electric vehicles are carefully designed not to shock you, but the sticker price on the rear window might. It may be higher than you have bargained for, but measured over the lifetime of these cars, the costs are likely to be cheaper than the other cars you have enjoyed or fantasized about owning. Cars, like a lot of the items you own, arrive with hidden costs.

The last razor or computer printer you bought came with a price tag that was deceptively cheap, but they subjected you to long investments in expensive blades and printer ink. The last car you bought exposed you to volatile gasoline prices and, possibly, a long relationship with your auto dealer's service department that you didn't expect and didn't budget for.

Well, think of the hybrid-electric or plug-in electric or fuel cell electric vehicle that may have aroused your curiosity as a kind of superhero, a track-tested revolutionary that has come to save you from some of the hidden costs. Because they have fewer moving parts, are more energy-efficient, and can run on cheaper, cleaner fuel, electric vehicles are creating a lengthening record of reliability and economic satisfaction that many drivers are now discovering.

Think of them as Indiana Jones on wheels. They are the product of thousands of adventurers, inventors, hot rodders, engineers, and risk takers who have relied mainly on America's high technology to challenge the auto industry's status quo. You need to do more than kick the tires to grasp the promise of these cars. but once you do, they will very likely give you a kick.

The roots of the first generation of electrics go directly back to one of the founders of the nation: Ben Franklin. His early experiments with electricity attracted a worldwide following that included a minor eighteenth-century Italian aristocrat, a reclusive dreamer named Alessandro Volta.

Volta, a public school administrator who fancied himself a physicist, was proud to describe himself as a "Franklinist." He performed magic tricks using static electricity and wrote poems in Latin and lyrical papers on electricity's mysterious properties and its possible future uses. When he described electricity as a miraculously invisible liquid, one of his mentors felt he had gone off the rails of science. He ordered Volta to "keep silent forever."

Instead, Volta went back to his lab. In 1799 he built a stack of silver coins, interspersing them with poker chip–sized pieces of zinc and circular pieces of water-soaked cardboard. After he soaked his hands in water and then grasped both ends of this strange apparatus, he was rewarded with a substantial electric shock. He had invented the first storage battery.

The discovery brought him worldwide honors, including a medal from Napoleon, and immortality as a unit measuring the potential carrying capacity of a line connected to an electric current: the volt. Alas, Count Volta never fully understood the complex electrochemical reaction that made his invention work. He has that in common with thousands of other pioneers who have spent their lives trying to fathom the continuing mysteries and quirks of batteries.

The pioneers' work eventually led to the Electrobat, a black,

1,650-pound coffin-shaped vehicle carrying on its skinny wheels a battery derived from those that powered Philadelphia's streetcars. It made its stunningly silent appearance on the lakefront in Chicago on Thanksgiving Day 1895. Electrobat was one of the standouts of the nation's first automobile race, even though it ran out of juice before the finish line and lost to a pack of noisy, fume-belching, gasoline-powered cars. The judges were so impressed they gave it an award for appearance.

Still, there were businessmen who saw electrics as the future. By 1900, the Electrobat morphed into the Mark XVII hansom cab. Although their batteries weighed nearly a ton, hundreds of these cabs zipped soundlessly along Manhattan streets at twenty miles per hour. They worked longer hours than horses could and did not poop on the streets. Plus, they provided an exotic thrill to passengers accustomed for generations to looking from the coach at the slowly churning backside of an animal.

"There is a sense of incompleteness about it," marveled Cholly Knickerbocker, a columnist for the *New York Journal-American*. "You seem to be sitting on the end of a huge pushcart propelled by an invisible force and guided by a hidden hand."

Most important, these cars made money. By the turn of the century more than twenty-seven manufacturers were making electrics. Among the leading customers creating the demand were society women, who disliked arriving at a reception in a cloud of dust in a vehicle propelled by explosions and steered either by a goggled chauffer or the man of the house.

The electrics offered a salonlike quiet and luxury refinements, including glassed-in enclosures, carved wood interiors, crystal flower vases, even patent leather fenders. Moreover, to go out for a spin, the woman did not have to negotiate with the chauffeur or her husband. She simply climbed in, pushed a button, and drove off.

Margaret Whitehead, the reigning society queen of Denver, drove her electric to opening nights, stepping out of her car perfectly composed to make her entrée. "One can wear the most perishable and delicately hued gown she possesses," she explained, "and the daintiest of footwear without giving it a thought, for when she arrives at her destination, she is unsullied and her coiffure is as unruffled as it was when she left home."

What appealed to women was that electric cars were simple and clean, with relatively few moving parts to break down. Advertising men took the story from there: "Takes no strength. The control is easy, simple," said an ad for the Columbus Electric, once made in Columbus, Ohio. "A delicate woman can practically live in her car and never tire."

Three gasoline-powered cars managed to cross the United States in 1903. Jouncing along nearly impassible and sometimes nonexistent roads, the cars had to be rebuilt en route by attendant mechanics who arranged for hundreds of replacement parts to be delivered by train.

By 1908, when O. P. Fritchle, the Denver chemist who designed and built Ms. Whitehead's car, made the first crossing for an electric vehicle, he needed only two new tires and a new lining for the brakes in his Victorian Phaeton, which stopped to charge up at dozens of electric utilities along the way. In some places he didn't need utilities because he found a way to recharge his batteries by converting the energy captured by the car's brakes into electricity. It worked, but the brakes wore out as he was coasting down the Alleghenies toward the East Coast.

In his reminiscences, Fritchle managed to wrap the struggle that tested the patience of first buyers of electrics on an almost daily basis in an aura of romance. He was a professional electrician who ran a garage that serviced electric cars in a fancy neighborhood. Well-heeled customers such as Ms. Whitehead paid him a monthly fee to keep their cars charged and to fuss with the pesky details.

The peskiness began with the fact that car batteries could weigh up to 1,200 pounds, often had to be removed for proper service, and formed a sludge at the bottom of their cells that caused short circuits if they weren't regularly cleaned. Poorly charged batteries might strand their drivers anywhere and overcharged ones might explode. That event could start with a flash as brilliant as an arc light, and then the amateur driver would be treated to a fine spray of sulfuric acid.

For people who weren't rich, the old electrics were a hard-to-acquire taste. The power lines needed to recharge them didn't often run into poor neighborhoods. More prosperous people without electricity could still buy electrics by first acquiring five-hundred-watt power plants driven by a water-cooled gas engine. They were specially designed to recharge electrics. Sadly, they didn't work very well. Charles Duryea, a gasoline-car enthusiast, was only half joking when he said: "A set of batteries was worse to take care of than a hospital full of sick dogs."

The man who killed off the first generation of electric cars was Charles Franklin Kettering, a freelance inventor who later became the founder of research laboratories for General Motors. On February 17, 1911, he delivered his battery-powered invention, an automatic starter, to Cadillac Motor Company.

No longer did drivers of gasoline cars have to bend over the front bumper and turn the engine over with a hand crank, which started the engine but could result in broken arms and dislocated shoulders or other disasters. (Sometimes when the car was left in gear, it started and then simply ran over the driver.)

Because women didn't like the hand crank, Kettering's starter introduced them to gasoline-powered cars. At the time they cost only two-thirds of the price of the more elegant electrics. The electric starter also had the unintended side effect of freezing commercial battery technology in the United States for almost a century. The gasoline-powered cars required only a simple, sixty-five-pound storage battery and not the behemoths that powered electrics.

The man who eventually threw the market for gasoline cars into overdrive was a country boy from then-rural Dearborn, Michigan, who came to Detroit to learn about machinery. "Dynamic and attractive, [Henry] Ford exuded a self-confidence that made him a presence whenever he walked into a room," was the way one biographer later described him.

Ford made himself an expert on repairing electric generators and rose to become the chief engineer for Detroit's utility Detroit Edison. His ultimate boss, Thomas A. Edison, became enthusiastic about Ford's hobby, which was tinkering with gasoline-powered engines. In the late 1890s, after seeing a sketch of Ford's first car, the "quadricycle," Edison told him: "You have it—the self-contained unit carrying its own fuel with it! Keep at it!"

Ford did. He worked with gasoline engines in his coal shed, his basement, and sometimes in his kitchen, where his adventurous wife, Clara, sometimes played the role of fuel pump. She poured drops of gasoline into a sputtering engine's intake after Ford had bolted it to the kitchen sink.

A rare combination of a meticulous engineer and a charismatic marketing genius, Ford attracted backers and left the electricity business to form his first automobile company, which soon failed. There were hundreds of tinkerers like him trying to get into the car business and Ford quickly diagnosed his problem: to gain visibility in this nearly all-male market, he had to do something dramatic and different. So he built a racing car and made himself a legend.

Racing has usually been the key to the emergence of new automotive technologies. In 1901 Ford challenged Alexander Winton, a Cleveland bicycle manufacturer who had built what was reputedly the nation's fastest car—the Winton Bullet. That set the stage for a ten-mile race before eight thousand onlookers in Grosse Pointe, Michigan.

Ford built a racer he called the Sweepstakes. When he couldn't find anyone to drive it, Ford—who had never been on a racetrack before—climbed into the driver's seat and pulled the throttle. When

Winton's car, which had almost twice the horsepower of Ford's, began belching smoke, Ford passed the Bullet to become the only car to finish the race.

"Boy, I'll never do that again," exclaimed the dust-covered Ford amid the hoopla at the finish line. He almost didn't get another chance because then his second car company, born out of the bankruptcy of the first one, failed.

But by this time Ford had achieved escape velocity. The headlines from his racing coup brought in more investors and drew reporters who, charmed by Ford's down-home humor and his gift for understatement, wrote glowing accounts of his struggles. All this led to a new racing car, the 999, named after a legendary, record-setting New York Central express train. This car was mostly engine attached to a tiny driver's platform.

Ford cheered from the sidelines as his hired driver, a daredevil bicycle racer named Barney Oldfield, drove 999 across the finish line on October 25, 1902, to win the Manufacturers' Challenge Cup and set an American speed record of nearly fifty miles per hour. That helped launch a third company, Ford Motor, which began by selling a few hundred cars a year.

After working through most of the letters of the alphabet, Ford and a committee of six men designed the Model T in 1908. It was lighter and simpler than its predecessors; sturdy enough to handle America's rutted roads and built on a moving assembly line at a pace that allowed Ford to cut the car's price from $780 to $360 by 1916. Mass production put it well within the range of the middle-class buyer. By 1918 half the cars in the United States were Model Ts. By 1927 Ford had sold fifteen million of them, creating a new national culture on wheels and leaving most of his competitors in the dust.

Ford had helped design one of the world's largest and most competitive industries and pioneered an enduring marketing plan that used visions of racing, acceleration, and durability as the sizzle that has driven hundreds of millions into the showrooms to see the "steak." "I never really thought much of racing," Ford would explain, shrugging to his admiring coterie of reporters. "But as the others were doing it, I, too, had to do it."

Makers of electrics didn't give up without a fight. They knew their cars were more energy efficient and could generate more torque or quicker acceleration than Ford's could. This inspired Baker Motor of Cleveland to launch the Road Torpedo, an electric car shaped like a rocket on wheels. It hit seventy miles per hour in a race on Staten Island in May 1902, but was then thrown off course by streetcar tracks and shot into a crowd of onlookers, killing two and injuring eight.

By 1916, the market economics and the looming war had driven nearly all electric car companies out of business. Woods Motor Vehicle of Chicago made a valiant last stand, rolling out the Woods Dual Power, an electric with unlimited range because it had both a battery-powered electric motor and a gasoline engine that recharged the batteries. This "hybrid," selling for $2,650, quickly followed the rest of the electrics into oblivion. Its problem was that it was ninety years ahead of its time.

What we are watching now is the second act of this story; the start of a trillion-dollar, worldwide race to see who will dominate what could become one of the biggest commercial upheavals of the early twenty-first century: the resurgence of the electric car.

It may seem odd to describe this part of the story as a "race," because it has been under way since the 1960s. But the pioneers in the race were only able to revive the corpse of an industry that had bloomed in the days of their grandfathers by staging a series of races that began to recapture public attention.

The first race was initiated by Wally Rippel, a bookish physics major at the California Institute of Technology, who challenged

Massachusetts Institute of Technology students to race electric cars across the country. The first car to arrive on the rival campus won. It created so much interest that both cars were later flown to the Smithsonian Institution in Washington for an exhibit touting the "cars of the future."

But the anticipated future didn't really get moving until an Australian, Hans Tholstrup, who is known to millions of Australians as The Adventurer, staged another race. He was famous for his exploits, which included jumping a bus over a bunch of parked motorcycles. He was fired up by the feats of an American, Paul MacCready, who had designed a solar-powered aircraft that flew across the English Channel in 1981.

Tholstrup designed a light electric-powered car and drove it across Australia. Then he drew up the rules for a solar-powered electric car, set for December 1987, that lured in Japanese electronics and vehicle manufacturers. General Motors, which wanted an opportunity to show off solar power and battery technologies that it had developed during the Cold War, accepted the challenge and beat all contenders with an expensive, exotic car called Sunraycer. The resulting worldwide publicity coup hooked GM on electric cars.

The drivetrains of the electric cars people are buying today were born in that race. In the next two decades they were improved by American inventions, including the lithium-ion battery and fuel cells, which came out of the U.S. missile and space programs. These breakthroughs led to a number of others by pioneering inventors and businessmen, including Alan Cocconi, Elon Musk, and Geoffrey Ballard.

Former vice president Al Gore did not invent the Internet, but he did have a hand in the birth of the Supercar, a U.S. Department of Energy program that had an unintended but electrifying result in Japan. It provoked the launch of Toyota's Prius, whose sales still dominate the growing electric car market today and whose success showed American carmakers that electric vehicles might be the car of the future after all.

Both polls and auto sales show Americans now realize there is much at stake in this race, but they know very little about the inventors, the hot-rodders, entrepreneurs, computer geeks, companies, regulators, and futurists who are part of this backstory because they paved the way for the reappearance of electric cars. The gamut of players in this drama is huge, running from the "father" of the Prius, an overstressed Japanese engineer named Takeshi Uchiyamada, to President Barack Obama, whose campaigns projected visions of American-made electric cars, to Amory Lovins, a futurist visionary, and to torque-addicted American hot-rodders such as John "Plasma Boy" Wayland, "Electric Louie," and "Big Daddy" Don Garlits.

One of the peculiarities of the race to perfect the electric car is that it quickly became global and is full of unexpected diversions. A recent phase of the story began in Vancouver, Canada, in the 1980s, when Geoffrey Ballard and a small team of researchers discovered that the design for fuel cells that electrified U.S. Gemini spacecraft in the 1960s was in the public domain.

They redesigned the fuel cells, made them more powerful and cheaper, and with financial, engineering, and political help from Daimler, the parent company of Mercedes-Benz, sold "stacks" of automotive fuel cells to automakers around the world. The resulting hydrogen-powered electric cars are just beginning to roll out of showrooms in the United States.

This sets up the present phase of the race, with hybrid-electrics, plug-in electric cars, and fuel cell cars all contending for a share of the trillion-dollar automobile market. Which technology will win? Which companies will dominate this market and which will be shoved to the wayside? Which countries will prosper as a result? And what could change the buying habits of millions of consumers and lure them into electric vehicles?

All of these questions are now hanging in the air, except for the last one. Automakers, parts suppliers, entrepreneurs, and advertisers see the future in the form of a new category of racing: Formula E. Its managers are staging electric car races in cities all around the world.

As electric vehicles begin to challenge speed records and race records long dominated by the internal combustion engine, the players in this race predict the electric car market will really take off in 2016, when the generic electric cars used in Formula E will be replaced by cars carrying automakers' brands. This will turn one of the most popular, pulse-pounding sports in the world—auto racing—into a showcase for a powerful, clean, new product that could change lives and give some badly needed help to the environment. Watching them win will help people who may still scratch their heads over the mention of an electric car.

ONE

The Great
Electric Car Race

What got Americans thinking again about electric cars started with the brownish blanket of smog that took shape over the varicose network of freeways growing out of Los Angeles in the 1950s. In the sixties the smog congealed into a semipermanent blanket of atmospheric filth that hung between the Pacific and the San Gabriel Mountains. Sunlight cooked its automobile exhaust and other ingredients into a more toxic stew as Los Angeles continued to sprawl.

Smog obscured the horizons. It sent a growing number of people to hospital emergency rooms. And it outraged students in the sophomore history class that Wally Rippel, a physics major, was taking at the California Institute of Technology in Pasadena in 1965.

The class discussion was about how the United States solves problems and it soon drifted into smog. Rippel, then a twenty-year-old day student, still remembers the rapid-fire questions: Why doesn't the government pass regulations? Why should automakers continue to sell vehicles that fouled the air? Why would people blithely ignore such pollution when America had the tools and the money to clean the air? Hadn't American scientists and engineers pivoted from the promise of the atomic age into the mind-numbing potential of the space age in a mere two decades? So why can't they fix this?

But the really galvanizing moment for Rippel came when one of the class's brighter and quieter members shouted three words: "We are they!" The room suddenly grew quiet.

Rippel lived in Hollywood. He was frequently prodded by his father to think of unconventional solutions and to believe that the American "can-do spirit" could solve almost anything. His father had not finished high school, yet he had become an NBC radio sound engineer and something of an electronics expert by reading a lot of books.

By 1965 most of the people who had worked on electric cars in the United States were dead, so the "we are they" moment in the Caltech classroom sent Wally to the books. Books often romanticized the earlier phase of electric cars as their "golden age." But romance meant little to Rippel, a physics major. He began with the basics: how much energy did it take to make a car go one mile? Soon he was scribbling multiple calculations: If every car in Los Angeles were electrically powered, electricity use would rise by 20 percent, but smog might drop by as much as 90 percent. That led to the next question: How would you go about making a modern electric car?

He initially thought of using fuel cells. They were much discussed in the sixties because they were being designed to power U.S. spacecraft. Rippel found them to be far too complicated and expensive. Batteries would be much cheaper and simpler, Rippel decided, so he read about those. They could power electric motors, giving them enormous spinning power or torque to propel cars. He discovered that transmissions were a problem in the earlier electric cars, making the cars jerky as drivers accelerated. But this was the space age and Rippel was sure that solid-state electronics could give these cars "glass-smooth acceleration."

So he set about to design an electronic control system, following a manual he'd gotten from General Electric. He invested eighty dollars in what seemed to him to be an elegant solution, a solid-state device called a thyristor that controlled the electric flow by cutting it into segments, hence its nickname: the chopper. Rippel managed to fry his chopper by feeding it too much electrical current. After many mind-numbing hours of trial and error and more spectacular destructions, he gave up. It seemed too hard. "Looking back, I didn't know what I didn't know—the worst kind of ignorance," he recalled.

But the other elements were there. Batteries had been used for over a century and chargers were readily available. Electric motors that were used in forklifts and other small industrial applications produced no emissions and were far more energy efficient. Stacked up against the gasoline engine, Rippel calculated, they had the ability to reduce emissions regardless of how the electricity they used was produced. After quizzing a number of his Caltech professors, Wally Rippel decided that he was going to be "they." So that summer he earned $1,000 working as a lab technician and invested $700 of it in a used 1959 Volkswagen Microbus that he set out to electrify.

One thing Rippel began to have doubts about during his junior year, when he began to assemble his electric VW, was equations that showed that it took almost a ton of lead-acid automobile storage batteries to get the car up to a mere thirty-five miles per hour. In theory batteries should be able to deliver fifty times more energy per pound than his did. Why didn't they? Rippel upgraded to a set of golf cart batteries.

When he asked his professors about batteries, they were evasive. Rippel had stumbled into a data gap. "Batteries were something we didn't talk about on campus. It was still a topic like sex used to be during the Victorian age," he recalled. After more research, Rippel concluded that his professors didn't know exactly what went on in electric batteries. The electrochemical reactions in batteries tended, as he put it, "to be very messy. There's a lot of stuff going on, so it's hard to write an equation for things like that." What was known about batteries came from trial and error, not from well-understood physical laws.

That brought Rippel back to brood on the "we are they" problem. After more frustrating experiments, in his senior year Rippel concluded that the grand solution to smog would require getting a lot of bright minds to focus on the problem at once. It would take a competition, one that was novel enough to capture public attention and outrageous enough to get young scientific minds focused on defeating the enemy—smog—by resolving the battery's many issues.

While he was thinking of enemies, Rippel came up with the one that would definitely grab Caltech's attention. That would be Massachusetts Institute of Technology, the Pasadena school's longtime East Coast rival. Rippel's school was the rising, younger West Coast upstart that had blossomed during the space age. When it came to innovative science, MIT graduates often seemed to feel they were the cerebral equivalent of the New York Yankees. They could be smug about their clout, which had been proven long before.

Other celebrated rivalries among the nation's universities might be tested on the baseball diamonds or the basketball courts, but where could engineering geeks go to have it out? Rippel started thinking up the rules for a cross-country electric car race. It would be Rippel's electric VW versus whatever MIT came up with. The idea was amusing enough to persuade the then-dean of Caltech to write his counterpart at MIT extending the challenge. The two schools had a long history of taking jabs at each other.

Partly because it was a Caltech idea, MIT's dean immediately rejected the idea. Who needed that? But then a newspaper clipping of his curt rejection tickled the imaginations of one of the university's unofficial fraternities, the Number Six Club. "Back in those days, we had a lot of time on our hands and we said well, why not?" explained Leon Loeb, a sophomore from Corpus Christi, Texas.

An engineering student with a dry wit and a flair for entrepreneurial ventures, Loeb became the leader and, as he put it, the "chief scrounger," of the MIT effort. The MIT faculty became interested because one of its members had designed a state-of-the-art, electronically timed induction electric motor. Here was an almost poetic opportunity to show how easily MIT could still leave its cross-country rival in the dust.

MIT had excellent corporate connections and Loeb approached companies for donations to the MIT effort. He accumulated more than a half-million dollars' worth of equipment, including Detroit's latest creation, a brand-new Chevrolet Corvair contributed by General Motors. It would be powered by nickel-cadmium batteries made by Gulton Industries, a New Jersey company. The batteries were big, normally used to kick over aircraft engines, and came with a special set of nylon tools that would hopefully prevent the MIT students from electrocuting themselves.

On paper, Loeb's team had the race already won. MIT's more powerful batteries cost $18,000 versus the $600 worth of car batteries powering Rippel's VW. The Corvair was far more aerodynamic, even with 1,800 pounds of batteries stacked where the rear seat was and jammed into the front compartment of the rear-engine car.

But in the garage the calculations began to work out differently. Loeb's team spent hours trying to coax meaningful life out of the futuristic induction motor that had been designed at MIT under a grant from the U.S. Department of Transportation. "The damn thing never did work," explained Loeb. "Then it became 'Oh, fuck it, we need something that will get us there.'"

MIT's car wound up with the same electric motor that Caltech had, normally used to power industrial forklifts. The last-minute switch meant Loeb's team had to spend all night before the race wrenching the final version of their Corvair together. They managed to mate the forklift motor with a four-speed transmission by leaving out the clutch, which would require drivers to do a lot of carefully synchronized shifting. "Boy, was it jerky," recalls Loeb. "I still have on my desk some of the gears that had the teeth knocked out of them."

On race day, August 26, 1968, Rippel's moment had come. Over a cross-country hookup attached to a public address system, the two teams managed to greet each other with sarcasm. Rippel told the engineers from Cambridge that he was sure to meet them at the Massachusetts border. MIT's riposte was that if Rippel's team made it that far, they would be happy to provide free towing because Caltech would surely need it.

Then the heavily laden VW bus whooshed away from the Caltech campus in Pasadena at 9:00 A.M. Pacific daylight time followed by two chase cars and an assortment of vehicles carrying newspaper reporters and local television crews.

At the same time the Corvair left MIT headed west. Electric utilities—which have long nurtured a dream of selling gobs of power to electric car owners—had helped establish a chain of fifty-five charging stations extending across the United States that the teams could use. They consisted mainly of linemen waiting with connecting cables brought down from overhead power lines.

Under Rippel's rules of the race, the first car to reach the other's campus would win. Both teams calculated it would take them five days to navigate the designated 3,398-mile route across the country.

Despite their desperate all-nighter spent reengineering their car, Loeb's MIT team appeared dressed in suits and ties for the prestart exchange of remarks in an attempt to establish a psychological advantage. They knew they still had a considerable edge when it came to the technology. Their car could go faster, recharge faster, and had a simpler, more aerodynamic design. But after that the posturing ended swiftly. There were cruel realities waiting for both teams out on the nation's highways, most of them having to do with batteries.

As a backup, the MIT team brought along a Corvette capable of towing the Corvair in emergencies. Caltech's car was followed by another towing a portable generator. The rules said that each side would be penalized by adding more time to their crossing if they used the tow truck or the generator. Each team was followed by judges and cars carrying reporters from *Machine Design,* a trade magazine that had volunteered to enforce the rules.

There were no cheerleaders waving pom-poms as the MIT team rolled out of the campus, but banners were flying and students were cheering as the electric Corvair disappeared in the distance. Getting out of sight was good because there were few witnesses to what happened twenty minutes later when MIT's high-powered batteries pooped out. In a short shakedown test the weekend before the race, Loeb's team noticed their batteries had a tendency to lose charge and overheat at the same time. Now they found the Corvair's electric motor overheated, as well.

As part of their all-nighter before the race, the MIT team thought they had a fix for the simmering batteries with a jury-rigged cooling-and-ventilating system. It began with bags of ice dumped on the batteries and copper coils that carried the meltwater through the front seat and into a "bilge" in the Corvair's trunk. Aside from the possibility of causing electrical problems, the melting bags of ice also leaked down the driver's neck. They fogged the inside of the windshield so there were times when he couldn't see.

But those were small issues compared with the batteries. Despite frequent attempts to charge them, their output remained so low that the Corvair had to be towed for two hundred miles to Buffalo, New York, racking up huge time penalties.

When they pulled into a service plaza near Buffalo the MIT team had been up for almost forty-eight hours. They had tried every trick they could think of to get the batteries to work better. None of them helped much. They called in a representative from Gulton Industries, who recommended overcharging the batteries, which seemed to Loeb and his team to be a dubious proposition. Overcharged batteries could blow up.

The psychological advantage, if MIT ever had one, seemed to have weakened. "By that time we had lost our idealism about what a battery really was," Loeb recalled. "At that time battery electrochemistry was witchcraft and to a great extent it still is. I still don't think that folks have got a very good handle on exactly what goes on in a battery."

Shortly after dawn the sleepy, scruffy MIT crew watched as utility technicians gave their ailing battery what amounted to a supercharge. For almost six hours the Corvair's batteries hissed, bubbled, and gurgled menacingly as the incoming juice from the power line split some of the batteries' liquid electrolyte into oxygen and hydrogen, which the budding engineers also knew might blow up. "It was at this point when spirits were as low as the battery charge," observed one accompanying judge from *Machine Design*. "It was a gamble and if it failed the MIT team would probably have called it quits. For them the race had become a go/no-go proposition."

At about the same time, 3:00 P.M. California time, Wally Rippel's VW was climbing mountains in eastern California. The uphill strain drained almost all of his battery charge, but the downhill replenished it because Rippel could coast and recharge them through one asset that most electric cars now have—regenerative braking. The system captured the energy from braking and turned it into electricity that fed back into the batteries.

On a downgrade just east of Seligman, Arizona, Rippel decided to drop the VW into second gear to make the batteries recharge even faster. There was a loud thud and the car rolled to a dead stop. One of the crew members got out and dashed around to the back, but Rippel knew that any frantic attempt to fix things now would be pointless. The extra RPMs from his downshift had blown the VW's electric motor apart. It was the middle of the night and all was silent on the deserted highway. "So we sat there, thinking," Rippel recalled.

Caltech's adventure with the electrified Microbus had been, up to that point, mostly a one-man show directed by Rippel. In his mind he ran through all the new problems; a blown engine would not only have to be replaced, but specially machined before it could be made to fit the unique transmission he had rigged up for the VW. What it all added up to, for Rippel, was failure. He broke the silence. "I said to the team, 'You know, I think this is over for us.'"

The first stirrings of a resurgence of the electric car now seemed stillborn. MIT was mystified and a little frightened by their batteries bubbling away in a gas station in Buffalo, New York, and Caltech was depressed and stranded along with pieces of their shattered engine on the road in the deserted mountains of Arizona.

The technology was too hard. There were too many voids in the knowledge that people had written in books. And the thousands of men and women who had done the trial and error that put an earlier generation of silent, clean electric vehicles on the road seventy years before this race were now silent themselves, or in no position to be of any help.

TWO

"Whatever Happens Will Happen!"

When Dick Rubinstein, a Caltech junior who had been riding in a chase car, heard that Rippel was going to give up, he exploded.

This jarred Rippel out of his gloom. Rubinstein was the quietest, most self-contained member of the team. Rippel can still hear Rubinstein screaming at him: "Look, we're going to Boston! The issue is how we're going to get there." Rubinstein seemed determined enough to push the car by hand, if that's what it took. "Or," he shouted at them, "we're going to drive it under electric power. . . . So we're going to get this done and whatever happens will happen!"

It was as though an electric charge had struck the car (that would happen later). The Caltech team came up with a plan. They would phone Electric Fuel Propulsion, a company in Michigan, and order a new motor to be delivered to Phoenix by air freight.

Robert Aronson, the owner of the company, modified an existing motor in a machine shop to fit Rippel's car. The Caltech team picked it up at the airport, but had to use an Arizona machine shop to make some final adjustments. Then they sped the new engine back seventy miles to the stranded VW. Along the way they put together a plan for how the five of them could work in tandem, yanking out the shattered two-hundred-pound motor and installing the new one in fifteen minutes.

The whole transaction cost them twenty-three hours and thirty minutes, but Rippel's VW was back on the highway, aiming for Cambridge. Rippel felt elated. "It was a lesson that I'll never forget. When you work with a team it's amazing what you can do if you really all agree on doing something."

But Murphy's law was running with them. Whatever could happen often did happen. A few hours later when they arrived in Amarillo, Texas, Murphy struck again. At charging areas there were three electric cables that had to be connected with large alligator clips to three points on the VW. There was a right way to connect them and a wrong way.

It was 4:30 in the morning. The Caltech team, again bleary-eyed from an all-night ride, didn't notice that two cables were reversed until an explosion and a brilliant electric arc lit up the surroundings as though someone had just used a million flashbulbs to take a picture of downtown Amarillo.

"A tremendous current surge resulted and diodes failed, which caused the surge to be even greater," explained Rippel. "I've never seen anything like that in my professional work, even though I've seen some exciting things."

Then he discovered that one of the two chase cars was missing. It was the one carrying the spares for the diodes that had just blown up and it was lost somewhere in Texas. The Caltech team called on the state highway patrol to help them find it.

Meanwhile the MIT team was breezing through the flat plains of Indiana. What Loeb called the "cure or kill" approach to fixing the Corvair's enormous battery pack had somehow shocked it back into life. MIT began cruising eighty miles between charges.

There was occasional radio communication between the two teams and MIT was thrilled to hear about Caltech's motor burnout. Loeb and his teammates were still gloating over that when they ran into Murphy.

They were charging the Corvair at a power pole in Elkhart, Indiana, when a short circuit between a battery and the car's body created an electrical arc that vaporized a 3.4-inch bronze motor terminal. It melted some of the copper tubing that the MIT team had rigged to cool the batteries. The gloating ended as the young engineers examined the smoldering ruins of their idea. The repairs cost them ten hours.

Loeb had a tendency to make light of what happened after that. He later wrote: "The long haul from the Midwest to the California line went quite smoothly. Except for getting lost in St. Louis, incurring a leaky cell by blocking a vent cover (creating another battery crisis), starting electrical fireworks at an Oklahoma power pole and being sirened to the curb by local police, we found the race no different than a Sunday drive in the family car."

In Tulsa the MIT car was driving off from a power station when a series of explosions from the battery pack sent the team in the Corvair and some bystanders running for cover. One of their jury-rigged battery cooling fans had emitted sparks that set off the hydrogen rising from the freshly charged battery pack. Fortunately there was no damage.

Then they received a telegram from the Caltech team, which had calculated the two teams would meet in western Oklahoma. Caltech, wary of more screwups caused by fatigue, was suggesting that they divert to Oklahoma City for twelve hours of rest and perhaps some time to compare notes. MIT interpreted this as whining. Determined to get the race over with as soon as possible, they rejected the idea.

Rippel's team had just finished charging at the designated power pole in Weatherford, Oklahoma, when the MIT Corvair pulled in.

The Caltech team consisted of five men. Rippel stared wearily out of the VW's window, watching the rival team's refueling process: "It was enough to scare someone out of driving an electric car. It was amazing; there were probably twelve people involved, girls rushing around, dropping big bags of ice on the ground, everything helter-skelter, confused. And they refused to stop to talk."

Perhaps at this point in the race, neither team wanted to disclose the little tricks that had gotten them this far. Women were a rarity at engineering schools in the 1960s, but even back then there were signs they might become essential. When the copper tubing on MIT's ice-powered battery-cooling drainage system became continually plugged up with sludge, one of the young engineers whipped out a pair of nylons and slipped them on the line as a filter.

MIT, using a hundred-pound bag of ice at almost every refueling stop, dumped the water through a hole drilled in the bottom of the trunk. The Caltech team, which had also started pouring ice on the VW's steaming batteries, used a siphoning system starting with a baby syringe they bought in a drugstore. Still, there was so much moisture in the air that if you touched the car while it was being charged, you might ground it, getting a strong electric shock. (Rippel's team developed the technique of jumping into the VW after charging without touching the body.)

MIT soon paid a price for shunning a night of rest. They stopped to recharge east of Newberry Springs in the California desert. They were elated, only about 150 miles away from Caltech! For them, victory was literally just over the horizon. Then somebody made the wrong connection with the power cables, blowing out the Corvair's charging system.

For four hours in the blazing sun, they attempted various fixes until a blue fireball erupted from the top of the power pole they were using. The fuse on the line had blown, so MIT was confronted with an agonizing decision. They concluded that the way to make the best show of this mess would be to tow their car all the way into Pasadena. Then they would make hasty repairs at some garage and cross the finish line under electrical power.

That might have worked, too, had somebody thought to take the Corvair out of first gear before starting the tow, but nobody did. The result was the electric motor spun beyond its limits and blew apart.

Loeb had to witness the ignominy of MIT's Corvair being towed across the finish line in Pasadena. The car's motor was shattered, its charging system was fried, and welds were beginning to pop on the car's chassis from the strain of hauling an extra ton of batteries across the United States.

"There wasn't an MIT cheering section there," Loeb recalled, but there were a number of people who had seen glimpses of the electric Corvair on television news reports. "They just wanted to see what the thing looked like."

But what later became known as the Great Electric Car Race wasn't over yet. MIT had accumulated a lot of time penalties by being towed in from the desert, but Rippel's VW was still in Ohio. Rippel recalls Dick Rubinstein penciling some new calculations.

"He said 'Wally, if we can improve our average speed by 8 percent and cut down our charging time by 6 percent we'll win this.'

"I was so tired I just wanted to get to MIT and sleep because of the tremendous stress," Rippel remembered. Nonetheless, the VW sped up, and so did the heat pouring out of its batteries.

According to the judges from *Machine Design*, technicians from the local utility in Erie, Pennsylvania, "shook their heads in disbelief" as the Caltech team raced in, clamped on the high-voltage power cables, and then piled more ice on the VW's batteries near the connection terminals.

Trying to be helpful, the technicians pointed out to the scruffy crew that there was a nearby first-aid room that had five empty cots in it. Rippel's team succumbed and took a nap "which almost cost Caltech the race," according to the judges.

But the Californians soon awoke and continued their mad scramble, accelerating the teamwork they used to cut recharging times, until they reached the last recharge point at Worcester, Massachusetts, where they learned the local utility wasn't set up to give them a charge. They had to use their portable generator, which should have given them a half-hour penalty, but they convinced their accompanying judges that this impasse was, for once, not their fault. The half-hour penalty was waived.

When the Caltech VW rolled onto the MIT campus at 7:40 A.M. on a Wednesday, they had been on the road for almost nine days. The MIT team had already been in Pasadena for more than forty hours, but they had accumulated so many penalties for being towed that the judges concluded that Caltech had won . . . by a half hour.

Rippel, Rubinstein, and the other adventurers from Pasadena were given a strained but gracious welcome by MIT's president, Howard Johnson, speaking at a campus press conference. A day later they were feted at a banquet organized at Tavern on the Green in New York's Central Park where Rippel was presented with a trophy by Edison Electric Institute and Reddy Kilowatt.

His VW was the first car in history to cross the country using only electric power. It took them eight days, nineteen hours, and forty-six minutes.

It was a victory that America wanted to hear about. In Pasadena a weary Leon Loeb was roused by a phone call. It was from the U.S. Secretary of Transportation's office. The secretary wanted the MIT car in Washington.

"I said we don't have a way of getting it there. They said to go to the San Bernardino Airport the day after tomorrow." There Loeb watched the battered Corvair being strapped down in the belly of a massive Air Force transport.

By the following Saturday it stood proudly beside Rippel's well-worn VW at the Smithsonian Institution. The exhibit was titled *Cars of the Future*.

THREE

The "Adventurer"

Despite the national publicity over the *Cars of the Future,* the race between Caltech and MIT would not lead to the commercial rebirth of the electric car.

At least that was the conclusion of a report by two car-savvy writers for *Road & Track* magazine after the race. They said the batteries were too heavy and the cars were too slow. They had little power and an embarrassingly short range.

But they did admit that the innovations and daring by Wally Rippel, Leon Loeb, and their teammates had struck a spark that might someday lead to a new era: "They did push back the darkness a little. Such has it always been with pioneers. We salute them."

It took another man and another celebrated race to turn the spark into a blaze. Most Americans are not familiar with Hans Tholstrup, a stocky, immensely competitive Australian who is the real father of the resurgence of the electric car.

In Australia his exploits are so well known that he is often described simply in news accounts as an adventurer. He is a former cowboy and auto, boat, and motorcycle racer who had little background in either science or engineering. And yet the intellectual and entrepreneurial bloodlines of most of the electric and hybrid cars running silently past you in the streets today can be traced back to this man and one of his many improbable feats.

Tholstrup grew up in Denmark, the son of a family grown wealthy by starting businesses that ranged from selling propane to blue cheese. As a teenager he had explored Europe by bicycle and moped and at nineteen he struck out for more risky adventures. He headed for Bangkok where the CIA was recruiting air crews to support its then-secret war in Laos.

He was going to be a "kicker" who pushed parachute-equipped supplies out of the rear of a C-130. However, his family vehemently objected, so Tholstrup diverted to Australia where he worked as a jackaroo (cowboy), a mine worker, and the driver of "road trains," muscular, fifty-four-wheeled trucks that towed three trailers across the country's vast outback.

In his early twenties Tholstrup was persuaded to settle down as an office worker for a propane business in Sydney, Australia, but he couldn't. He still had the itch. This time it wasn't just a craving to explore; he was determined to do things that no one had ever done before. For example, no one had ever circumnavigated the continent of Australia—a 9,147-mile journey—in a small, open motorboat.

So Tholstrup spent his savings on a seventeen-foot boat, the *Tom Thumb*. He loaded on an eighty-horsepower outboard motor, some Australian Army coastal survey maps, and a compass. That, plus food and other supplies, left him without enough money to buy gasoline. When he asked a gasoline dealer if he could buy it on credit, the dealer shook his head. "If you succeed," he told Tholstrup, "we'll give you the gas."

Seventy-seven days later Tholstrup, then twenty-five, reentered Sydney in triumph. His face reddened and blistered by a relentless sun and battered by flying fish, he proudly piloted the *Tom Thumb* into the harbor behind an escort of welcoming yachts. No one had ever done that before. Reporters thronged around him. How did he do it? "It's keeping Australia on your left," explained Tholstrup.

His gift for understatement and his flair for setting implausible records led to Tholstrup's customary one-word description in the Australian press. The adventurer plowed through the troughs of the Atlantic in a twenty-foot outboard from Europe to New York. He won round-the-world races in cars and motorbikes and circled the globe in a small plane without the need for navigational aids.

In 1980, after the American daredevil Evel Knievel came to Australia to perform stunts and commemorate a 1975 show in London where he attempted to jump his motorcycle over thirteen single-decker buses, Tholstrup joined a publicity-loving friend, Dick Smith, in a double-decker bus. The idea was to drive it off a ramp and jump fourteen motorcycles.

"That was far more dangerous than it looked," recalled Tholstrup, who built a six-foot ramp and had a V8-powered Land Rover helping to nudge the bus up to sixty miles per hour to give it some extra oomph when it hit the ramp. Smith, a journalist who thought the stunt was just going to be a joke, became alarmed. "I said we're supposed to jump the motorbikes, not just run them over," Tholstrup recalled. "I thought he would jump out of the bus, but he stayed in."

In record-crazed Australia, Tholstrup's name meant gold to his sponsors, allowing him to engage in a more serious pursuit, which was to convince Australians that they needed to use less oil. The Arab oil embargo of 1973 had roused the idealist in Tholstrup, who began leading a series of long-distance challenges, competing with other drivers to see who could get the best mileage out of cars and trucks. He found that more fuel-abstemious driving habits and more aerodynamic vehicles could reduce oil consumption by as much as 30 percent. But that didn't deter Australians from racing their gas guzzlers or vying to beat Tholstrup's bike-jumping record. In January 2003, a stuntman performing under the name of Lawrence Legend attempted to hurdle twenty-one motorbikes in a double-decker bus. (Legend's bus mashed the final three bikes, but it was still enough for a new record.)

Tholstrup continued to brood over the implications of the oil embargo and increasingly discussed the possibility that production of the world's oil supplies had peaked. In a country with dwindling oil supplies, modern agriculture would become impossible. How would nations feed themselves? "I didn't think the world was treating the oil situation with the respect it deserved," he explained. What would really grab people's attention, he was thinking, would be to find a way to show Australians that they could cross their continent without using any oil at all.

It is usually impossible to trace something as complex and evolutionary as the modern electric car to one man. It is much more often a matter of one influential man nudging another and then another—a kind of daisy chain of inventiveness. That turned out to be the case with Tholstrup.

In 1981 newly elected president Ronald Reagan decided to show what he thought to be the folly of relying on solar power by dismantling the Department of Energy's programs for developing it. That outraged Paul MacCready, a California meteorologist, businessman, and former world champion glider pilot. So he built an ultralight, solar-powered aircraft, the Solar Challenger, and in July 1981 it flew across the English Channel.

There was the missing piece for Tholstrup. He set out to build a solar-powered car. "I figured if he could fly on the stuff, we could drive on it."

He needed a sponsor to provide the cash to build a solar car and finance the event. It turned out to be an oil giant, BP, which was then being picketed by antinuclear green groups in Australia for buying shares in an Australian uranium mine. Eager to restore their environmental credibility, they gave Tholstrup $25,000 to put their brand on the car.

In 1982 one of Tholstrup's friends, a race car driver and engineer named Larry Perkins, built the car with his brother. It looked like a bathtub on bicycle wheels that carried a big door on top. The door carried an array of solar cells that powered two twelve-volt auto batteries. Minus the driver, it weighed 330 pounds. They powered it with an off-the-shelf Bosch motor. "It was so bloody simple that it couldn't have been any simpler," recalled Tholstrup.

Because it made no sound, he dubbed it the Quiet Achiever and sat down to concoct a story line for the press: His goal was to beat the first crossing of the Australian continent in a motor vehicle, which was done by Francis Birtles in 1912. Birtles did it in twenty-eight days.

Followed by observers from the Confederation of Australian Motor Sport, which verified that only solar power was being used to charge the batteries, the two men took turns driving the Quiet Achiever across Australia from west to east in December 1982, braving the heat of the continent's summer, which provided an assortment of thunderstorms and four 110-degree days.

They crossed in twenty days—shaving eight days off of Birtles's record—propelled by the amount of electric energy used to run a portable hair dryer. This was something that Australians were more interested in than in mere energy efficiency, Tholstrup concluded. Crowds appeared, waving and cheering, at many stops. It was as if the "whole world had burst into a smile," he recalled.

Aside from a brief flurry of Australian headlines, the response to the Quiet Achiever's achievement was, well, quiet. Tholstrup had not stirred the world into action. "I naively thought that people would say yes, we need to develop a world that can survive without oil."

Having established that a solar-powered car could cross Australia, Tholstrup started thinking about what, to him, was the next obvious step. It would be a solar car race and he planned to invite the world's best universities and the globe's automakers to compete.

He drafted forty-four pages of rules, setting the allowable size of solar arrays and the daily schedule of racing, which would begin at 8:00 A.M. and end at 5:00 P.M. Racing teams would only be allowed to charge their batteries for two hours before the race and two hours after. The course was a 1,877-mile highway that stretched from Darwin in the north to Adelaide in the south. Teams of judges would follow each car to make sure car batteries were charged only with solar energy.

Tholstrup set the race date for December 1987 and recruited BP to sponsor what would be called the BP Solar Challenge. In December 1986 he sent out invitations to everyone he could think of who might want to enter. He got what he was hoping for: responses from prospective entrants from around the world.

Then the trouble began. The Confederation of Australian Motor Sport, a member of the Fédération Internationale du Sport Automobile (FISA), an international organization that sanctioned auto races, rejected his rules. "These sorts of activities are new and they have to be done right from the start, if they are to gain credibility," stated John Keefe, the confederation's chief executive officer.

"We were running an education event, a brain sport, and it was meant to be a challenge not a race, so I felt I could circumvent them," recalled Tholstrup. He knew that if FISA rules controlled the race, losers could appeal and a final decision would be made in Paris. Appeals could sometimes take months. "I wanted the sun to decide the winner."

The confederation took its case to BP, which withdrew its sponsorship and its money from the race. So eight months before the race, Tholstrup had a race, multiple contestants on the way, and no one to pay for it.

On April 28, however, Tholstrup got what he needed to get his newest venture off the ground: a very big push. General Motors, then the world's largest automaker, announced it would enter the race. Meanwhile Pentax, the Japanese camera company, hoping to film the exploits of Mitsubishi, a contestant in the race and an affiliated company, agreed to be the sponsor. An accommodation was reached with FISA to permit what was quickly renamed The World Solar Challenge.

On the day of GM's entry, Tholstrup told the *Australian Courier-Mail* that the big Detroit automaker's move had "put the whole event back on the rails."

Within GM, some of its many wheels had been turning on the matter for several months. The invitation had come from Australia in December 1986 to Roger Smith, the freewheeling chairman of GM, who had never heard of Tholstrup. But GM had just purchased Hughes Aircraft, then the world's leader in solar cells and electronics. Hughes had built its expertise selling space satellites and missile guidance equipment to the U.S. military and NASA. Now that the Cold War was over, GM was looking for peacetime markets for Hughes's high technology.

Smith sent the invitation and Tholstrup's packet of rules to Howard Wilson, a vice president of Hughes, who was given the job of finding the new terrestrial opportunities. As he looked through the packet, Wilson, based in California, was thrilled. "This was just a perfect deal so I promoted it on that basis."

In the few months Wilson had had to study how to navigate GM's ponderous bureaucracy, he learned that the fact that he was forwarded the information from the chairman's office meant nothing by itself. He needed to find an ally, a sympathetic ear among the top executives. It had to be someone with the clout to help him promote the idea and the budget to help him develop a more formal proposal.

He visited GM's executive offices in downtown Detroit, where Lloyd Reuss, head of GM's North American operations, received his idea coolly. What, he asked, would a solar car race in Australia do for him in the United States? Wilson was back walking the corridors. He passed Bob Stempel's office, saw the door was ajar, and that Stempel, then head of international operations, was in there. Wilson walked in and made his pitch.

He found his ally. "He [Stempel] was basically a very enthusiastic guy, so he bought into it right away," recalled Wilson. He left with a promise of $75,000 to develop a proposal for a solar race car and a deadline of three weeks.

Back at Hughes in California, Wilson consulted a friend, one of the company's top engineers. He was a Caltech graduate who said, "Hey, I know a guy back here that really wants to be in this race." That turned out to be none other than Paul MacCready, a fellow Caltech graduate and the inventor of the Solar Challenger. Here was the man who had lured Tholstrup into solar cars in the first place.

If there was no exact polar opposite to Hans Tholstrup in the world, MacCready would have made a good substitute. A small and quiet man, a bird-watcher sometimes described as birdlike, a businessman with few obvious business skills and a habit of forgetting names and faces, MacCready had one big thing in common with the adventurer: When it came to contests, they both knew how to win. Tholstrup would throw himself into strange competitions, gut it out, win, and then dazzle people with his charisma. "He [Tholstrup] is six-one and weighs two hundred and twenty pounds," recalled Chester Kyle, a bicycle racing consultant who later worked for MacCready's company and met Tholstrup in Australia. "He looks like a Viking warrior, very handsome guy. . . . If you stand next to him he makes a tremendous, powerful presence. Not an ounce of fat on him. He's somebody you'd like to have on your side if you get in a fight." MacCready, described by one of his biographers as a "calculating machine with idiosyncrasies," was a man who could work the equations in his head about how fast you could go with a particular amount of energy in a certain kind of vehicle. Then he would design it and win.

It was not clear to those who knew them whether MacCready and Tholstrup would get along. MacCready was also a man that the garrulous Tholstrup might breeze right past at a cocktail party. Even if he had been introduced to him, that would make little difference to MacCready, who probably wouldn't recall the adventurer. But MacCready, sixty-two, had nurtured a skill that both GM and Tholstrup now had to have: he knew how to build extremely lightweight, low-powered vehicles that were almost preternaturally aerodynamic.

In an age of big cars and increasingly voluminous aircraft, MacCready was a fervent minimalist. The best engineering minds in Britain had failed for seventeen years to win the Kremer prize, put up by Henry Kremer, a British industrialist. He promised nearly $100,000 for the first sustained, maneuverable, human-powered flight. In 1976 MacCready won it on the first try. His craft was the Gossamer Condor, a bicycle-powered hang glider with long Mylar wings reinforced by aluminum tubing and piano wire. Minus the pilot, it weighed seventy-two pounds. It was ridiculed by some of the losers as a "flying laundry bag."

The Royal Aeronautical Society, hoping to stay in the awarding business for another decade or longer, offered a second Kremer prize for the first human-powered aircraft to cross the English Channel. MacCready won that with an updated version called the Gossamer Albatross in 1979. Then came the Solar Challenger, which had given Tholstrup his inspiration.

MacCready, who died in August 2007, assembled a team of experts at his company, AeroVironment, in Monrovia, California, that included the best and the brightest people he knew at making and propelling lightweight vehicles. His protégé at AeroVironment was Alec Brooks, a fellow glider and bicycle racing enthusiast and civil engineer from Caltech. Brooks recalls three intensive weeks of spitballing and computer modeling to come up with a car that had lightweight electric motors, a solid-state, supersmooth electronic control system, and potent space-age solar cells and batteries.

Wilson, MacCready, and Brooks brought their plan back to Detroit and described the vehicle that GM would later call Sunraycer to a group of senior executives. They were men who had risen to the top in GM in an age of chrome trim, soaring tail fins, and stylish but heavy muscle cars that got eight miles to the gallon. Here was a car with no trim and no decorative styling that didn't use any gasoline. Including the driver, it would weigh about five hundred pounds.

"To our surprise they basically approved it in that room and at that time," recalled Brooks. Wilson recalls GM's initial commitment to be somewhere in the neighborhood of $1.5 million.

Brooks found himself excited and perplexed at the same time. "The thing that was interesting was that this was new. When you're developing the first car, you had no idea what you'd be racing against. So we were doing the Sunraycer really in fear that we were going to lose. GM was putting a lot of money in this, so we had to win, but we had no idea what the other guys were doing."

FOUR

Charging Toward Night

A more detailed version of Sunraycer began to take shape on an Apple Mac at AeroVironment in California. Although it was still mostly a digital image, in many ways it was already a dream machine with financing and technology far beyond what MacCready's people or any other groups of high-tech experimenters might have for peacetime projects.

Sunraycer was about to become the rolling embodiment of swords to plowshares. Thanks to the largesse of GM and the expertise of Hughes and at least nine other GM affiliates, it would have a curved array of 7,200 gallium-arsenide solar cells that Hughes used in space satellites. They were twice as efficient as those used for civilian purposes.

The solar cells would feed electricity into silver-zinc batteries with double the storage capacity of conventional auto batteries and, still more important, one-fifth of the weight. Combining lightness and speed was the Holy Grail at AeroVironment, located near the foothills of the San Gabriel Mountains on the edge of the smoggy sprawl of suburbs radiating east from Los Angeles.

The batteries had delivered the electricity for intercontinental ballistic missiles in the Cold War and later for NASA's first Apollo space rockets. Few consumers in the United States had ever seen them because they were superexpensive and would wear out after ten or twenty charging cycles. What made them seductive to Mac-Cready's team was their short but exciting life. They expected the race to last ten days.

The batteries, in turn, would power a new super-lightweight electric motor, using GM's patented Magnequench magnet technology. It was later used in a wide array of military weaponry, including drones and homing torpedoes. All of this had to be crammed into a minimalist frame made from aluminum tubing and a body made from Kevlar, the same material used for canoes and bicycle helmets.

The whole car—with the driver lying under the solar array in a nylon-mesh hammock much like a rider on a recumbent bicycle—weighed 575 pounds. It would roll on skinny, twenty-inch slick tires, the kind used on racing bikes. Sunraycer, which would be only three feet high, was designed to make a knifelike cut through the air. The exterior, shaped something like a pumpkin seed or a cockroach's exoskeleton, was developed with the help of NASA computers and GM wind tunnels. It was the most streamlined body ever designed for a land-based vehicle.

In his later years MacCready turned over the details of his many projects to younger men. The head of Sunraycer's team was Brooks. He paid particular attention to the connectivity between the driver and the technology. There were safety issues. The battery pack, sized to take in and deliver maximum power under Tholstrup's racing rules, was located directly behind the driver, making him or her vulnerable to fires, burns, and shocks from short circuits and explosions from escaping hydrogen gas.

Brooks, who would become one of Sunraycer's team of eight drivers, also oversaw the design of an elaborate instrumentation and telemetry system that would allow tacticians riding behind Sunraycer in a computer-crammed Winnebago to monitor the condition of the batteries and the electronic drive system. That allowed them to see the symptoms of potential problems and fix them before they happened.

The next question was who could put all of this together and make it work by December? That was a tough one. Brooks had already brought in Wally Rippel as an advisor. For organizing and winning the electric car race between Caltech and MIT, Rippel had become a legend at Caltech. He had also personally experienced most of the screwups that could occur while racing an electric car.

Both Rippel and Brooks had already met the man they felt could master the mysteries of Sunraycer's elaborate electronics. Alan Cocconi, another model airplane and bicycle racing fanatic, had specialized in power electronics starting when he was a student at Caltech. Brooks gave him a call. But Cocconi, who had paid his way through Caltech by working summers in GM laboratories, was not intrigued. "I said that I'm really not interested in cars, I prefer airplanes, but he talked me into it and I got involved."

Drawing in the skinny, bespectacled Cocconi, who resembled an Italian version of the young Woody Allen, was not easy. He was not motivated by money. He would not work on military-related projects, and he was definitely not a team player, preferring to work on his own. Both Brooks and Rippel worried about whether Cocconi could work with GM's engineers, who tended to be very proud and rigid about the specific technologies under their control. According to Rippel, Cocconi was more like MacCready, a visionary. During the discussions at AeroVironment about how to put together Sunraycer, he was usually thinking three steps ahead.

"Alan has this instinct for sniffing out the trouble spots. It comes across as negative, but it's not. He's probably one of the most honest people I've ever met. But Alan doesn't tolerate exaggeration. He is adamant about that. He's not a people person," recalled Rippel.

Cocconi signed on because the electronic drive system for an electric car hadn't been done with state-of-the-art technology before and that attracted him. He was also attracted by the fact that in the waning days of the Cold War, when many U.S. engineers applied new technologies to weapons systems, Sunraycer was for peaceful use.

The son of two Italian nuclear physicists who had come to the United States after World War II, Cocconi had his early education in Switzerland where he picked up a strong antiwar sentiment. His passion as a teenager and when he entered Caltech was model airplanes and aeronautics, but in the late 1970s he discovered that all the career paths in aeronautics led to work for the military. So he dropped his aeronautics major without taking a course and began taking classes in power electronics.

"I sort of liked the physics and engineering aspects of it. Somehow it's the area I got into. It intrigued me and I was roughly good at it, so that was my career." Cocconi graduated in 1980 with a specialty in high-power processing circuits, in controlling motors, power supplies, and in switching power supplies. It was very new in the seventies; now it is reflected in every laptop, computer, and electric car.

But Brooks and Rippel were right. Cocconi soon got into several fights with researchers from GM's electronics labs. "There were some pretty heated arguments there," Cocconi admits. In the end he found a way to keep the GM people quiet about circuit designs. "I'd say, look, if you think you have a better approach that's going to be more reliable, here's the interface. The connectors have this pin out. Then you have to bolt them to this spot. Go ahead and do it. If I'm wrong and you're right, then we'll use yours." The GM people rarely built their versions of Cocconi's circuits because his usually worked and the rapidly approaching deadline for the Australian race left little time to make alternatives.

Where everyone agreed in the constantly expanding GM team was on testing. GM decided that two Sunraycer vehicles would be built by AeroVironment, one as a spare in case of an accident. In September, the first one was tested for four thousand miles at the GM Desert Proving Ground outside Phoenix, Arizona.

An AeroVironment meteorologist had already scouted the entire length of Stuart Highway in Australia, where the race would be run. The GM team knew the weather patterns and had videos of places in the outback where the road sometimes narrowed down to a bumpy, one-lane gravel pathway.

As Rippel, Cocconi, and MacCready knew, stuff happened, things blew up. One day in October after a motor tore itself apart leaving the Sunraycer team stranded in the 115-degree desert heat, MacCready seemed pleased about it. "This is exactly what we wanted to happen," he told a reporter. "Better the motor should go kablooey here and give us a chance to correct it, rather than somewhere in the middle of Australia."

Because Sunraycer's drivers would also have to learn to weave their way through city traffic in Darwin and several other places along the route, GM had the car made street legal and tested it in California.

On October 8, 1987, when the first sheriff flagged down Sunraycer near El Mirage, he approached it cautiously, thinking it was some kind of giant, radio-controlled toy. After hearing him yell "Is there anyone in that thing?" GM engineer Molly Brennan, the car's red-headed driver, flipped open Sunraycer's gold-plated top (designed to shade the driver from Australia's vicious summer sun) and gave him a dazzling smile. The sheriff later posed for photographs, pretending to write the first ticket awarded to a solar-powered car.

GM's substantial public relations team was already hard at work, flying reporters out to the normally closed Arizona test track and letting it be known when Brennan, one of Sunraycer's drivers, set a solar car world speed record of 35.22 miles per hour operating on solar power alone with no batteries onboard. This news positively thrilled technicians at Ford and other companies preparing for the Pentax World Solar Challenge, but GM had failed to mention that the record was set on a cloudy day. By then they knew Sunraycer could go 50 percent faster in bright sunlight.

J. Bruce McCristal, then director of public affairs for GM's Hughes Electronics, recalled that "the big question at GM was if we enter this, we can't afford not to win." It was go in big or stay home and by October, McCristal had already gone in big. He had scouted Stuart Highway, noting places where he could set up satellite phone communication for the press as the race progressed. He even had hired an Australian automotive writer, Bill Tuckey, to write a book about the race and, assuming GM would win, made arrangements to have it published six weeks after the race.

GM had rented helicopters so television crews could film the race and so GM's meteorologist could scout the weather ahead as the race progressed. GM public relations teams had already touted the race to newspapers and brought films of Sunraycer to television stations around the country. "It [Sunraycer] turned up in virtually every newspaper in the country just prior to the race," recalled McCristal.

The second Sunraycer emerged from AeroVironment and began doing practice runs on the massive parking lots of nearby Santa Anita Racetrack in October; it incorporated the hard lessons learned in Arizona and California by the first car. Then they were both flown to Australia for another six hundred miles of testing on Stuart Highway, the site of the race. Australians often refer to it as "the track" because it is the main north-south route through the center of the country.

In Darwin, the northern starting point, the contestants got their first good look at one another because each car had to be tested to see if it could withstand the sharp blast of air they would receive from the big road trains, which used the highway as their "track." Thanks to MacCready, who even argued with GM over a tiny bump that the company's blue-striped logos raised on the body of the car interfered with its streamlining, Sunraycer hardly felt a ripple of windy bow waves of the behemoth trucks.

The GM team figured their closest competitor would be Ford's Sunchaser, which looked like a Formula 1 racing car with a surfboard mounted on top carrying the prescribed maximum area of solar cells. The car could tilt the panel to the side to feed its batteries the maximum possible power generated from the sun.

Then there was Mana La, a Hawaiian entry that carried massive batteries and heavy motors. It was sponsored by an American shampoo manufacturer, John Paul Mitchell Systems, and its crew of "reformed hippies" often did war chants around their car. The Team Marsupial was an entry put together by an Australian team, headed by Dick Smith, Tholstrup's double-decker jumping bus companion.

A roster of college teams ranged from MIT and its Swiss equivalent, the Biel School of Engineering and Architecture, to Missouri's Crowder College, a two-year technical school that put together a car made of bicycle parts.

Then there were four Japanese entrants, which amazed the Aero-Vironment team because they appeared to have paid almost no attention to streamlining or weight reduction. One car looked like a World War I fighter plane with the driver's helmeted head sticking out of the top. Another looked like a folding door on wheels, and a third, the Southern Cross, resembled two halves of an airplane body connected by a thin rail that carried a door-size panel bearing the solar cells.

"The Japanese didn't have a clue about motor efficiency, aerodynamics, whatever you wanted to look at," recalled Chester Kyle, an aerodynamics expert who designed the wheels and the hubs for Sunraycer. He remembers Japanese reporters and engineers excitedly taking pictures of the GM car when it appeared. "But it didn't take them long to figure things out. Things like that happen in a hurry. Technology transfer can happen very fast."

Strange things that Rippel was familiar with began to happen even before the race. The battery of a German entry exploded. Then Solectra, the MIT entry, caught fire on a Darwin street. The car's carbon-fiber seat shorted the battery and the resulting arc slightly burned the driver, who was on his way to speed trials.

But these accidents didn't mar the start of the race on November 25 as the twenty-five entrants streamed through crowds stretching for thirty miles on the highway heading south from Darwin. Perhaps the best description of it was written by Bill Tuckey, GM's hired book writer:

"The whole thing was a chain of eerie apparitions, the odd geometric shapes contrasting weirdly with the dun-green tropical foliage, the red of the earth, the hard blue sky, the dark gray bitumen. And there was the lack of noise—just the sounds of chains or the bodywork or suspension joints clacking or rubbing as the bicycle or motorcycle wheels hammered over the surface."

The first day was sunny and thermometers hit 112, but GM's meteorologist saw rain clouds heading in from the south, all the more reason for the Sunraycer driver, John Harvey, one of two Australian race drivers GM had hired for the tough parts of the race, to stomp on it. Molly Brennan, in the first chase car, watched him zip past out in the country.

She radioed the GM Winnebago, equipped to receive ninety channels of telemetry from Sunraycer. There MacCready, Brooks, and six others were manning their computer screens, but they were stuck in traffic back in Darwin. It was Molly who gave them their first electrifying jolt.

"He's way out ahead! Wow . . . he's just flying . . . there's no one else in sight."

Indeed there wasn't. At 5:00 P.M. when Tholstrup's rules said they had to stop, Sunraycer was 322.5 miles south of Darwin and had used only half its charge. Behind them, strewn almost all the way back to Darwin, were the other contestants. The Swiss team was seventy-one miles behind them. And farther back were multiple disasters.

MIT's motor had burned out. Hoxan, a Japanese entry, had melted a battery. Ford had a software glitch that showed their battery was full when it died, and their gearbox was stuck in third gear. And another Japanese team, the Southern Cross, limping along at six miles per hour, barely made it out of Darwin. The Hawaiian team, even with its big batteries, had run out of juice.

GM's Winnebago and a crew of Australian outfitters caught up with Sunraycer as it began charging its batteries from the waning sun. There was a strategy session as Cocconi, the mother hen of Sunraycer's electronics, checked out its wiring, ducts, connectors, and warning lights and the outfitters produced tents and cooked dinner in the desert for the excited GM team.

At the end of day two the teams were strung out over 646 miles of Stuart Highway and Southern Cross, the slowest Japanese team, had made it only forty miles from Darwin. Ford's Sunchaser, sponsored mainly by Ford's Australian marketer, had started to speed up when its battery died again. Mana La, the Hawaiian entry, had to stop for forty hours to recharge its massive batteries.

The GM weatherman predicted a sunny day for day three, so the Sunraycer took off with only half a charge. What Brooks and the other drivers found was that, when the road trains weren't around, it was so quiet that animals and birds feasting on roadkills hardly moved until the almost soundless Sunraycer was upon them.

On day four, Sunraycer was in desert country, charging up on the hot summer sun, as most of the rest of the contestants foundered in the rain behind them. The Hawaiian team dropped out with terminal mechanical problems. McCristal, Hughes's public relations chief, was ecstatic because most of the press covering the race were in the comfy bus he had rented, where they could phone in their stories about how far GM was out in front.

Day five was cloudless. Molly Brennan was hitting sixty miles per hour when the news came that the Spirit of Biel, one of their nearest competitors, had struck a car while entering a parking lot. Cocconi did another of his meticulous checkups. Aside from a few flat tires, Sunraycer seemed fine. The team began pulling on sweaters because it was getting cold.

Day six was, for Sunraycer, a two-hour drive to the finish line at the outskirts of Adelaide. There was a press entourage traveling behind them and they met more media and police cars as they came triumphantly into Adelaide. There a party had already started at the Seppeltsfield Winery where Bob Stempel, now GM's president, was buying the drinks.

Tholstrup still insists that the best part of the race, for him, was meeting MacCready, Wilson, and Cocconi. "Paul [MacCready] proved that what we had set out to do could be done." He also had kind words for GM. "What has happened with this unique event is that GM has shown that a huge multinational corporation can care about the world."

Six days later, when the trophies were handed out, he discovered that ten cars had dropped out. Ford, which arrived two and a half days later, was second, the Spirit of Biel was third, and Australia's Team Marsupial was fourth. Three Japanese teams had finished, but it took some help from Tholstrup to accomplish that. He had to drive the members of the Southern Cross team to Adelaide to get their visas extended before they could finish. They came in last, thirty-two days after GM.

"It's good to be here," said the team manager, Shinji Imato, after his car pulled up to the finish line at Town Hall in Adelaide. The

Japanese quietly enjoyed a bottle of champagne and then left, saying they would be back.

"We have many jobs waiting for us in Japan," Imato explained to the press.

FIVE

The Dream

In September 1987 Hans Tholstrup's dream of somehow jarring the world into thinking about emission-free electric cars had seemed far-fetched, even as preparations for his Solar Challenge were under way.

Three months later, on November 6, it was beginning to happen on the lawn of a winery in southern Australia as jubilant members of GM's Sunraycer team held an impromptu press conference suggesting that the day of the electric car was just around the corner. What was then the world's largest carmaker was in a celebratory mood and reporters were eager to hear and write about the new automotive future as the wine flowed. Then a tidal wave of well-managed publicity from GM's lopsided victory began to circle the globe.

Howard Wilson, a vice president of GM Hughes, cautioned that a solar-powered car might be "five to seven years away." But, he added, "Solar cars for short commutes could be available now. You drive it ten or fifteen miles to work. It sits in the parking lot all day and the solar cells charge it up. The technology is here already for that."

While cautioning that the electricity from a limited array of solar panels was nowhere near enough energy to power a family car, Paul MacCready, whose company AeroVironment had built Sunraycer, got caught up in the bullish mood of the day. Because of the use of lightweight materials, streamlining, high-efficiency electric motors, and the electronics that went with them, Mac-Cready explained, "What we have learned makes practical battery and hybrid-powered vehicles more feasible."

As soon as Alec Brooks, the leader of the Sunraycer team, arrived back in California, he was told to repack his bags; GM was going to fly him and the winning Sunraycer to Capitol Hill in Washington, D.C., where congressmen would line up to sit in it. Later it was parked in front of the Lincoln Memorial, where traffic-jammed commuters inching toward Memorial Bridge on their way home could get a long look at what was being billed as the car of the future.

In January, Sunraycer flew back to California where Brooks led the Rose Bowl parade in the flower-bedecked car. It carried a sign that read PACE CAR OF THE FUTURE.

This was just the start of a twenty-five-month public relations extravaganza that put the two Sunraycers on display at 250 events in the United States, Canada, and Europe. In all, GM estimated, ten million people had seen the cars by the following June. Descriptions of the car and its victory had been mentioned in nearly every major newspaper in the world. An estimated 250 million people had seen the car on television.

Six weeks after the race the book GM had commissioned was published and Bruce McCristal made sure that the first copies were handed out to members of GM's board. Videos and slide shows of the race were making the rounds of the nation's universities, often narrated by a member of the team of Sunraycer drivers.

McCristal is retired now, but he still keeps a copy of the book—*Sunraycer*—on his desk at his fishing lodge in Ontario. "I read this and I still say, wow, that was one hell of a deal!" Just what it cost GM to win the Pentax World Solar Challenge remains a mystery. Newspaper accounts estimated up to $8 million. "We never put a number on it," explained McCristal. "It was enough to win."

Interestingly, the statement that Roger B. Smith, chairman of General Motors, put out after the race was vaguely worded about what the victory meant: "What we learn from Sunraycer may be useful in solar-powered, electric, or other kinds of vehicles for the future."

In the spring of 1988, Howard Wilson, the GM Hughes vice president, and Brooks made another trip to GM headquarters in Detroit. AeroVironment wanted to build a two-seater electric car based on the same philosophy used to build Sunraycer. It would have the same intense focus on efficiency and new technology, but it would be relatively inexpensive and simple, using lead-acid batteries, for example, instead of the exotic, space-age batteries used to power Sunraycer. The effort, the latest attempt to produce a commercial electric car, would be called Project Santana.

Stunned by the ongoing flood of publicity from Sunraycer, younger members of GM's management team were intrigued, but not Roger Smith, who said he was inclined to pass. Sunraycer had gotten all the public relations boost that GM could possibly want from electric cars. It was time, Smith felt, to move on.

But Bob Stempel, the newly chosen president of GM and former champion of the Sunraycer project, kept pushing, and in September 1988 Smith relented and approved a $3 million budget for the prototype and a fifteen-month deadline for the prototype car. That put the freewheeling AeroVironment team back into contact with GM's bureaucracy, particularly the Advanced Concepts Center in Newbury Park, California, where company stylists had their own version of what a sporty two-seat electric car should look like.

According to Brooks, it was just the beginning of a series of new battles.

"I said, let's work our way from the inside out," recalled Brooks. "And they said, oh, no, no, no. We can't do that. We have to have something that has the feel of the car. They had worked up something that looked like a fighter jet with the wheels in the middle of the car." Wilson gave permission for AeroVironment to develop its own design, but then GM flew an executive, Don Runkle, to California to demand that the two warring groups agree on one design for the electric car, which was eventually baptized as the GM Impact.

Meanwhile Alan Cocconi, who insisted on working from his home, was battling with GM over the Impact's electronics. He built several inverters, complex electronic devices that convert direct current electricity coming from the batteries into alternating current needed by the car's motors.

They were scaled up from the Sunraycer's electronics and they worked, but GM engineers complained they couldn't easily be replicated because Cocconi had made each one by hand. He accompanied them with hand-drawn notes that documented his work, but they were not detailed enough for the Hughes Aircraft part of the team to work with.

When GM's manager of the project asked for more time, Roger Smith, GM's chairman, responded with a new deadline. By now he had become excited about the prospect of having a GM electric car and said he was going to introduce it as a concept car for the Los Angeles Auto Show in January 1990, which was six months away.

Younger executives worried that would give competitors an early signal and also rouse the interest of California's smog regulators, the Air Resources Board (CARB), which might turn around and mandate an electric car. But Smith, a former GM financial expert, ignored them. He had developed a certain disdain for automotive types at the company, who seemed to be forever fussing over details. "Most engineers would still be working on the 1971 Chevrolet if someone hadn't grabbed it away from them," he later explained. "I just figured it was time to get this thing out of the chute."

In the auto industry, concept cars can be little more than fancy designs, stagecraft, and puffery, but after a series of all-nighters at AeroVironment the prototype of the Impact rolled quietly out into the darkened backstreets of Monrovia at 1:00 A.M. on November 28. It was a sporty-looking two-seater.

Impact was the first concept car to carry the GM brand, rather than one of its vehicle nameplates, and it was given the show's pole position, right at the edge of the Oldsmobile exhibit, next to the main aisle leading from the entrance door. Because GM had succeeded in keeping its debut a secret, it created the desired buzz among showgoers and radiated shock waves into the ranks of GM's competitors.

But now Smith wanted more than just a prototype. In April 1990, on Earth Day, the GM chairman announced that the Impact would soon become a GM production model. That meant hundreds of GM engineers had to converge from different divisions to figure out how to mass produce the car. One result was more advice, second-guessing, bureaucratic infighting, and regimentation than Cocconi could stand. He left his job as a GM consultant at AeroVironment and resolved to go back to building model airplanes.

"I said, okay, my job is done. I don't want to be part of this big conglomerate. And I didn't fully agree with some of the decisions they made on my project. . . . I gave them some input. I started them off with some working hardware and they took it from there," he explained.

According to Alec Brooks, who was still running the project for AeroVironment, he and some GM executives drove to Cocconi's home and GM attempted to negotiate a looser consultancy arrangement that would give Cocconi more free time to work on his own projects, yet kept him as an advisor on the Impact's electronics. As a sweetener, the GM team leaders were going to offer Cocconi GM designs for electric motors, which they knew he wanted for his own vehicle project.

They pulled up in the driveway of Cocconi's suburban house, which is often cluttered with model airplanes and electronic parts for his various projects. They had the designs in their car's trunk, ready to hand over. Parked just ahead of them was Cocconi's latest project, an electrified version of Honda's sporty CRX, an early indication that the inventor might emerge as a competitor in the electric car business.

That day Cocconi certainly played the role. He wouldn't bargain and did not invite the GM team into his house. "And he left them there, standing in the driveway," recalled Brooks.

Jon Bereisa, then heading the Impact's propulsion team, was aware of Cocconi's quirks. A fellow power electronics expert, Bereisa had started his career working for Aerojet General on a contract with the Atomic Energy Commission and NASA to build a nuclear-powered space rocket powerful enough to land a large vehicle on Mars. When that project was canceled, he joined GM to work on electric cars. One of his first projects was the Electrovette, an electric version of the Chevrolet Chevette. Powered by twenty twelve-volt batteries, it was canceled after fifteen years of tinkering.

A tall, heavyset man who understood not only the batteries and the electric motors but the computers and software that controlled them, Bereisa kept a sharp eye out for other electrical engineers and had recruited Cocconi at Caltech to work as a summer intern for GM. He had been proud of his catch. "I had to fight with other GM divisions to make sure Alan came to work for me," he explained.

He had put the young engineer to work designing the first computers to control electric drive systems. He still remembers his protégé sitting in the front seat, tweaking the computer as the car drove along. Although Cocconi had infuriated some of his colleagues with his snap judgments and eccentric work habits, Bereisa defended his work on the Impact.

"Alan built that [the electronic drive system] to move the wheels; he didn't build it to be environmentally friendly. That was up to someone else." But it definitely needed more work. When development engineers drove early Impact prototypes home, they looked like Geo Storms, but had electric drivetrains.

But there was one thing about them GM could not disguise. When the engineers attempted to recharge the vehicles at home by plugging them in, they created a big electronic buzz in the neighborhood. Electric garage doors suddenly opened. Television sets went haywire. "They had snow and haze on their TVs. We had to figure out how to shield that," recalled Bereisa. "We were running a gigantic radio transmitter."

That was a small issue compared with Bereisa's other problems. Under pressure from Chairman Smith, the Impact team grew and there was infighting between Hughes and various other divisions within GM over turf when it came to who did what on which part of the car. There were continuing battles over how much the car should weigh.

But the finances for the drive system went through Bereisa, who needed teamwork to meet his deadlines. He tried to crack the whip, threatening at one meeting to be a tyrant. "I have all the goddamn money and none of you has any recourse."

Then, in September 1990, an unexpected jolt from California's Air Resources Board (CARB) made his job still harder. It came in the form of a footnote amended to the board's schedule for phasing in different types of low-emission vehicles to phase out California's smog problem.

According to Analisa Bevan, chief of CARB's sustainable transportation technology branch, it happened on the spur of the moment after GM's chairman, Roger Smith, introduced the Impact as a concept car at the Los Angeles Auto Show. "So, with GM making these statements," she explained, "our regulatory staff at that time decided, well, let's throw in a requirement for zero-emission vehicles."

It appeared in a footnote at the bottom of a timetable: if car companies' California sales were above a certain level, then 2 percent of their vehicles had to be zero emission by 1998. By 2010 the level would rise to 10 percent. If they didn't make them, they could be fined $5,000 for each car that they sold in the state. The rule applied to what became known at CARB and the industry as the "lucky seven."

That meant the clock was ticking not only for GM, but also for Ford, Chrysler, Honda, Toyota, Nissan, and Mazda. Suddenly GM's rivals had a big incentive to catch up with GM's lead in the technology. The footnote also triggered a prolonged civil war within GM, whose lobbyists had battled in Washington for decades to uphold the principle that it was the market and automakers, not the government, that should decide which cars to build and sell in the future.

"All of a sudden I had half the company trying to fight the mandate," recalled Bereisa. He worried that a successful government intervention would also signal GM suppliers to jack up their prices for electric car parts. "They would figure that car companies had no choice but to buy this stuff." And that, in turn, would result in an expensive electric car that few would buy. "Cost always rules."

Few carmakers could afford to abandon the lucrative California market. So, while American carmakers and some of their Japanese competitors lined up to oppose what became known as the ZEV (for zero-emission vehicle) rule, a second, quieter round of activity also got under way. Carmakers began working on electric cars as a fallback position. California's ZEV announcement had given some of GM's toughest competitors a substantial wake-up call.

GM's electric car venture had begun with its stunning victory in the Australian Solar Challenge in 1987, but rather than spend the money to compete in subsequent versions of this race, GM's president, Bob Stempel, used it to sponsor solar car races for college teams. His hope was to build a cadre of young American engineers who were familiar with electric cars.

But Tholstrup's next races proved to be a window into what was going on in the secretive experimental labs of other members of the lucky seven. In 1993, a team from Honda shattered the record set by GM. Its cockroach-shaped solar car crossed Australia in 35.38 hours, nine hours and thirty minutes faster than Sunraycer had done it.

Honda's team manager, Takahiro Iwata, announced that the car's technology would help Honda meet California's ZEV standard, which could most easily be met by an electric-powered car. "We'll be there by 1998," said Iwata, who explained that Honda's solar racing car had taken three years and $10 million to perfect. Honda, a company that had grown large on racing, first motorcycles and later cars, had joined this race with an eye on California's big auto market. They called their car The Dream.

SIX

Who Makes the Rules?

Could one American state convince the globe's automakers to produce electric cars? In 1991 that seemed preposterous to what was then the Big Three American car companies and most of the other major players in the $1.6 trillion global industry.

Major oil companies and foreign automakers eventually joined them in a lobbying juggernaut intended to crush the rule. The battle has gone on for almost a quarter century. The juggernaut made a few dents. At times CARB has modified or delayed its timetable, but the rule, recently reinforced, survives. When it comes to electric vehicles, CARB's headquarters in a modest corner office building in downtown Sacramento remains the tail that wags an enormous dog.

Like GM, many carmakers flirted with the idea of electric cars in the late 1960s and early '70s when smog rules kicked in and soaring gasoline prices unsettled consumers. But when gasoline prices began to slump in the 1980s, many of these plans were shelved. Meanwhile the gasoline-powered auto had steadily become more efficient, but most of the new efficiency had been swallowed up by making cars and pickup trucks heavier, bigger, and faster.

But in 1991 California drew a line. That October nine other states, including most of New England, raised the stakes. They adopted California's mandate.

The experts were ecstatic. "The ZEV mandate may be the single most important event in the history of transportation since Henry Ford. . . ." wrote Daniel Sperling, founding director of the Institute of Transportation Studies at the University of California.

But the political support for the regulators remained sparse and wobbly. What propped up CARB in the early days were environmental groups and even getting them on board took considerable doing, according to Stewart Brand, one of the early leaders of the Greens and author of the *Whole Earth Catalog*. He credits one man with lining them up: Amory Lovins. Brand says many early environmentalists were "romantics," people mostly opposed to technological or market-based solutions. "He [Lovins] single-handedly converted them from loathing the auto industry to engaging with it."

Lovins's ascent as the guru of modern electric cars started in July 1991, when the National Academy of Sciences decided to hold a workshop in Irvine, California. The question was how much could the efficiency of cars and light trucks be improved. A battery of experts and lawyers from Detroit was set to defend the status quo of the industry.

Ralph Cavanagh, a lawyer representing environmental groups, couldn't think of anyone in the environmental movement who might be able to poke holes in their arguments. By default he came up with Amory Lovins.

Lovins was smart; there was no doubt about that. But he was not a car expert. He had dropped out of Oxford University in early 1971, giving up a planned doctorate in physics because at the time Oxford didn't consider his proposed topic—energy—a fit subject for academics. (It does now.) Lovins's real passion was finding solutions to avert climate change.

A young man with wild hair and thick, dark-rimmed glasses, Lovins first emerged as a national figure in 1975 when he wrote a prophetic article for *Foreign Affairs* magazine outlining a "soft path" toward an energy future that stressed energy efficiency and solar and wind power over further dependence upon coal and oil. Lovins was among the earliest figures who saw coal as the main producer of man-made "greenhouse gases" such as carbon dioxide, which artificially warm up the planet by trapping more of the sun's heat in the atmosphere.

Cavanagh knew that automobiles were also major producers of carbon dioxide—40 percent of California's greenhouse gases came from cars. But he was more than a little worried about Lovins, who was not a scientist or an engineer, but more of a futurist who seemed to veer off into the unknown at times. His credentials were articles and books he had written for Friends of the Earth, a U.S.-based environmental group, but Lovins, Cavanagh knew, had only three weeks to bone up on cars. The Detroit witnesses were going to jump all over him.

"Amory breezed in in his usual way," recalled Cavanagh, "saying we can have hundred-mile-per-gallon cars at competitive costs. He began showing them car designs."

Detroit pounced. Its lawyers cross-examined Lovins, pointing out that he didn't even have a science degree. Lovins calmly cited piles of studies and engineering data, some from their own auto companies showing how cars could be far more efficient. "He [Lovins] has a way of talking about the future as if it was aimed in his direction. It drives people crazy," Cavanagh recalled.

After the automakers' experts had asserted that their companies had already tapped out most of the cost-effective ways to reduce energy efficiency, Lovins brushed their claims aside. "I've heard that before." While their argument might have been right five or ten years ago, he argued, "It's wrong today."

Lovins went into the main advantage of electric motors: they are far more efficient than internal combustion, which converts most of their energy to heat, not motion. He pressed for wider use of tough but light carbon fiber—a material pioneered for jet fighters—and plastics that could bring the weight of vehicles down to below 1,400 pounds. He outlined ways of assembling cars by using prefabricated lightweight body panels that snapped together and that could bring the cost of cars down.

He described what he called "elegantly frugal" ways to build a car by eliminating a lot of hardware that current cars were lugging around and suggested switching to hybrids, cars with small engines that charged batteries.

"Today's car efficiency isn't like a three-hundred-pound man who's lost a hundred and fifty pounds and can't lose much more; it's like a six-hundred-pound man who reduced to four hundred and fifty pounds before gaining much of the modern knowledge of nutrition and exercise that can get him down to one fifty," Lovins went on. "And now that he can get out of his chair and start moving around, the next three hundred pounds will be easier than the first one fifty."

In sum, Lovins said there were many ways some automakers could "tunnel through the cost barrier" that prevented companies from rolling lighter, more efficient cars into their showrooms. There was money to be made, he suggested, and warned that defenders of the status quo had better "hope none of your competitors is faster."

Lovins finished by noting that some of Detroit's own prototypes pointed in the direction he just described. Then he noticed a man sitting in the back row who later cornered him for a chat. He was Don Runkle, GM's vice president of advanced engineering. He led a team of engineers that oversaw the building of concept cars. They had some involvement with Sunraycer and its pending spinoff, the Impact. They were the iconoclasts at GM, known as Runkle's Wild Men.

He invited Lovins to visit GM's secretive skunkworks in Warren, Michigan, where Runkle said there was a car that might interest him. Lovins accepted and became one of the first outsiders to have a chance to closely examine GM's futuristic Ultralite, a four-seat concept built from carbon-fiber panels that snapped together.

It weighed 1,400 pounds, had a top speed of 135 miles per hour, and got a hundred miles per gallon of gasoline. It was designed with a removable engine pod that would allow it to switch to a hybrid-electric engine, but as it was it could accelerate to sixty miles per hour in eight seconds.

"One year we were sort of sitting around having a beer and saying, what would be a good project," Runkle recalled. "I said, let's do a hundred-miles-per-gallon vehicle, now how would you pull that off? I don't want a dumb little car with terrible performance."

GM hired Burt Rutan, the legendary American aerospace engineer and lightweight aircraft designer who had put together Voyager, the first plane to fly around the world without stopping or refueling. He did the engineering and development of the Ultralite's body.

The idea, Runkle said, was to develop a car that "pushed the envelope" for company engineers, and it did. "It was the concept car that I'm most proud of in my long, forty-year career in the industry," Runkle recalled in an interview.

Ultralite was built in a hundred days, but after a brief star turn as a concept car, it drove into history. Although it had what Runkle called a "reasonable chance" at meeting U.S. safety rules, including crash tests, GM's marketers determined it couldn't be sold at a price that buyers would be willing to pay. People wouldn't crowd showrooms to look for energy efficiency or to green the planet.

Runkle, who quickly rose through GM's ranks during the era of muscle cars, has since retired from GM. But he still agrees with that philosophy. "Whenever you try to defy economic gravity it costs," he explained. "You get the green beans and movie stars to fall for these things, but you run through those people pretty quickly and then you're down to people like you and me who ask, 'Does this make sense? I'm not trying to save the world against CO_2.'"

So the Ultralite remained in a storage room at GM until several months later when an action movie producer, Joel Silver, contacted Runkle. He needed a futuristic-looking car for *Demolition Man,* a movie set in 2032, where Sylvester Stallone, a Los Angeles cop, confronts Wesley Snipes, a criminal mastermind. Runkle sent him several truckloads of concept cars and the producer liked the sporty-looking Ultralite with gull wing doors that flipped upward. They made more than twenty plastic shells of its body and put them over Volkswagens for the car chases and traffic scenes in the movie. "Joel is known for blowing things up and invited me out to the filming. I said, Joel, please don't blow the original up. I think we've got about $20 million in that one."

Demolition Man appeared in 1993 and grossed $159 million worldwide. Ultralite returned (intact) to the oblivion of its storage room.

If there was a movie to be made about Lovins, the energy geek, and Runkle, the car guy, it would be a sequel to *The Odd Couple.* "From the Ultralite, Amory and I became very good friends," explained Runkle. "I brought him around GM, but people hated to talk to Amory because he is so provocative."

For Lovins, it was the beginning of a new branch of his many-limbed career as a technology provocateur. He took GM's Ultralite concept and elaborated on it, working with GM and several other automakers around the globe. In his papers and his lectures—which he sometimes delivered to college students wearing a pointy hat made from carbon fiber—his message has been that rather than fear the future, people can change it. The formula for that, Lovins explains, requires "chutzpah and humility, eager enthusiasm and relentless patience."

He went to great lengths to detail the many synergies that can result from light, streamlined, easy-to-assemble bodies and electric-powered motors. His intention was to put them in the public domain and thus remove them from patent-dominated secrecy. He has made repeated visits to automakers and academics in China, England, Japan, and Germany to stoke the fires and suspicions of an increasingly competitive global industry.

Lovins called his way of changing the automobile of the future the Hypercar. As he described it, his mission with Hypercar was to "open up the concept and get a lot of people fighting about it." And so they are. VW, BMW, and Toyota are among those that have since produced concept cars that have a lot of features that embody Lovins's ideas. Most of the world's major automakers have developed business ties with carbon-fiber manufacturers.

As the electric car business slowly matured, Lovins has spun off some for-profit companies from his nonprofit think tank, the Rocky Mountain Institute in Snowmass, Colorado. So far none of them have caught fire or made big money in the auto industry.

"That's not Amory. That's not what he does," explains James Woolsey, a Washington-based consultant and former head of the Central Intelligence Agency who has worked with Lovins on defense-related projects. "He plants ideas, then goes on and plants some more."

Occasionally Lovins still plants some more with Runkle, who has a house in nearby Aspen. Runkle is not sure that carbon-fiber car bodies will ever be competitive with steel, but he still enjoys having dinner with Lovins. "Amory provides the right sort of inspiration; he pokes you in the ribs," says Runkle. "He's been a very helpful pundit of high efficiency. I think he's done a service to his country."

The bottom line for Runkle is that if a car such as the Ultralite or Hypercar ever hits the road, it will require more help from state and federal regulators. "Emissions are something that people can't grasp. You've got to have some regulations on emissions, and industry needs to know a target."

California's rule makers continue to pay close attention to the accelerating technology changes going on within the industry, where "lightweighting" has become a commonly accepted way to meet tougher future federal mileage standards. California delayed their ZEV mandate to allow companies to get more credit for plug-in hybrids, which can run totally on electricity. But in 2012 CARB raised the ante again.

Because of the regulators, Ultralite—either the original gasoline-powered version or an electric—may return for another curtain call. By 2025, 15 percent of the cars sold in the state will have to be pure ZEVs. By 2050, according to Analisa Bevan, chief of CARB's sustainable transportation branch, all cars will have to be ZEVs to meet California's ever-tightening carbon-emissions standards.

The regulation is reviewed every two years. And the input that regulators get will soon change. Back in the 1990s when Ultralite hit the screens, CARB relied pretty much on what auto industry representatives said that the public wanted, Bevan explained. What's changed since then is that tens of thousands of drivers in the state are discovering hybrids and plug-ins. "In the coming two years we plan to ask new car buyers, did you know about EVs? Did you buy one? Why not, and things like that," explained Bevan.

SEVEN

Quest for a Better Battery

The puzzle that California had now placed before the automotive industry and the federal government's scientific establishment began with a dead frog.

In 1786 Luigi Galvani, a professor of anatomy at Bologna, Italy, put a dead frog on a metal plate. He put his scalpel into it, starting to dissect it, when he saw the frog's leg twitch. What did that? Like many scientists of his day, Galvani had experimented with static electricity, but he had provoked this reaction with just a knife, a frog, and a plate. He decided that the muscle in the frog's leg had electricity stored in it, which was released when he completed a circuit between the frog, the scalpel, and the plate.

Galvani was the first of a long line of experimenters with stored electricity, a line that extends up to the present day. They shared one attribute in common: when it came to explaining this strange phenomena, they were frequently wrong.

It was not long before Alessandro Volta, a minor Italian aristocrat and amateur physicist, found Galvani's error. Influenced by

Benjamin Franklin's methodological curiosity, Volta restudied various parts of Galvani's experiment and concluded it wasn't the muscle, it was an electrical charge that had moved between two dissimilar metals.

He began exploring different pairings of metals and found silver and zinc provoked the strongest reaction. So he assembled a stack starting with a silver coin, a piece of wet cardboard, and a piece of zinc, and repeating the process until he had an assembly that produced an electric jolt. In his time it was known as a Voltaic Pile. We think of it today as the first storage battery, a moving stream of electrons conducted between dissimilar metals, one serving as the anode, the other the cathode. The wet cardboard was the conduit, or what scientists came to call the electrolyte.

The result electrified Volta's career. He toured Europe performing what amounted to electrical parlor tricks. He made ghostly lights appear with him onstage. He pressed a switch that ignited a pile of gunpowder before the astonished eyes of Napoleon, who promptly made Volta a count. The clamor for more electricity tricks was so strong that it left no time for scientific study of the electrochemical process that Volta had harnessed, explains Henry Schlesinger, who tells this story in his book *The Battery*. The reason for the lingering mysteries surrounding the battery is that people were too busy exploiting it: "The fact that it worked was enough."

The lack of a scientific establishment, reigning theories, or accepted procedures, though, left the field wide open to amateurs. Many of them were self-educated technological adventurers who were bright and intrepid enough to go where this shadowy trail led them.

In the early nineteenth century, Humphry Davy, son of a failed Cornwall farmer, used the Voltaic Pile to achieve electrolysis, producing enough of a charge to separate water into its constituent elements, hydrogen and oxygen. While electrifying more complicated compounds, Davy released and identified pure lithium, a light, highly reactive metal that seemed to have no earthly value at the time.

In the 1820s, Michael Faraday, the son of a blacksmith, found his first employment as a bookbinder. He used his spare time to experiment with the battery and eventually set up a magnetic field in which a wire could be made to rotate. He had invented a simple electric motor.

Fame followed. When William Gladstone, a future English prime minister, asked Faraday what his discovery might be used for, Faraday was said to have responded grumpily: "I have no idea, but no doubt you'll find some way to tax it."

In 1831 Faraday went on to discover the principle behind the electrical generator. Later that decade a self-taught American inventor, Joseph Henry, used a powerful version of Volta's battery to develop the first big electromagnets.

And finally, in the middle of the nineteenth century French engineer Gaston Planté took the time—thirty years—to reflect upon this odd technological trail. He finally developed the first practical, rechargeable, lead-acid storage battery using, among other things, pieces of his wife's petticoat.

It was elaborations of this battery that powered the first generation of electric cars, and it is a simplified, lighter, more efficient successor of this battery that electrifies most automobiles today. The man who succeeded in freezing this technology for better than a century was another inventor: Charles F. Kettering, a former school teacher with poor eyesight.

He became an electrical engineer and invented the electric ignition system that eliminated the treacherous hand crank needed to turn over the engines of gasoline-powered cars. When that was introduced in Cadillacs in 1912, the market for gasoline-powered cars began to explode.

Thomas Edison, another in the long line of self-educated battery makers, once thought storage batteries were a fraud used by stock swindlers. But in his later years, in the first decade of the twentieth century, he began tinkering with them, encouraged and financed by his former employee and friend Henry Ford.

He was among the first to appreciate how little was understood about the way they worked and awed by the many variations that were possible. When he was ribbed by friends for his many failed battery experiments, Edison reportedly responded: "No, I didn't fail. I discovered 24,999 ways that the storage battery does not work."

He finally perfected the alkaline battery, which had multiple uses, but the work of Kettering and Henry Ford's cheap, useful Model T made the possibility of using them to power electric cars moot. Electrics had all but vanished from America's roads by 1920.

In the post-Kettering era, all that was needed was a simple battery with enough charge to turn over a cold gasoline engine and power the lights. For his reward, Kettering became the vice president of General Motors Research Corporation in 1920, setting the course for the company's engineering for twenty-seven years.

Ted J. Miller, a senior manager for battery research at Ford Motor, explains that for decades making car batteries became a humdrum business. Big battery makers bought out the little ones. "Nobody cared how it worked or how to make it any better. It was sort of making profits by the half cent kind of thing . . . putting anything into R and D was a waste of time."

In the 1980s Ford's executives began to push its suppliers for better batteries. The more they began thinking about future electric cars, the more they realized that these could not be simple, state-of-the-art batteries. Because they were the heart of an electric vehicle, batteries would have to be dependable for the lifetime of the car. That was a tall order.

"Because the battery is an electrochemical-thermal device with all these things wrapped up into one, it's not a simple system," said Miller, who explains there are multiple reactions going on simultaneously. "I think the challenge is still, in general, how and why do these things deteriorate."

While there had been frequent demands from the U.S. military for better batteries, the U.S. automobile industry had not formally sought help from the Department of Energy laboratories that did the research until 1990, when General Motors began to make the rounds in Washington. It had an electric vehicle, the Impact, in the works but the bulk and heft of conventional lead-acid batteries made it too heavy, made its range between charging embarrassingly short, and took up too much room. GM had nothing in its pipeline or in its elaborate network of suppliers to fill the bill.

Ford had been experimenting with sodium-sulfur batteries that were three times more powerful than lead-acid batteries, but expecting them to last for the lifetime of the car seemed like magical thinking. They had an annoying tendency to catch fire in the laboratories. Chrysler, which was trying to convert a minivan to run on nickel-cadmium batteries, was well behind GM and Ford in its research.

The idea that the Big Three might not be able to stop California's Zero Emission Vehicle mandate from kicking in for 1998 model cars had begun to sink in. So they joined in a plea to the first Bush administration for help. The White House responded favorably and in January 1991, the U.S. Advanced Battery Consortium (USABC) was formed to develop a better battery by the late 1990s. DOE, its laboratories, and the Electric Power Research Institute, which represented the electric utility industry, were also part of the consortium.

The research arm of the National Academies of Science, which reviewed the consortium's progress five years later, paid witness to the fact that the carmakers' battery research cupboards were bare. And, despite billions spent on nuclear weapons research and the space program, the United States had very little mass-produceable hardware at hand to help them. "Technology capable of meeting the [California] mandate did not exist when the USABC was founded and there was no obvious path to it. The USABC's experience has confirmed that there are major technical difficulties and challenges in developing batteries for EVs."

The start of the consortium was not auspicious. On October 25, 1991, the three automakers met at the White House where a prototype Impact, a battery-powered Ford Ecostar van, and a Chrysler minivan were on display. After picking a car by drawing lots, President George H. W. Bush jumped in the minivan, turned the key, and nothing happened. (Chrysler's mechanics later got it to start.)

Things tended to go downhill from there. Ford and Chrysler, worried that GM had too great a lead on electric car technology, tended to favor delays in making decisions, beginning with a fight over who would be named chairman. Some elements of GM agreed, worried that any breakthrough in car battery technology would be interpreted to show that California's standard could be met.

There was research money to be spent. The United States put in $130 million and the automakers contributed the same, but a lot of it remained unspent because there were long wrangles over whom to give it to. Finally the members of USABC agreed to give an $18 million contract to Energy Conversion Devices, a company that was clearly a dark horse among the more obvious candidates.

But its founder, Stanford R. Ovshinsky, had the right credentials to fit in in the long, eccentric tradition of successful battery experts. He was the son of an Akron, Ohio, junk dealer and most of his post–high school education came from reading books in Akron's public libraries when he wasn't working in a local machine shop.

A confident, thin, nattily dressed man who died in 2012 at the age of eighty-nine, Ovshinsky liked to flaunt his lack of scientific credentials. "I learned on my own and at my own pace, faster than I could get it in school." In the evenings he would pack a load of books to take home. "They [the libraries] were very strict. The rule was you could only take out two books, but they let me take out any book on any subject and as many as I liked."

In 1960 he and his wife, Iris, who had a doctorate in biochemistry from Boston University, set up their corporation in a Detroit storefront. They wanted to exploit the potential of what scientists call "amorphous materials," little-studied alloys made out of elements such as cesium, tellurium, and germanium. These are metals that don't have the ordered crystalline structure of most metals. While scientists regarded them as too messy, they seemed to the Ovshinskys to have enormous potential for batteries and solar power.

Ovshinsky, who helped his family survive the Depression by doing odd jobs, had watched the U.S. economy revive. "I felt America was a can-do country," he explained in a 2006 interview. "We felt new technology was essential. We wanted to start new industries and solve serious societal problems."

What was remarkable about the Ovshinskys was that their joint effort often backed up their proposals with impressive and commercial results. Their thin film photovoltaic arrays, which produced solar-generated electricity more cheaply than others, impressed Larry Kazmerski, who managed the solar energy program for DOE's Renewable Energy Laboratory. "When you bought Ovshinsky, you got two Ovshinskys," explained Kazmerski, who was among those who were impressed by how Iris helped organize her husband's scientific papers and sometimes even finished his sentences.

And their contender in the battery business, the nickel-metal hydride battery, impressed GM, Ford, and Chrysler because it was a true breakthrough. Bench tests showed it could give an electric vehicle virtually double the range of a conventional lead-acid battery. The batteries were also relatively cheap, including materials from recycled scrap.

The Ovshinskys were courted by many corporate CEOs and signed partnership agreements with Atlantic Richfield, Standard Oil of Ohio, BP, and the U.S. subsidiary of Canon, the Japanese camera and copy machine maker. But no CEO was more taken by them than GM's Robert Stempel, who saw their powerful battery as the solution to the Impact's problems.

Stan Ovshinsky, in turn, was eager to find someone who could quickly get his batteries into the Impact for testing because he suspected that, as a group, Detroit's Big Three would prefer not to have a breakthrough that made them more vulnerable to California's ZEV rules. But 1992 turned out to be a bad year for Stemple to make deals. The previous year GM posted $3 billion in losses and had to cut 74,000 jobs. Six of the auto giant's thirty-three assembly plants were shut down and Stemple was replaced as head of GM's executive committee by John Smale, a former CEO of Procter & Gamble.

It was the year when the first hand-built prototype Impact was completed, but in October the management committee decided the Impact cost too much. Over Stemple's objections, the group voted to delay production for two years. Shortly after that, Stemple and other high-level backers of America's first new electric car in almost seventy years resigned.

In early 1993 GM began informal negotiations with Chrysler and Ford and the newly arrived Clinton administration in Washington to see if there might be joint support for a "Team America" approach, a government-industry consortium that would jointly produce an electric car.

EIGHT

Supercar

There were moments in their meandering race to develop the electric car where Detroit automakers might have felt certain that they were being haunted by what they considered to be ghosts of their technological past. A lot of them came during the Clinton-Gore administration, which began its efforts with a rhetorical flourish from the White House on September 29, 1993. Led by Vice President Al Gore, the new administration had brokered a deal with GM, Ford, and Chrysler to work together with U.S. government agencies and laboratories to develop a five-passenger sedan that could get eighty miles per gallon, tripling the mileage of most family cars of the era.

The new vehicle would be called Supercar. There were elements of GM's Sunraycer in it: it would be lightweight and have close to zero emissions. There were also fingerprints of Amory Lovins's Hypercar on the concept because it was aimed at revolutionizing the fat, middle, gas-guzzling segment of the car market. The theory was that carmakers and government scientists and engineers would jointly explore new materials, motors, and batteries that could drive a reliable, cleaner, affordable family car into the showrooms within ten years.

It was a new world of acronyms that seemed repugnant to old-time "car guys." The leverage that had pushed Detroit into the Partnership for a New Generation of Vehicles (PNGV) came from the Corporate Average Fuel Economy Standard (CAFE), a federal regulation approved by Congress in 1975 in reaction to the long gasoline lines and chaos brought about by the 1973 Arab oil embargo.

The United States and Canada had the lowest efficiency standards for automobiles among the world's developed countries, and the regulation, which applied to passenger cars and light trucks, was intended to raise them. In his campaign for the presidency, Clinton proposed that it should be raised from the scheduled 27.5 miles per gallon by 2000 to forty miles per gallon.

Gore had made reducing global warming emissions a major issue in his Senate career. He had the temerity to call for the elimination of the internal combustion engine in twenty-five years in his book *Earth in the Balance,* published in 1992. His deal with the automakers would delay the proposed tougher efficiency rules if they agreed to tackle the auto emissions problem head-on.

The PNGV rules called on the automakers to decide on appropriate technologies for the Supercar by 1998, implement them in at least one concept car by 2000, and prepare one or more cars for production by 2004. As an additional sweetener, taxpayers would contribute $170 million a year to the program if the industry matched it. The government money was appealing because it would also help the industry deal with another tightening regulatory noose, California's zero-emission standard.

Initially GM and Ford had rejected the idea, but when Chrysler expressed interest in the Supercar, the industry's hopes for solid opposition had crumbled. The CEOs of the Big Three had come to the White House for the late September meeting to hear President

Clinton compare their new partnership to the Apollo moon shot and Star Wars. America had pulled together to meet serious challenges before and here was a great opportunity to do it again.

Not long after the ceremony, Toyota, the biggest of Japan's Big Four automakers, applied to join PNGV, but the Clinton administration rejected the idea. Japan's more efficient cars were taking an increasing bite out of the American car market. One of the political selling points for the Supercar in Washington was that it was intended to improve the competitive stance of American car companies.

There was probably no one more interested in the progress of the Supercar in Washington, D.C., than Charles Gray Jr., a chemical engineer who directed the U.S. Environmental Protection Agency's advanced vehicle technology program. It was EPA's job to test whether a given car complied with CAFE rules and Gray, a seemingly folksy scientist who grew up in Fountain Hill, Arkansas (population 175), played a major role in developing the process.

Gray was used to running against the grain. Back in the 1960s, when most teenagers were trying to get more speed out of used cars, Gray was tinkering with engines in his backyard to see how they might go farther on a gallon of gasoline. It had become a lifelong passion and when he joined EPA in 1970, he found its laboratory in Ann Arbor, Michigan, to be the perfect place to pursue it.

EPA had started what amounted to a small skunkworks of technicians at the lab to work on ways to improve automobile efficiency and Gray soon became the leader. One of his first ideas was a car driven by a hybrid electric-gasoline power system, but his team was pulled away from that to work on how to remove the lead from gasoline.

In the late 1980s Gray was back experimenting with another hybrid that would use a small alcohol-fueled engine coupled with a system that captured the energy wasted in braking a car to compress nitrogen in a steel cylinder. Then, when the driver wanted to accelerate, the nitrogen would be released, adding its turning power to the engine's.

Gray was certain that Detroit would eventually turn to hybrids and EPA supported his efforts. "We never wanted to be a hobby shop, working on things that nobody wanted," Gray explained to the *Wall Street Journal*.

During the late 1980s he found support in the White House where C. Boyden Gray, legal counsel to President George H. W. Bush, wanted to know what the possibilities were for more fuel-efficient vehicles. After studying the weight and the inefficiency of family cars, Charles Gray (no relation) concluded that it might be possible to triple their mileage with a hybrid-powered drive system.

He had briefing books already prepared for the concepts because he hoped his laboratory would get enough federal funds to build such a car and when the Clinton administration arrived in 1993, he found fertile ground for his idea. But Charles Gray had watched the U.S. battery consortium closely and knew that, left to themselves, the automakers would be jockeying for corporate advantage, trying to hold back their best technology and stalling the moves of their competitors. He also worried that the Japanese might try to leapfrog their American competitors by developing Supercars of their own. So he continued to refine his idea for a hybrid even after the Supercar was launched. As far as Gray was concerned, a fourth Supercar candidate would prod the other three along. This was no time for delays.

It soon turned out that his first hunch was correct. A cautious game of show-and-tell had begun among the Big Three on January 13, 1993, when GM invited Ford and Chrysler to its laboratories to view a prototype Impact and meet the team that had developed it. Ford and Chrysler reciprocated within a few weeks. But during the first year of the PNGV deal the automakers abandoned the collaborative approach, with each intending to design a Supercar of their own.

Ford had held back a more sophisticated version of its Ecostar Van. GM continued to roll out its handmade, prototype Impacts, each costing roughly $340,000 including parts and labor. Meanwhile one ghost from the past, Stan Ovshinsky, had begun to make headway in his campaign to test one of his nickel-metal hydride batteries in an Impact.

He'd hired GM's former president Bob Stempel as a consultant. Jon Bereisa, GM's architect of the Impact's drive system, agreed to the experiment and conducted some tests at GM's secrecy-shrouded proving grounds near Mesa, Arizona. Ovshinsky's batteries proved to be durable and could more than double the seventy-to-ninety-mile average range of the Impact, which could drop down to less than fifty miles between charges in cold weather.

In March 1994, GM's board tentatively agreed to revive the Impact, but this time they resolved to keep the renewed effort secret. The strategy was to dash within eighteen months to production of the Impact; to try and recover the half-billion dollars or so the company had invested in it; and to retain their lead in electric cars by blindsiding their competitors, both in the United States and in Japan.

Ovshinsky made a $25 million deal to provide batteries to the Impact and continued to tout the advantages of nickel-metal hydride batteries by letting California's Air Resources Board test one. Then he sued three Japanese battery manufacturers for infringing upon his patent. They capitulated and agreed to buy licenses to manufacture the batteries.

By 1994 engineers from the Big Three were making some headway with weekly meetings in Detroit, discussing the best technologies they might use to reach eighty miles per gallon, but there continued to be distractions and surprises. One distraction was another ghost from the past, Alan Cocconi, the reclusive genius who had put together the original Impact electric drive system. He turned up in Detroit in a four-passenger Honda Civic that he'd converted to electric drive. It had a range of 118 miles.

But there was more to it than that. Tom Gage, an electrical engineer who had worked with Chrysler and consulted with Honda in California on electric cars, still recalls his initial meeting with Cocconi, who promptly invited him to drive the converted Civic. Gage hopped in, took it to a freeway, and pressed the accelerator. When he looked at the dashboard, he was shocked to realize he was doing eighty miles per hour!

Cocconi, sitting in the passenger seat, then instructed Gage to drive to an empty parking lot. "He said, stop here. Now flip that switch and floor it. I did. The front tires erupted in smoke. The torque was so massive we did a huge burnout. . . . That really changed my outlook on EVs!"

Gage liked the competitive aspects of the little Civic, which could put most Detroit muscle cars to shame, and of Cocconi, who was determined to find a financial backer for his latest creation. Gage, who decided to accompany Cocconi on the visit to Detroit, recalled that the car really had unlimited range because it towed a small gasoline-powered generator that amounted to a range extender.

Cocconi had already tested it by driving it cross-country on pure electricity to Washington to meet with the government officials running the PNGV program. "They wanted a car that got eighty miles per gallon, so Alan says to them, well, this car already does it because the more you plug it in the less gas you use," Gage explained. But Washington didn't seem interested. So Cocconi drove the Honda to Detroit where he and Gage showed the converted Honda to the PNGV teams working there.

"We made the rounds of Ford, Chrysler, and GM, and it was not a hostile greeting, but you know it was far from embracing what we were doing at the time," Gage recalled.

So he and Cocconi drove the electrified Honda back to California, where they began raising money to expand the business of AC Propulsion, a San Dimas, California, company Cocconi had started. The intention was to exploit the market for converted electric vehicles.

One of the ways Cocconi raised money was by selling the converted Honda Civic back to Honda for $40,000. Soon, other carmakers, including Volkswagen and BMW, began making the trip to San Dimas, on the outskirts of Los Angeles. They wanted copies of the electric drive system he'd used for the Honda. "Many carmakers bought one or two samples from us and that was a way for us to survive, to sell relatively expensive prototypes," Cocconi explained.

A year later, the PNGV teams were jolted by a big surprise. Toyota introduced a new concept car at the Tokyo Auto Show on October 27, 1995. It was a four-door sedan, a hybrid electric-gasoline powered car that Japan's leading carmaker had decided to call Prius, a Latin word probably intended to send Detroit a message. It translated to "go before." Toyota claimed it could get seventy miles per gallon.

Ted J. Miller, senior manager of Ford's energy storage program, had just started working in Ford's electric-vehicle program. He recalls the announcement as a stunner. "It had a surprising effect; suddenly all the things we had done in research, Toyota was putting into production. It was more like whoops! And honestly the auto industry and in particular Ford says, 'Oh, my God, we'd better get busy. This isn't [just] research anymore.'"

The following year, in January 1996, GM announced its surprise at the Los Angeles Auto Show. One of the hand-built Impact prototypes rolled out onstage. The car had been renamed EV1. Jack Smith, GM's CEO, said it was ready for production by the following September and would be the first electric car to emerge in modern times. "This is not a concept car. This is not a conversion," he emphasized. "It is a car for people who never want to go to the gas station again." The selling price would be around $35,000.

The surprises, particularly the Prius announcement, did not sit well with Charles Gray, the head of EPA's advanced vehicle laboratory. By this time he had obtained enough money from the PNGV program to redesign his hydraulic drive Supercar. The bulky nitrogen storage tanks were shrunk and taken out of the car's backseat.

He switched to a relatively clean-burning diesel engine and began giving auto company engineers tours in the laboratory parking lot. It still looked mostly like a dune buggy, but it had power and durability. Best of all, it did not need a big heavy battery to store its energy.

Gray eventually got what he had worked so hard for, a contract with Ford to split costs and help develop his hydraulic hybrid. Because Gray was part of the PNGV program and the agency held a number of patents on his Supercar, some industry experts found the arrangement distasteful, but there were no formal complaints.

Finally in January 2000, PNGV announced its own surprise. All three automakers rolled out more or less the same technology, diesel-powered electric hybrids, as their chosen prototypes for the Supercar. There was the GM Precept (which got eigthty miles per gallon), the Ford Prodigy (seventy-two miles per gallon), and Daimler Chrysler's ESX3 (seventy-two miles per gallon). Vice President Gore appeared at the unveiling, examining the cars. "This is truly a mountaintop moment for America," he announced.

It turned out to be a tiny mountain, though, because the reception to these diesel-powered cars was cool. Environmental groups didn't like diesels because they were dirty, although one of PNGV's successes had been to make them cleaner, according to the National Research Council.

A much more serious problem was that the auto industry felt the cars would be too expensive to produce. The following year

Detroit pressured the incoming George W. Bush administration to cancel PNGV. So the final and crucial step of the Gore-Clinton program—selecting an eighty-miles-per-gallon car for mass production—never happened.

Instead the second Bush administration overhauled the program. It would now be called FreedomCar and it would concentrate on an electric car that produced power from fuel cells. There was no deadline for production and Detroit breathed a sigh of relief. (Production model fuel cell–driven cars didn't arrive until 2014. The first arrivals were made in Japan.)

So the first three prototype Supercars went back to their storerooms. But all was not lost: the fourth prototype, Gray's hydraulic hybrid, was still on track, thanks to Ford's interest and financial help. Ford announced it would use the EPA technology to improve the fuel economy of light-duty trucks and sport-utility vehicles. Ford and EPA engineers developed a hydraulic hybrid Ford Expedition, a big SUV that got more than twenty-seven miles per gallon in city driving. But in 2004 Ford withdrew, opting instead for a licensing agreement with Toyota that allowed it to build hybrid-electric vehicles.

"We definitely think hydraulic hybrid has merit," explained Nick Twork, a technology spokesman for Ford. "We just decided that it wasn't going to be on the top of our list." He called it a financial decision that was most easily resolved by exchanging patent licenses with Toyota. Toyota got to use Ford's patents to make catalytic converters. Ford was able to use the electric drive system pioneered in the Prius.

After nine years of relentless pushing for an American Supercar, Charles Gray and the other government scientists who worked on the program were dejected. "You can't imagine the grieving we did when Ford left," Mr. Gray recalls. "We were that close to production."

Still, there was some interest. United Parcel Service formed an alliance with a heavy-duty truck manufacturer, Daimler Trucks North America, and Parker Hannifin, a maker of control technologies, to design and produce a hydraulic hybrid transmission system for the big brown UPS parcel delivery trucks. In October 2012, UPS began testing forty of them on delivery routes in Baltimore and Atlanta. According to the company the trucks, which do an enormous amount of stop-and-start driving, can reduce fuel use by 35 percent and cut carbon dioxide emissions by 30 percent.

Mr. Gray, ever the optimist, thinks his invention—the last vestige of the Supercar—will still, someday, find its way into the family car. "There is a good chance of that happening if people look at the UPS truck sitting next to them at a stoplight and realize that it's getting better mileage than some of the vehicles they're driving."

NINE

Crash Program

The Toyota Prius concept car that was shown at the October 27, 1995, auto show was a fraud. It is a tradition in both the United States and Japan to roll out futuristic cars surrounded by advertising hoopla and press releases loaded with puffery, but Prius was a journey into the unknown.

In the place where the gasoline-electric hybrid's largest power source—the battery—was supposed to be was an electric condenser, a piece of hardware that had no business being there except that it might make people think it was the car's exotic battery, which was still under development.

The following month, when a version of the battery was installed and the first prototype was rolled out for testing, technicians for the handpicked team working on the car couldn't get it to start. It remained stone dead for forty-nine days, according to Takeshi Uchiyamada, the head of the development team. "And then it only went for five hundred meters [547 yards]," he explained, before it broke down again. "We didn't know which system was wrong.

"What we finally produced was a completely different concept from the auto show prototype," added Uchiyamada, referring to the Prius that Toyota later unveiled to the world in late 1997.

In a way, the Prius project was also a fraud on Uchiyamada and the ever-expanding elite team of Toyota managers, engineers, and technicians who were thrown into the effort by top management. The first deadline for production of the radically different, fuel-abstemious car was vague, somewhere around the year 2000, then later he and his other team members were told it was to be 1998. Still later, under a management directive calling on department heads to "instill a mood of crisis," the deadline was pushed up to late 1997.

"Some of this wasn't fun," Uchiyamada, sixty-nine, admitted in a recent interview. But the fact that he met the deadline and produced the best-selling hybrid in the first decade of the twenty-first century has something to do with the fact that he later became chairman of Toyota, which overtook GM as the globe's largest automaker in 2007.

The history of Toyota and electric cars goes back to Sakichi Toyoda, founder of Toyota Industries. Because Japan had no oil, but plenty of hydroelectric dams, he set up a research laboratory to work on batteries for electric locomotives. His son Kiichiro Toyoda later set up a new research facility to make batteries for automobiles.

In the 1960s, after the company rose from the rubble of World War II, work on an electric car resumed, but accelerated after the 1973 Arab oil embargo when the country imposed its own version of the U.S. Clean Air Act and set the toughest tailpipe emissions standards in the world.

Toyota's electric car development effort became a crash program in 1993, the same year the Clinton-Gore administration and U.S. automakers announced the PNGV program, a national effort to produce an eighty-miles-per-gallon passenger car. A Toyota vice president, Yoshiro Kimbara, called for a G21 project, which was intended to set up the architecture for a smaller, more fuel-efficient car for the twenty-first century.

Uchiyamada, a slender, soft-spoken man who had a reputation as being something of a dreamer, was picked to lead the effort. His father had once been chief engineer for the company and Uchiyamada, whose education had been in applied physics, did not want to be shunted into a specialty. His ambition was to work on something that oversaw the development of an entire car.

Older people in the company suggested that research on vibration, ways to make cars quieter and give them a more solid feel, would be the route to go. After leading a research team to the United States to study its bigger, faster, quieter cars, Uchiyamada was picked to head the team for the secretive G21 project.

At first the company assigned them to a red-carpeted room at Toyota headquarters and gave them carte blanche. There was no corporate scheme for the structure of the car, except that the company wanted original research, nothing copied from existing cars, and whatever resulted had to get 50 percent better gasoline mileage than the company's fast-rising Corolla brand.

It was known at Toyota that the American PNGV program, which Toyota was told it could not enter, might be focusing on a hybrid-electric vehicle. Uchiyamada had already looked at the idea and rejected it. He decided the batteries that would give the car an acceptable range weren't available and that a hybrid would be too expensive.

His team went ahead to work on a prototype for a gasoline-powered, four-seat economy car that would improve mileage by 50 percent, but in November 1994, this project had a premature death. The overseer of the G21 project, vice president Akihiro Wada, rejected it, pointing out that the company had decided to give a preview of the G21 car at the 1995 Tokyo Auto Show.

"I don't want to build just another economy car. We have to rethink development and if that means building a hybrid car that gets twice the fuel efficiency of any other car out there and exhibiting it at the Motor Show, that's what we'll do," Wada told him.

Uchiyamada was shocked. He had developed an elaborate argument why a hybrid wouldn't work. He trotted out another reason. Toyota's engineers told him the hardware for both a battery-powered and an electric car could not be crammed into a body the size of the Corolla. Prius had to be a bigger car. Wada swatted that down, too. It had to remain a small car.

Uchiyamada's team had no experience with hybrids and now they had a year to put together a concept for one. The 50 percent better gas mileage rule was also part of the rubble of his earlier scheme. Now it had to be double, or 200 percent.

According to one account, that was when Uchiyamada lost his celebrated cool.

"But that's outrageous!" he told Wada.

"Then come up with another system that won't be outrageous," Wada replied.

"It is too risky," Uchiyamada replied.

Then Wada told him if he couldn't do a hybrid, the G21 project would be disbanded.

Having the gears of his project shifted on him in the early days of the Prius "was major pressure, the most intense I had ever experienced," Uchiyamada recalled much later.

Uchiyamada said he was never told why management had become fixated on hybrids. David Hermance, executive engineer for Toyota's advanced technology center in California, later shed some light on it in 2006. He told a *Wall Street Journal* reporter: "It would probably be accurate to say we reviewed PNGV goals and considered them in our [Prius] development process."

Studies showed that there were eighty different possibilities to combine a gasoline engine and an electric drive system. The G21 team decided that the ideal combination would be arranged in what was known as a parallel system that offered the possibilities of combining the best attributes of both systems.

Gasoline engines had a point where they hit peak efficiency, a sweet spot. Electric motors had the ability to develop instant acceleration. In a parallel system both motors power the wheels, backing each other up depending on driving conditions and upon which combination achieved the most efficiency and what the driver wanted.

The stunning number of possible options posed an enormous control problem and the answers, like almost every other solution the G21 team came up with, involved computers and software. The car's onboard computers would figure out which system should be doing what.

Uchiyamada's team came up with four possible engine-motor drive systems. Since they didn't have the time to prototype each one, it had to be a virtual competition. They simulated them on an elaborate software program obtained from a U.S. company.

The simulations worked just fine, but in November 1995, when it came time to road test the first prototype, the car refused to move. Two months of anguish followed.

"We had more than nine computers on the car talking to each other," explained Uchiyamada. But they used different software protocols, so the electronic conversation that worked on the simulators wasn't really going on between the controls, the gasoline engine, the two electric motors, and the inverter. Prius remained brain-dead.

On the forty-ninth day of testing, technicians got the Prius to start and it went for about a city block before conking out. Part of this was attributed to battery problems. The Japanese were determined to use Stan Ovshinsky's nickel-metal hydride battery, but it was producing only 50 percent of its advertised power.

Here was another headache. Toyota, like U.S. automakers, had decided that the battery should last the lifetime of the car. They were working with Panasonic to make the battery perform better and longer.

Around this time Totota's newly installed president Hiroshi Okuda told Vice President Wada that he wanted the car to arrive a year earlier, by the end of 1997. The chairman of Toyota, Shichiro Toyoda, felt it had to arrive early. Otherwise "We will miss becoming the first company to launch a hybrid vehicle. Toyota has been second too long."

Okuda threw more resources at the project, opening up a hybrid prototype production line for engineers to experiment upon for twenty-four hours a day. There were more times when Uchiyamada felt overwhelmed, the company was giving him no room for running into a technological impossibility, and he was looking at the possibility of several of them.

He found himself thinking about impossible deadlines and how some teams, such as the one that directed the U.S. Apollo moon launch, had found the grit and the grace to overcome them. Then he stumbled upon a version closer to home: a crash program near the end of World War II to develop a rocket-powered fighter that could launch quickly enough to intercept and destroy American B-29 bombers that were incinerating Japanese cities.

Given the assignment, Mitsubishi, the designer of one of the best fighter planes of the war, the famed Zero, assembled a far-flung team that produced five of the so-called Shusui or Ki-100 fighters in the six months before the war ended. Uchiyamada found himself studying the team's logbook and realized that leaders of other projects with seemingly impossible goals and unmeetable deadlines had stood in his shoes before. The conclusion he drew from all of this was: "You can achieve the impossible when you really have to."

Uchiyamada developed ways that could focus more of Toyota's brainpower on the clusters of problems facing the Prius. He launched a contest for the vehicle's final design, which was won by Irwin Liu of Toyota's California design team in Newport Beach.

He found the battery engineers on his team were deeply demoralized because battery failures often fouled up more elaborate tests. Members of other teams were claiming the battery team didn't know what it was doing. Battery experts replied that there were at least a hundred years of experimentation behind the gasoline engine, but the nickel-metal hydride battery's operations were "based on chemical reactions, many aspects of which were still unknown."

Technicians from Uchiyamada's team hooked up the battery specialists to the company's fledgling intranet. This allowed the testers to describe the symptoms of the failures they were plagued with to thousands of engineers at the company. Some solutions came back instantly, but more important, criticisms of the battery team stopped. The other departments now had a sense that these problems weren't simple.

But the train of problems and failures with the car seemed endless. Toyota began making more of the car's electronic components itself, by downsizing the power train that had been used earlier to electrify a version of the company's smallest SUV, the RAV4.

Feeling the pinch of the deadline, young engineers on the team (which consisted of mostly young engineers) began pulling all-nighters to resolve their problems. Uchiyamada began to show up at night. One engineer pleaded with him to go home. "Mr. Chief Engineer, you are distracting us by appearing so late at night. We will let you know the results in the morning. Please leave us alone."

At the core of the inverter unit, which switches the battery's direct current into alternating current for the electric motors, Toyota's engineers had decided to use exotic transistors, called IGBTs, which had first been used for Japan's bullet train. They were critical components, each car relied on one, so Toyota decided it had to make them.

When prototype modules were assembled for bench tests, the engineers found that a small surge in electric power caused them to explode. As one author of the Prius history put it, they were both methodical and dramatic. "Every time they thought they had the problem figured out, the module would break and explode like a firework, with light bright enough for a photo shoot. For a while every staff member was dumbfounded as similar failures occurred more than ten times in a row."

After months of nightly fireworks, Toyota engineers decided that the original Japanese version of the chip had been made incorrectly. They ordered special transistor-making equipment from Orthodyne Electronics, then a privately held company in Irvine, California. The Toyota people had difficulty identifying the machinery they needed because under the strict secrecy that enveloped the Prius, they were not allowed to explain why they wanted it.

Still, batteries continued to be the root of most of the dramas. Ovshinsky's batteries had been fine for the RAV4, but Toyota had to find a way to shrink them by 90 percent to make the Prius work. It began working with Matsushita Electric to make a downsized version, which could weigh no more than one hundred pounds.

In the summer of 1997, as the deadline for production grew nearer, technicians found the new battery had a chronic tendency to overheat. In the United States, Vice President Al Gore used to talk proudly about "mountaintop moments" in the progress of the Department of Energy's Supercar. Meanwhile, Toyota's engineers were having one of their own. For them it was more of a desperate struggle to save face. After the head of the Prius hardware team, a young engineer named Satoshi Ogiso, was stranded in a test Prius on top of a mountain, technicians were ordered to figure out why the car's finicky battery still failed.

They were busy readjusting the three cooling systems needed for the Prius: one for the air conditioner, one for the gasoline motor, and one for the battery and other electronics, which included the inverter and the two electric motors.

That was when Toyota's president, Mr. Okuda, arrived. It was one of the warmest days in the summer and he wanted to drive the prototype that the company's reputation would soon be riding on. A technician told a manager to steer him away. "You shouldn't drive the car in this condition."

"How can I tell him that?" said the manager. "Just let him take it."

Later Okuda sat grinning behind the wheel of the prototype. It had worked perfectly. He told the apprehensive manager who had escorted him: "Fujii-kun, one day everyone will be driving a car like this. You people are working on a great mission." Mass production of the Prius began in September 1996 at one thousand units a month.

A marketing team was working to develop a sales rationale for the Prius in Japan. They settled on global warming. In the 1990s transportation generated about 20 percent of the greenhouse gases flowing into the atmosphere. In the next century the percentage would begin to soar as China and other developing countries built their own car markets. Meanwhile fossil fuels were being used up. That meant the old ways of making cars had to change. Prius, the first modern hybrid car, would help point the way. That message would sell in Japan according to the marketing team.

More exhaustive testing in the late summer and fall of 1997 included pushing the prototypes for seven days of nonstop, 24-7 driving. After this testing, the company felt that Prius, the reluctant debutante—mentored by nine interdependent computers—had acquired the skills and the staying power needed for its introduction to the world.

The debut came on an October evening in the ballroom of the posh ANA Hotel in Tokyo's upscale Roppongi district. The first Prius with Uchiyamada at the wheel, Wada in the passenger seat, and Okuda, a six-footer showing off the spaciousness of the car's backseat, appeared. The car, in electric drive mode, rolled over the posh carpet and then stopped before the waiting battery of television cameras.

There was no sound. There were no carbon dioxide emissions, either, unless there was a way to measure the sudden exhalation of the thousand or so Toyota employees who had beaten into submission some of the most beastly engineering problems in modern automotive history. Their Prius was launched.

TEN

Doing Less with More

In early 1997, Chris Paine, the owner of a start-up Internet company in southern California, walked into a Saturn dealership in the San Fernando Valley and signed an agreement that changed his life.

He was looking for a second car and what he really wanted was GM's newly launched all-electric car, which had been rebranded as the EV1. The son of an engineer, Paine had followed the wayward progress of the car from the early 1990s when Paul MacCready's company, AeroVironment, delivered the first prototype of the lightweight, electric-powered Impact to Detroit.

"I loved his [MacCready's] whole thing about doing more with less. That appealed to me on a lot of levels. It was sort of a vision of the future," recalled Paine.

Now, here it was. The technology heir of the fabled GM Sunraycer, the focal point of the creative tension that gave birth to the Impact, the EV1 was parked on the other side of the showroom window as if it were waiting for him.

It seemed to Paine that he already knew this car. It was built to accelerate, with a lightweight, mostly aluminum frame and sleek, aerodynamic body panels that were made of light, dent-resistant plastic instead of stamped steel. It had superlight magnesium alloy wheels and tires with low rolling resistance specially developed by Michelin. Paine was impressed by the fact that it used a keyless entry and ignition system; you just punched a combination of numbers into its computers.

But he wasn't really hooked until he drove one. "The acceleration just blew my mind. I thought, wow, this is so fun."

Many other prospective buyers for the EV1 were turned off by GM's peculiar contractual arrangement—you couldn't buy one, but you could sign a two- or three-year lease for somewhere between $399 and $549 a month. But Paine just signed the lease and drove home in the silver EV1 that had caught his eye.

It was supposed to be Paine's second car, but he soon found himself leaving the family's first car, a Ford Explorer, in the driveway. EV1 became his first love.

GM already knew the EV1 had audience appeal. Focus groups done with people who had driven the hand-built GM Impacts showed that men liked the torque, and women liked the environmental benefits of the first modern zero-emission car. Moreover, the public fascination with the car didn't appear small. In a 1994 program called PrEView, where fifty hand-built Impacts would be loaned to selected families to drive for periods of one to two weeks, more than ten thousand had called in to participate before the phone lines were closed in Los Angeles. In New York City, there were 14,000.

But the stage set for the launch of the EV1 in 1996 turned out to be cramped and the selling arrangements were nonexistent. The cars were only available for lease at Saturn dealerships in the Los Angeles area and in Phoenix and Tucson, Arizona. A year later the market expanded, but only slightly. EV1s became available in San

Francisco and Sacramento, California, along with a small program in the state of Georgia.

Moreover, it wasn't really designated as a launch but "a real-world engineering evaluation and market study" being undertaken by GM's Advanced Technology Vehicles group. One likely reason for the restricted debut was that in the previous year, 1995, California's powerful Air Resources Board had voted to relax its zero-emission vehicle mandate. This opened discussions that might allow for more fuel-efficient gasoline cars and hybrids that got still higher miles per gallon to get credits that would remove some or all of the burden on manufacturers to make ZEVs.

The argument within GM's hierarchy had been between those who felt launching EV1 might help the company seize and develop a market niche for later, more advanced electric vehicles and a faction that continued to feel that any sign of EV1 success would undercut the company's strenuous lobbying to force CARB to abolish the ZEV mandate.

To some the plot was almost opera-like, a fabulous venture flirting with doom. EV1 had been put on a small stage under tightly controlled terms that made failure likely. CARB's move in 1995 had strengthened the anti-ZEV faction within GM, according to Jon Bereisa, who had designed the car's electrical power system.

"EV1 was ordained inside GM as a poster child for failure. It was a formula for career disaster, I can tell you that personally. It was basically lampooned within the company," asserted Bereisa, who has since retired from GM.

The upshot was that the first vehicles were never intended to be sold. "They were too expensive at the time," explained Bereisa. "In hindsight, perhaps they should have been sold later on. That's what Toyota did with the electric RAV4."

GM had to go a long way to recoup the money that it and the U.S. government had put in those cars. Some of its executives doubted it would ever become profitable. Their concerns were backed up by others who were fearful that it might become profitable and thus threaten GM's main product lines. According to Bereisa, EV1's batteries alone cost around $40,000. Bob Lutz, a later vice chairman of GM, placed the total value of the car at $250,000. However the value of the car used in the calculations for the lease was $33,995.

Still, in southern California, where GM had sponsored an $8 million advertising campaign to tout the car, even a leased EV1 seemed like a good opportunity to buyers like Chris Paine. Standard operating procedure in the car business is to get new cars into the hands of celebrities and "influencers," and GM reached out to hundreds of those. Mel Gibson and Danny DeVito were already cruising the freeways in EV1s when Chris Paine began driving his. So were film producers and others from Los Angeles's major industry—movies.

Paine loved their company. "In the early days GM took such great care of us. They held special parties. . . . We all got to know each other this way," recalled Paine. "I became an enthusiast." GM gave them EV1 jackets, coffee mugs, and trained EV1 specialists to interact directly with customers. Enthusiastic tech-savvy EV1 drivers even set up listserves so they could stay in touch via e-mail.

That's where Paine eventually began hearing rumors that were not so comforting. When his first lease expired, he had signed up for a second. When he read the wording, though, it seemed much less renter-friendly. At the end of these leases, GM would reclaim the car and any EV1 renter who resisted would be responsible for GM's legal fees in repossessing them. Continued resistance could make them subject to prosecution for grand theft auto.

Around 2001 rumors began to circulate that the returned EV1s were disappearing. In December 2002, Paine took his car to an Inglewood dealer to have its brake lights fixed. When he returned to pick it up, he was told he couldn't have it and that it had been shipped away to a "recovery center."

There were still three months remaining on Paine's lease, but the folks at the Saturn dealership remained unmoved. "They said, here, we have this nice gas-powered Saturn. Take that. I called them back and said, 'Hey, my gym bag is still in the trunk.' They eventually retrieved my gym bag but I never saw the car again intact."

It was around then that Paine began thinking of making a movie. It would be about GM's mishandling of the EV1 program and the cancellation of the entire program in California. Having sold his Internet business he had some extra money. He had produced a documentary about motorcycle racing and studied documentaries at Stanford University with Jon Else, so he had some idea of how to do it. And, thanks to GM, he had contacts with many other EV1 owners who shared his passion for EV1s and wanted to keep theirs.

The plotline seemed ripe. Here was a multibillion-dollar environmental engineering program that was being scrapped with almost no media coverage. Chargers had been installed around the state with public money and there were nearly five thousand electric cars on the road.

He tried to interest television networks in the story, but found no takers. "They just didn't get why the story transcended California." In July 2003, Paine decided to stage a media event, a mock funeral starting with a rented hearse followed by a procession of twenty EV1s driven by the remaining lessees in the area that Paine found hadn't (yet) had their cars carted off to the "recovery center."

EV1s were becoming extremely rare because only 1,117 had been produced before 1999, when GM shut down their production line, so Paine felt there might be some media interest in that. To spice up the coverage he had some of the pioneers of the modern American electric car give eulogies when the procession of silently rolling mourners reached the cemetery.

The speakers included Ed Begley Jr., who had driven his EV1 in the procession, covered in black crepe. "Everybody knew I drive an electric car," cracked Begley, "but not many knew where I got it.

They all went to Saturn dealers who said, you don't want that car, let me show you another."

Even Paine's boyhood idol, Paul MacCready, his silver hair blowing in the wind under the mourner's tent, took his turn at the lectern. Wally Rippel, one of the inspirations behind Sunraycer was there, and Eric Garcetti, a five-year EV1 driver and Los Angeles City council member (who later would become the city's mayor), drew a laugh from the crowd when he said he will continue to drive his EV1 "until December, when GM will have to pry it out of my charger's dead, cold hands."

Just in case the local media didn't show up, Paine had his own film crew covering the event. After the funeral, the questions kept growing. Where were the repossessed EV1s going? The listserve began reporting some intriguing rumors. A trucker posted a picture of EV1s that had been crushed before being hauled to the proving grounds.

Then came a tip from a salvage company near Mesa, Arizona, that said specialized car batteries were coming in, probably from GM's nearby proving grounds, which were off limits to the public. In the months to come, as EV1 drivers protested at GM's facility in Burbank, two drivers even followed a transport truck to the Arizona border before being turned back by police.

Paine and another sufficiently outraged EV1 owner rented a helicopter and flew over the proving grounds. There, near the celebrated track where the first Sunraycers and the prototype Impacts had been tested, they saw fifty EV1 bodies that had been crushed into cubes that were stacked up in flatbed trailers.

They managed to film some of the process. "Although it was a terrible day for me as an EV1 driver (I may have even seen my car), it was a good day for the movie," Paine recalled.

His film was going to be called *Driving with the Brakes On* or *EV Confidential*, but that was before he realized he would need considerably more money than the $50,000 he had invested in it to tell the story properly. He began to hunt for more investors.

A chain of Internet and film industry contacts led Paine to Dean Devlin, a producer of two blockbuster movies: *Independence Day* and *Godzilla*. It turned out Devlin's father had leased one of the first EV1s to arrive in California. As his son later told a reporter for About.com, an Internet newsletter that covers the movie business: "I thought my dad was just being an old hippie and I thought this was some goofy little golf cart he was buying. I got in and my dad said, 'Hit the gas pedal.' . . . The thing took off like a rocket. I couldn't believe it. It was the most fun car I'd ever been in and I said, 'I've got to get one.'"

When Paine was introduced to Devlin and showed him a brief trailer for his movie, Devlin didn't need to hear a further pitch. He said, "Look, man, I'm in," and put up $1 million to finance the film. The result was *Who Killed the Electric Car?* It was produced by Devlin, who managed to insert a film clip of his father driving his beloved EV1 out of the showroom.

The documentary begins with Paine's funeral scene and as GM was concerned, the funereal tone continued downhill for GM from there. Paine said he tried to get all sides of the debate over clean cars—California regulators and the auto industry—in the movie and, indeed, a lot of the players are in the film.

But in the end the viewer is buried under an avalanche of criticism of GM, from Ralph Nader getting yet another chance to damn the big auto company to Stan Ovshinsky berating Detroit's leader for shutting down production of the EV1, later versions of which graduated to Ovshinsky's battery. "It [the shutdown] was wrong, but more wrong was the reason for it," asserted Ovshinsky. Ovshinsky may have been alluding to a decision by the GM board to abandon electric cars and focus instead on the Hummer, the large SUV modeled after the U.S. military's Humvee. Although Ovshinsky's battery had been selected in a competition involving some sixty companies, GM's decision was that future profits would come from the Hummer rather than electric or hybrid-electric cars. The Hummer was discontinued in 2010.

Some of the players in the movie, including Wally Rippel, the hero of the first U.S. cross-country electric car race, went on a publicity tour to drum up an audience for the movie, which opened in November 2006. Some of the audiences seemed to Rippel to be "left of center," but when he tested that theory one night by giving a sermon about how America's "can-do spirit" can produce and sell a clean electric car, he got a standing ovation.

A GM spokesman, Dave Barthmuss, made one last attempt to buttress GM's stance on the EV1 before *Who Killed the Electric Car?* was launched. Despite the fact that the company spent more than $1 billion, including "significant sums" in marketing the car, a waiting list of customers prepared to lease the car shrank from five thousand to fifty. "Because of low demand for the EV1, parts suppliers quit making replacement parts, making future repair and safety of the vehicles difficult to nearly impossible," he added. While Barthmuss said he personally regretted that GM couldn't find a way for EV1 lessees to keep their cars, GM felt that the only way to reduce safety and breakdown risks over the long run was to remove EV1 from the market.

It turned out that Barthmuss wasn't the only one at GM who had regrets. In 2006 Rick Wagoner, GM's former chief executive officer who shut the program down, said it was his worst decision as CEO. "It didn't affect profitability, but it did affect image," he told a reporter from *Motor Trend*.

ELEVEN

Selling

The Toyota sales force working in the United States—then the world's largest and most stable car market—wasn't quite sure what to make of a small, lightweight, electric/gasoline hybrid, when the first demonstration models began arriving. Bob Carter, senior vice president for automotive operations for Toyota in the United States, recalled that the Prius reminded him of an orphan. It was an "odd-looking little bundle left on our doorstep back in 1997."

At the time Toyota was beginning to invade markets long dominated by GM and other U.S. companies. The most profitable vehicles were big pickup trucks and sports utility vehicles and as the market for them grew, so did the vehicles.

"We weren't sure about this Prius thing. We weren't sure what to think of it," Carter admitted at a symposium. "But we knew we wanted it. We wanted anything!"

The Toyota brand was hot. Dealers were running out of inventory, so they would take anything with a Toyota emblem on it. But figuring out how to sell Prius to a U.S. market was a problem that seemed formidable. There was no niche market for a "green" car. Worse yet, the only versions of the Prius that appeared in the United States in 1997 were right-hand drive models used in Japan.

To make selling it even more interesting, the $19,950 compact four-door sedan came with an eight-year, 100,000-mile warranty, but the car was strong on features that U.S. buyers weren't known to be seeking. During a year when the price of a gallon of gasoline dropped as low as 99 cents, the fact that a Prius got forty-one miles per gallon didn't generate much enthusiasm.

The car's other revolutionary feature was an electric power drive system. That was something that mainstream buyers weren't clamoring for either, recalled Carter. "In fact, they were suspicious of it."

So the first job for the Toyota sales force was to tease out the minority of car buyers who might be interested in a car that would produce lower emissions and make their visits to the gasoline station less frequent. That triggered a search for technology geeks, members of environmental groups that had slowly begun to raise the awareness in the United States of climate change, and health and organic food enthusiasts.

The job of finding them fell to Geri Yoza, a woman of Hawaiian ancestry who had been with Toyota Motor Sales USA for ten years. She held an MBA from the University of Chicago and had been through new Toyota product launches before, but on this one she saw a big handicap: the consumer data didn't exist. "It was going to be hard to determine who would want one and how to reach them," she explained. She plunged into what data there was, using Internet searches to find profiles of people who defined themselves as "environmentally friendly" or as "tech pioneers."

Yoza and her staff began showing up at Earth Day events across the United States. She collared health food enthusiasts in Whole Foods parking lots. Would they be interested in buying a Prius? The

Toyota team also concentrated on the entertainment industry, looking for celebrities and other "influencers" who had expressed environmental concerns.

What began to surprise Yoza was that some of the celebrities sought her out. There was the producer who had begun to shoot *Curb Your Enthusiasm,* HBO's improvised comedy show starring Larry David. The producer wanted to borrow a Prius for one segment, but later decided to write the car into the script for the whole season.

Yoza had only been given five demonstration vehicles for the United States, but she parted with one of them. To place the remaining four she sponsored an Internet essay contest for families who wanted to drive a Prius for a week or two. She received more than eight thousand applicants. Their names were added to Yoza's list of prospective Toyota buyers, a list that reached 43,000 by late 1999 as more Prius demonstrators (this time left-hand drive models designed for American roads) began to arrive. Toyota was also ready with a national advertising campaign for 2000, the year of the American launch, but then canceled it after demand soon outstripped the number of Priuses slowly becoming available from Japan.

Carter, who had taken a leave of absence from Toyota's national staff to help run two Toyota dealerships on Cape Cod, was still skeptical. "It sold better than we thought." But then he began to focus on how it was selling. A retired department store magnate on Cape Cod bought a Prius. Then he began prodding his friends into the showrooms. After that he began drumming up support from federal and state park agencies manning Cape Cod's beaches.

Word-of-mouth sales can mean gold for car dealers. "That one customer sold that first year probably 80 percent of the Priuses we sold in the two dealerships," recalled Carter. "It was sort of beyond words. He convinced other people and the thing started feeding on itself."

Toyota began creating partnerships with environmental groups, with health groups such as the American Lung Association, and a network of cities that promoted cleaner air. The presidents of World Resources and the Environmental Defense Fund began driving up to events in a Prius. An environmental group arranged to have Harrison Ford and Calista Flockhart step out of a Prius at the 2003 Oscar Awards, a picture that dominated the front page of the *Los Angeles Times* the next day.

A few celebrities, beginning with Cameron Diaz and Leonardo DiCaprio, bought the car, but there was still something missing in the U.S. sales strategy. Sales in Japan were climbing above 12,000, but the American market seemed stuck at around one thousand cars sold for each of the first three years.

Toyota's U.S. sales team began to worry about crossing what they call the "chasm," a problem in selling high-tech problems to mainstream Americans. Once the zealots, the celebrities, and the geeks have bought theirs, there is an ominous waiting period to see who might follow them. In some product lines, no one does.

Toyota was in no mood to wait and see what happened. By the end of 2000 a team of research and development engineers began arriving in the United States led by Satoshi Ogiso. He had been one of the youngest assistants to Takeshi Uchiyamada, leader of the unit that had put together the original Prius.

Ogiso's goal was to quickly develop a second-generation Prius that was more closely matched to the needs of the American buyers. In Japan, what that might require remained an unknown. "At that time everyone said in the United States no one cares about gasoline and no one thinks about the environment," recalled Ogiso.

But what he learned from first-generation Prius owners was surprisingly different from the impression he gained in Japan. They cared deeply about gasoline mileage and environmental impact, but they also wanted a somewhat larger car that was more aerodynamic and "futuristic."

After three trips to the United States, Ogiso put together plans for a slightly larger car, a five-door hatchback that was more aero-dynamic. It had a longer wheelbase, more interior space, and got still better gasoline mileage. It had a fancy new electronic shift lever and a push-button starter. Toyota wanted that ready by the fall of 2003.

There was also, Ogiso admits, pushback from Japan. "So many top executives said to me, Ogiso-san, what are you doing? What we should be doing is reducing the costs, but why are you spending money adding more high-tech items?" Whether it was because of the earlier marketing outreach, or because Ogiso—with help from Dave Hermance, Toyota's executive engineer for advance technology vehicles in the Unites States—had hit on the right formula for improvement, the second-generation Prius found the acceleration to leap the chasm. Between 2003 and 2007 almost three hundred thousand were sold in the United States. By 2006, twenty-six Oscar hopefuls were silently rolling up to the ceremony in a Prius or another of a growing array of Toyota hybrid-electric cars. By 2007 gasoline prices had peaked at what was then an all-time high of $3.46 a gallon. "It was a great time to be in the hybrid business," said Ed LaRocque, national brand manager for Toyota's advanced technology vehicles in the United States.

Geri Yoza's marketing team had many occasions to celebrate. There was the formation of the Prius "smile," pins representing buyers on a map spreading down the West Coast, down the East Coast, and then crossing the country through Denver and Chicago. There were more advanced signs that their car was finding ways to explore the many byways of American culture. Millions of television viewers saw Larry David have a meltdown on *Curb Your Enthusiasm* because other Prius drivers weren't waving back at him, giving him the special sign because he drove a Prius. The producers of *South Park,* Comedy Central's animated cartoon show for adults, topped that by writing a small car called a Toyonda Pious into one of their scripts. One of the characters drives all over town to show it off and gain attention, but he soon decides *South Park* isn't worthy of the car and moves to San Francisco, where there are more frequent "smug alerts."

Undaunted by any amount of satire, there were Prius "Hypermilers" who tweaked their driving habits to get well over a hundred miles per gallon out of their cars by using a technique called pulse and glide. They frequently lift their foot off the throttle at speeds over forty miles per hour, gliding down to twenty-five miles per hour, then accelerating back to forty, keeping the car in fuel-saving all-electric mode more of the time.

Toyota took full advantage of free placements of the Prius in movies and on television. It also paid for placements when it was clear that they would bring home the message that a new American brand had arrived. Toyota was one of several companies that paid to achieve a presence in a new version of Parker Brothers' Monopoly game. Some of the older player tokens had been modified so the Prius took the place of the race car, a New Balance sneaker took the place of the shoe, and a bag of McDonald's French fries helped round out the new set of players. Mary Nickerson, a marketing manager for Toyota, told *The New York Times* the token-sized Prius was "great from a marketing perspective because it creates an opportunity for conversations to take place in the home about hybrids."

Needless to say, there were people who did not celebrate when the Prius vaulted into America's mainstream, a list that begins with most of Toyota's competitors. It is a time-honored tradition at Honda to beat Toyota at whatever the biggest Japanese automaker was attempting. Honda, which got its start with fast, efficient cars in Formula 1 racing in the early '70s, built the first laboratory to research how to meet California's zero-emission mandate and built the first prototype electric Civic in June 1992.

The launch of the Prius gave Honda a splendid opportunity to do it again. Six months before the production model Prius began arriving in the United States, Honda's Insights began rolling into Honda showrooms.

They were two-seaters, aluminum-bodied cars that used a small gasoline engine to back up an electric motor powered by Stan Ovshinsky's nickel-metal hydride batteries, which had found great favor in Japan. "Our main technology was in a way more elegant than Prius because we got about 80 percent of the benefits at two thirds of the cost," recalled Robert Bienenfeld, an assistant vice president for American Honda Motor.

But getting the Insight out of the Honda showrooms proved to be much more difficult. Aside from Amory Lovins, who kept his Insight parked proudly outside his Colorado home for more than ten years, most American buyers weren't terribly impressed by the smallish, spartan two-seater.

Tom and Ray Magliozzi of NPR's popular *Car Talk* radio show summed up what they saw as the difference: "The Insight is a vehicle for people whose first and foremost goal in life is to get the best possible gasoline mileage, everything else be damned. And the Prius is a great little car that happens to get outstanding gas mileage."

Selling them "was hard, hard work," Beinenfeld recalled. Later Honda tried to pep up sales by putting a more powerful version of the hybrid power train in the high-selling Honda Civic. Those did better, but by this time the Prius was way out in front.

Bienenfeld's theory is that people who pay $3,000 or $4,000 more for a greener car want a certain amount of cachet, a distinctive car design, for example, and not just a little chrome sign on the body that says hybrid. Honda knows this, he explained, because it later held focus groups with hybrid owners and found that Prius owners wanted to make a statement. They were against big oil companies. They were against sending U.S. troops to protect oil-rich nations in the Middle East. At least that was the message they gave in the Honda focus groups.

"We were just astonished by this," continued Bienenfeld. But later on, the company began to see a pattern that left Honda at a disadvantage. "Once Al Gore's movie *An Inconvenient Truth* came out, Americans were awakened to the idea of climate change. So right around this time you've got Leonardo DiCaprio stepping out onto the red carpet at the Oscars from a Prius."

Suddenly, he asserted, California's regulatory focus had shifted gears, moving from cleaning up the smoggy California air to cleaning up the invisible carbon dioxide emissions from automobile engines. The result was that Honda, which had tried to impress California regulators with some of the world's cleanest-burning internal combustion engines, was still stuck with a major regulatory issue because its cars burned gasoline.

Honda buyers still prized more efficient cars, but Toyota was promoting Prius as a kind of environmental political/fashion statement, a sign the driver was committed to fighting carbon dioxide. In California, where regulators were allowing the Prius to drive on the freeways' limited access lanes, the trend was palpable, explained Bienenfeld. "There were times when driving a Prius in Santa Monica was the only thing to do."

James Press, who worked for thirty-seven years for Toyota Motor Sales in the United States and left in 2007 to become vice chairman at Chrysler, threw gasoline on this smoldering debate in March 2008. In a wide-ranging interview with *Businessweek* editors and two reporters, Press, who had been the American face of Toyota for years, asserted: "The Japanese government paid for 100 percent of the development of the battery and hybrid system that went into the Toyota Prius."

Press did not say how the payment was made and later refused to elaborate on his remarks. Toyota denied the accusation, pointing out that it contradicted what Press had earlier told the U.S. media and had said in testimony to Congress. Japan's Ministry of Economy, Trade and Industry (METI), which had previously gained a reputation for encouraging various incentives for making Japanese products more internationally competitive, including lower tax rates and cheaper bank loans, also made a denial.

The Japanese government's role in launching the Prius, whatever it was, is certainly not an isolated case involving a government helping its auto industry to shift gears. Germany has certainly been responsive to its automakers. And the United States sometimes spends a considerable amount of money to help American carmakers be more competitive. The most recent example was the Clinton administration's Partnership for a New Generation of Vehicles (PNGV, see chapter eight), which cost taxpayers $1.5 billion and did not result in a commercially competitive car.

But some American automotive experts had heard what they wanted to hear. John Newman, a retired University of California chemical engineer and battery expert, was serving on a committee of scientists overseeing the Clinton administration's PNGV program, when he heard the chairman of his committee conclude that the success of the Prius came because Toyota was able to subsidize the price of each car by $10,000.

Newman doesn't believe that. The success of the Prius, after being locked out of the U.S. PNGV program, "is something we've all puzzled over." He attributes Toyota's success to something else. "There's a mental approach. Some of these companies just say, by God they're going to do it. That's what Toyota did. One of the things we can start with is a different mental approach."

The current U.S. mental approach to technological breakthrough, Newman asserts, is to back away from it because it is the market, not government agencies, that is supposed to work on near-term commercial projects. "In DOE [the U.S. Department of Energy] if you have an inkling something would work in the next fifty years, the attitude is, we don't want to hear about it. I think you should be putting 80 percent of your resources into things that are working. Everyone wants a game changer. You have to dive in and work on a project."

Exactly what it cost Toyota to launch the Prius remains a mystery. Bob Carter, Toyota's senior vice president for automotive operations in the United States, said the car became profitable in the spring of 2003 when the second generation was launched. "I can't go beyond that."

But, if nothing else, the development and marketing of the Prius shows that a company can "dive in" on an environmental problem in the United States and make a considerable pile of money. According to the company, more than seven million Priuses have been sold in the world and U.S. dealers have rung up more than two hundred thousand in sales each of the last two years. Beyond that, according to Carter, Prius evolved into what the industry calls a "halo car" that inspires sales of other cars in Toyota's lengthening lineup.

What's interesting is that, despite the fact that the Prius is still made in Japan, consumers all over the world have shared in the benefits. According to Toyota its hybrids have reduced global emissions of carbon dioxide by thirty-four million tons, the equivalent of 132,527 railroad cars' worth of coal. In the United States the Prius alone has saved Americans $3.8 billion in fuel costs.

There is, as yet, no "finally" with which to conclude the story of this complex, futuristic car, once thought of as an orphan, whose cachet continues to lure Americans into Toyota showrooms. Ford, GM, and other major automakers have driven down Toyota's pioneering trail and hybrid-electrics now make up about 3 percent of the U.S. auto market.

"After ten years, the Prius still feels like what comes next," asserts Dan Neil, car critic for the *Wall Street Journal*.

TWELVE

The EV Grin

In the spring of 1998, John Wayland, a postal clerk hailing from Portland, Oregon, was in a hurry to get to a drag race in Phoenix and made a mistake. He whipped off the rubber insulating blanket covering the twenty-eight storage batteries he had wired together in the trunk of his boxy, white 1972 Datsun. He had one more connection to make, but in his haste he dropped the brass connecting rod he was holding. Before he could retrieve it the rod bounced from battery to battery, making a random trail of short circuits. Sparks flew. Electricity arced. In the sudden bursts of acetylene-like light and heat brass connectors and batteries began to melt and fuse together.

A hot, bluish cloud with streaks of gold in it formed over the Datsun's trunk and began hissing at Wayland as he and a fellow hot-rodder began to feel the skin burning on their faces. They threw a wet towel over the cloud. The towel disappeared. They tried fire extinguishers. Nothing happened.

"John came running into the house," recalled his wife, Cheryl, who'd seen her husband bull his way through many strange crises during his long adventure with electric cars. This time he was in a panic. He wanted her to call the fire department. "I looked at John. Do they really need to come? He said yes. For the first time I was afraid."

A fireman wearing a moon suit finally put out the blaze, saving the Waylands' house. The little Datsun, an electric drag racer Wayland called the White Zombie, was covered in soot. The plastic side panels lining its doors had melted. "The car looked like a roasted marshmallow," recalled Wayland.

Still, he loaded it up on a trailer and hauled it to Palo Alto, where his chief electronics advisor, a high school dropout named Otmar Ebenhoech, was waiting in his shop with a crew that specializes in converting gasoline-powered cars into electrics. They spent all night putting the White Zombie back together.

But first they had a little fun. "I told all my guys in the shop we need to prepare for John. We pulled out dark sunglasses, put marshmallows on sticks. When he rolled up, we all ran out and danced around the car, as if it were a bonfire." From then on Wayland became known in the small but far-flung world of amateur electric vehicle racing enthusiasts as Plasma Boy.

"We just do this for the joy and ideals," explained Ebenhoech. "Some of us will work out a way to make a living in the process."

In the late 1990s, when it looked as though Detroit automakers might pull away from electric vehicles altogether, others began to rally to the cause. One of them was George F. Hamstra, a retired computer scientist, who had begun to worry about the future of electric motors in the United States. "There were a tremendous amount of talented experts that we lost in the last generation. These are the old slide rule guys that used to design motors. There's very few of these people left," he recalled.

Hamstra began exploring the market and discovered that dragsters like Wayland used modified forklift truck motors, which are based on an 1890 design. He formed a partnership with Wayland and with an Illinois forklift manufacturer in his pursuit of a better motor. "We started back in 2000 and kept blowing up motors."

He later formed NetGain Motors, of Lockport, Illinois, which sells motors for EV conversions and for electric-powered boats. Hamstra hopes more Americans get interested in EV hot-rodding before the electric car market drifts away from U.S. producers.

The competition in drag racing increases opportunities for backyard inventors and provides the long hours of wear and the stress that helps test new engines and control systems, he noted. "We need guys who can develop the electric vehicle transmission to get higher efficiency and get us away from gasoline-powered drivetrains. We can compete, but it's going to be a tough road for us."

Competition might well be John Wayland's middle name. He learned drag racing on the streets of Portland in the 1970s when he and his older brother Chris began souping up old Datsuns, sometimes putting in bigger gasoline engines with turbochargers. "My brother loved the fact they'd make fun of his Japanese cars," recalled John Wayland, who remembers him pulling up to a throbbing 1970s-era muscle car at a stoplight and betting $200 he could beat them. "The other guy would say you better see what's under my hood. I got a 440 cubic inch V-8. My brother would look at him and say, 'You're going to need two of those.'" Then the lighter, more powerful Datsun would peel away, leaving strips of burning rubber on the pavement as Chris shifted through the gears. The muscle car drivers often lost more than $200 as they watched the Datsun fade into the night. "In those days getting beaten by a Japanese car reflected on your manhood," recalled John Wayland.

The younger brother decided to raise the surprise factor by taking the gasoline engine out of a 1972 Datsun coupe altogether and replacing it with three beaten-up car batteries. "Off I went at ten or fifteen miles per hour. I'm giggling like crazy. I am moving without gasoline! I am just thrilled. Then a woman cop tried to pull me over, but I couldn't stop because I didn't have an off switch. She got on her loudspeaker: 'I told you to pull over!' I got to my house, jumped out of my car and pulled the cables. She pulled a gun on me and then looked under the hood and says, 'Where is the engine?'"

That was Wayland's introduction to the difficulties of controlling electric power. Gasoline engines, or "gassers" as he calls them, have to wind up to reach maximum torque. Electrics can deliver it to the rear wheels instantly. In Wayland's early races "I hit it and it was on full power. You just held on."

Then he began meeting people who could help him. He met Ebenhoech during one of his early appearances at the Firebird International Racetrack near Phoenix, Arizona. Ebenhoech later delivered the first version of a solid-state controller he designed to Wayland's home in Phoenix.

Ebenhoech, whose father was an electrical engineer, loves electronics, but hated high school and other forms of what he considered to be regimentation. "I didn't fit into the structure well. I like to focus on one thing."

He explained that the invention he brought to show Wayland could be compared to a very large dimmer switch. It uses electronic circuitry to phase in electric power in segments, depending on what the driver does with the accelerator. Wayland installed the device in the White Zombie and stomped on the accelerator.

"The car went sideways down the street smoking the tires. I kind of got control and said, there is a monster under the hood. It's Godzilla! Otmar looked at me and says: 'Who is Godzilla?'" After the Waylands bought him comic books portraying Japan's most inspired monster, Ebenhoech grew accustomed to the idea of using it as a brand name, but he later shortened the name of his product to Zilla.

The innocent-looking White Zombie won a lot of drag races in Portland. It was also awarded a fair number of speeding tickets, but not as many as Wayland had feared. The skeptics in Portland included the police department. He recalls watching two officers measuring a long line of burned rubber on a street that he'd left the previous evening. "There is no electric car that could lay down a strip like that," he overheard one of the officers conclude.

Eventually Wayland began discovering more kindred spirits in the Northwest. There was "Electric Louis," who built an electrified go-cart and kept getting thrown out of racetracks because he won so often. There was Roderick Wilde, son of an automobile mechanic, who also began racing his electrified Mazda RX-7 as the Maniac Mazda against muscle cars in Portland. "Dad always said the internal combustion engine was a stupid design," explained Wilde.

One of Wilde's more memorable vehicles was Going Postal, a converted post office mail delivery truck that he loaded with 1,600 pounds of batteries to out-drag a Lamborghini. When a German television crew showed up at his home in Port Townsend, Washington, looking for his "research facility," Wilde, who runs an electric vehicle parts business, pointed them to his front yard, where he works on his electric cars.

Wayland and his buddy Roderick eventually formed the National Electric Drag Racing Association, which began holding its own races. The big crossroads for electric hot-rodders in the mid-1990s was Firebird International Raceway near Phoenix, Arizona, where electric car buffs from the Northwest could encounter Californians. Sometimes they ran up against a man they all revered: Alan Cocconi, the designer of Sunraycer and later the GM Impact, who had started his own company, AC Propulsion.

The acceleration in electric car racing produces something that both Wayland and Wilde refer to as the EV grin, the result of an unexpected surge of power. "It's like being shot out of a cannon," explains Wayland. Sometimes even the anticipation of being shot out of a cannon produces the grin.

Part of the etiquette of a drag race begins with a phase called the burnout, where drivers spin the rear wheels so fast that they don't achieve traction but generate a cloud of burning rubber in the attempt. Drag racers do this on purpose because the friction makes their tires hot and sticky, better prepared to grab the pavement when the green light signals the start of the drag. Wilde has vivid memories of watching Cocconi doing a burnout in the Firebird parking lot before the race began and watching the electric car idol be disqualified for breaking the rules. "We were all upset about that. When you see him [Cocconi] he's kind of a computer geek guy. But to see him with a grin on his face burning those tires was great!" recalled Wilde.

Wayland did a huge burnout at the beginning of his race and recalls people cheering him as the cloud of gray smoke enveloped the stands at Firebird. He later encountered Cocconi, who recognized him and told him he thought the burnout was "an irrational amount of time for a tire ignition sequence."

By the late 1990s, Cocconi admits, his company, AC Propulsion, of San Dimas, California, was going through a rough patch. He insisted in an interview that he was not into competition the way EV hot-rodders were, "but if you've got an electric car product, you've got to do some of that because we wanted to show our stuff was better than others."

His company was selling Hondas that were converted to electric drive systems. He was also converting cars from a variety of other automobile manufacturers into electrics including Volkswagen, BMW, and other companies that needed them to qualify for California's zero-emission mandate. The manufacturers were also eager to examine Cocconi's inventions.

Cocconi's experiments continued to attract outsiders bitten by the EV bug, particularly his efforts to put his powerful electric drive system in kit cars that resembled sporty, two-seater roadsters. Cocconi called the experimental car Tzero.

Meanwhile, Wayland continued his more modest innovations in

Oregon with his two Datsuns. There was White Zombie and then a small sedan, Blue Meanie. But the work stopped in 2003, when he was laid off from his most recent job at an Internet start-up company. Oregon had the highest unemployment rate in the country. Wayland saw an ad in the newspaper for a technician at Northwest Handling Systems, a company that sells and repairs forklift trucks. He drove over and applied. Asked for a résumé, he said he was driving it. When eyebrows raised, Wayland alerted the job interviewer to the blue Datsun he had parked outside.

Wayland noted that it had a forklift engine that he had rebuilt and modified. "He said, 'How fast is this car?' I said, get in and I'll give you a ride." By this time most of the mechanics in Northwest's office were out in the parking lot, a phalanx of dubious men in coveralls waiting to see what happened next.

Wayland saw a sign on the back of a parked forklift that read HOW'S MY DRIVING? He wasn't sure what he should do until the man who wanted to ride with him asked: "Aren't you going to stomp on it?" Wayland found himself grinning. "I took him on a sixty-miles-per-hour trip through the parking lot, leaving a lot of burning rubber. He hired me. I'm still there. I'm the corporate trainer. They partially sponsor my races."

Drag racing in Portland has tamed. Instead of hustling illegal drags on downtown streets, anyone who feels the need to "stomp on it" can drive out to Portland International Raceway, where there's a drag strip with timing machines that is open to the public. Wayland still appears there with the White Zombie. He looks over the nightly lineup with the practiced eye of a predator. He has hired a younger man, Tim Brehm, a forklift mechanic at his company, to do the driving. ("I'm not a teenager anymore.") A lot of drivers in Portland are now aware that Wayland's boxy little car, now approaching antique status, is still one of the fastest street-legal dragsters in the country, so some nights he has difficulty finding challengers.

Not long ago, in the company of a *Wall Street Journal* reporter, Wayland sized up the evening's crowd at the raceway. There was Robert Akers, the owner of a souped-up 2005 Corvette, the hottest looking car at the track. After the burnout, it wasn't close. "Oh, man, right off the line he had me," said Akers, shaking his head. "I knew it was an electric car, but I wasn't sure what that meant."

The Zombie finished off the evening by trouncing a 2002 BMW and then went on to defeat a classic muscle car, a 1964 Pontiac Tempest with a massive 455 cubic inch V-8. The protocol at the end of a drag race is often for both contestants to open their hoods. Jim Barham raised the hood of his Pontiac to show off what seemed like an acre of gleaming, chrome-plated engine accessories. "It's all old school," explained Barham, a mechanic who had done all the work himself. Wayland, ever the showman, opened the Datsun's hood to reveal two relatively tiny electric motors (the batteries were in the trunk). "What kind of transmission does it have?" asked an awed teenager. "It doesn't have one," said Wayland, grinning.

THIRTEEN

A Difficult Birth

Martin Eberhard, an electrical engineer, was coming out of a messy divorce in 2001. So he decided to cheer himself up by buying a sports car. He had made some money selling a software company that developed one of the first electronic books. He was thinking about getting something fast and exotic.

But after studying the market and calculating various factors on a spreadsheet, he decided it had to be an electric car. "The more I looked at it, I came to believe that this problem of global warming was real. It was to me becoming obvious and I felt it was terribly irresponsible to go out and buy something like a Porsche that gets twenty miles per gallon, so I started looking around."

But it seemed the cards were stacked against him. He thought the ideal car would have been an EV1, but GM had made them impossible to buy and was preparing to recall its leased electric cars and junk them. "All the electric car manufacturers had pulled out. You couldn't get anything,"Eberhard recalled.

Then, in an Internet search, he stumbled across Alan Cocconi's latest experiment, the Tzero. Cocconi was installing his electric drive system in sporty-looking fiberglass-bodied two-seat roadsters he had obtained from a manufacturer of kit cars.

So Eberhard became one of a number of pilgrims who have made the drive to the industrial park in San Dimas in the far-eastern suburbs of Los Angeles, where AC Propulsion puts together its electric cars. Since his days as the top electronic engineer for GM's Sunraycer, Cocconi had always been on the cutting edge of electric vehicle technology, and that's what Eberhard was hoping to find.

Instead he discovered Cocconi's company teetering on the edge of bankruptcy. "They had laid everybody off except for six or seven people and they weren't paying salaries to anybody. If you went into their building it was a ghost town. There were just these empty cubicles, empty coffee cups lying around, and nothing there."

There were three sleek-looking Tzeros, but Eberhard was told that two had been sold and the company didn't have the money to build anymore. Lightbulbs started coming on in Eberhard's head. He offered to bail out the company by buying stock and offered to buy the remaining Tzero if they would replace the existing lead-acid batteries with a pack of new lithium-ion batteries.

"And then a weird thing happened. They basically kicked me out of the office," recalled Eberhard.

Eberhard had been following the steady advance of Li-ion batteries since Yoshio Nishi, an engineer with Sony, the Japanese electronics manufacturer, commercialized them in the early 1990s as lightweight, longer-lasting, rechargeable batteries for video cameras, cassette players, and other portable devices made by Sony. Within a few years laptop, cell phone, and power tool makers made it into a multibillion-dollar global industry. Li-ion batteries could deliver the same amount of electricity as lead-acid batteries, but because they were based on lithium, the lightest metal, the batteries were smaller and weighed only half as much.

To be sure, Li-ion batteries—like their older relatives in the growing family of batteries—had some formidable quirks. Their basic ingredients were inherently flammable and once protections were engineered for that, technicians found the batteries had a tendency to grow strange internal filaments called dendrites that could eventually create short circuits that made the batteries blow up.

"In a battery you are basically trying to take two very reactive materials and get them to react slowly rather than blend them together. Inherently both parts are explosive," explained Robert P. Hamlen, once manager of electrochemistry at Exxon, which developed the first commercial lithium-ion batteries back in the early 1970s in Linden, New Jersey.

Hamlen recalls there were at least six fires at the Linden plant. "Finally the fire chief comes to me and said, if we have to come again, we're going to charge you for the chemicals" that were necessary to put them out. Soon Exxon decided to drop out of the Li-ion battery business. "We said this is a good $50 million business. They said, hell, that's too small, let's get rid of it. They wanted only $1 billion businesses." Eventually the rights were bought by Sony.

"The difference here is that you had a Japanese company willing to invest long-term and most Americans in the battery business were not," explained M. Stanley Whittingham, the inventor of the first versions of Exxon's battery. Whittingham is currently a professor of chemistry at State University of New York at Stony Brook.

The chain of U.S. inventors who managed to tame and perfect prototype Li-ion batteries ended with John B. Goodenough, a University of Texas physicist who also helped train an engineer from Sony in his laboratory. As Dr. Goodenough later put it: "I have always been happy to receive good people who are funded by a home laboratory to which they will return. I don't have many sources of funding."

But Eberhard knew that there were still other commercial uses for the batteries that hadn't been tried. His calculations showed if you installed enough of them, they could be used to make a very responsive, lightweight sports car, but so far no automobile manufacturer had dared to touch them, which is why he had made the pitch to AC Propulsion. Two days after that his phone rang. It was Cocconi inviting Eberhard back to talk some more.

In his office at San Dimas, Cocconi pulled a basic Li-ion battery pack, called an 18650, out of his desk. It was a small assembly of cells, each not much bigger than a standard AA battery. He confessed to Eberhard that he had been using the batteries in his model airplanes and was thinking about putting them in the Tzero.

"But they weren't sure they wanted to talk to me about it," explained Eberhard, who then tried to forge another deal with AC Propulsion. He invested more money, but the company later told him it had spent the money, but still hadn't completed the upgraded Tzero.

In June 2003, Eberhard decided to form his own company with a partner, Marc Tarpenning. They named it Tesla Motors, after the Serbian American inventor and rival of Thomas Edison. Tesla had invented the alternating current induction electric motor, the kind used in Tzero.

Tesla developed a business plan that would license AC Propulsion's technology and provide AC with enough money to install 6,800 Li-ion cells in the Tzero and test it. In the late summer of 2003 Eberhard borrowed the upgraded version and began driving it around California, looking for venture capitalists to invest in producing the car. This car was definitely capable of producing the EV grin; it could go from zero to sixty miles per hour in 3.6 seconds.

It was a prototype with batteries stuffed in the sides, but "it demonstrated what you could do with an electric motor if you weren't trying to make a cheap car, but a fast car," recalled Eberhard. He and Tarpenning, his partner, showed it off at the Los Angeles auto show and wound up with a deal from Lotus, the British automaker, to provide the bodies and assemble the car in the United Kingdom.

At about the same time that Tesla was created as a corporation, J. B. Straubel, a recent Stanford University energy systems engineering graduate, began making his own pilgrimages to AC Propulsion to learn what he could about advanced battery technology. He had started this odyssey when he was fourteen years old and rescued an electric golf cart from a Wisconsin junkyard and restored it. In his senior year at Stanford, studying energy systems, he restored a junked Porsche 944 and converted it to electric power. He drove the electrified Porsche to San Dimas, where he learned about the Li-ion-equipped Tzero.

Straubel was still uncertain about his career path. He had also been working with Harold Rosen, an aerospace inventor trying to sell the Pentagon an electric drone that could function as a cheap substitute for a spy satellite. One day Rosen invited him to lunch with Elon Musk, the owner of SpaceX, a company developing private space launch vehicles for the National Aeronautics and Space Administration. It turned out that Musk had very little interest in the drone, but when Straubel mentioned the Tzero, Musk grew very, very interested.

The youngest son of a South African engineer, Musk had grown up with the idea of coming to America and becoming an entrepreneur. He started college in Canada, but was offered a scholarship to attend the University of Pennsylvania's Wharton School of Business, where he earned undergraduate degrees in physics and economics. It was there that he was first smitten with the idea of making electric cars.

"I'm not a car guy, for cars' sake," Musk explained in an interview. "I think electric cars are important for the future of the world. It's just a more efficient way to convert energy into motion than a gasoline car, like by far. It's not even close." To pursue that dream he came to California in 1995 to learn more about electronics in graduate school. His goal was to solve the battery problem by developing new "ultracapacitors"—smaller, lighter, and faster electronic devices that could store and discharge electricity.

But he dropped out of Stanford two days later. He knew he needed capital to launch a car company, so he set about making a fortune buying and selling Internet start-ups. By 2003 he was worth hundreds of millions and owned a Porsche and a McLaren F1, top-of-the-line sports cars. Now he, like Eberhard, had been bitten by the electric car bug. Musk wanted one that was good-looking and fast.

Musk was a man who usually got what he wanted. Exactly why this happened has baffled a number of people, beginning with Marge Musk, his mother. "I have two brilliant children, but Elon's a genius," she once explained to a reporter from *Esquire* magazine. "I can explain Tosca [Musk's sister] and Kimbal [Musk's brother] pretty well. I can't explain Elon."

The job of dealing with Musk at AC Propulsion fell to Tom Gage—an earlier engineer/pilgrim who had come to San Dimas hoping to get involved with electric cars. By 2003 he had become the chief executive officer of AC Propulsion. Cocconi, the owner, was suffering from prostate cancer and had withdrawn from most of the business side of the company.

So it was Gage who climbed into the hot, Li-ion equipped Tzero and drove it to SpaceX's office in El Segundo to negotiate with Musk. Musk offered to buy the Tzero on the spot. Musk recalls Gage rejecting that out of hand.

"I said, well, you haven't said what the price would be. How about a quarter of a million dollars? It was, like, no, they don't want to make any more Tzeros." Musk says he offered to pay AC Propulsion to electrify the new Porsche 911 he had just bought. Gage said no. "We kept in touch and I kept pushing. I said you should really make a production car. I pushed Cocconi. He is a strange cat. It's, like, hard to determine what his motivations are. But, for sure, the idea of going into production with anything is not Al's idea of a good time."

Gage, according to Musk, made a counteroffer. He wanted Musk to invest in another AC Propulsion project, converting boxy Toyota Scion minivans to electric drive systems. Musk balked. "I said, 'Look, Tom, if you're not going to make an electric sports car, I'm going to go do it.'"

In early 2004, Gage suggested that Musk negotiate with Eberhard and Tarpenning, the co-owners of Tesla. By April, Musk had bought his way into the company. Now he was chairman of the board of Tesla Motors and J. B. Straubel was working for the company as an engineer.

That, according to Eberhard, is when the company's troubles began to accelerate. They discovered that AC Propulsion's motors and inverters had to be redesigned in order to mass-produce them. "Their designs were very primitive. It was very old school, so we wound up not using much of their stuff." But the effort of sorting through AC's technology to see what wouldn't work in a commercial car, he added, "was an education for us. It was a teaching tool."

Bringing on more engineers also proved to be a learning experience for Tesla, according to Eberhard. "In the early days it was quite difficult for us to hire people that had any automotive experience because, I mean, everybody knew that electric cars are dead and stupid and who'd work for a company that's doing that?"

So Tesla decided to launch a public relations and advertising campaign. "We came out with our prototype roadsters when we were more than a year away from production because I needed to show that there was a real deal, so we could actually hire people and we could also get suppliers to come and talk to us."

The hardest part, he recalled, was negotiating with automotive equipment suppliers. In that market, Tesla, with its few thousand planned roadsters, was very, very small potatoes.

He recalled trying to buy air bags from Siemens's U.S. affiliate.

"I was on bended knee. The guy from Siemens described it very clearly: 'You guys are going to buy a few thousand of these things. Our typical customer buys a few hundred thousand of these things. And if somebody gets killed in one of your cars, who's going to get sued? We're the deep pockets here, not you.'"

Difficult as that turned out to be, finding a supplier for air bags turned out to be a piece of cake compared to ordering a transmission to be built for the Tesla roadster. At first big suppliers rejected the Tesla order out of hand. Then a smaller company that built racing car transmissions tried to scale up to mass produce the transmissions and eventually failed, leaving Tesla without a transmission.

A bigger company finally signed a production contract but then pulled their best engineers out of the project later on to shift them to a larger customer. Again, the Tesla roadster was left without a transmission.

Sitting at the helm of Tesla, Elon Musk had no track record as a passive investor. He got heavily involved in the day-to-day activities of the companies he had previously run. He was also a battle-scarred veteran of the fast-paced rough-and-tumble world of Silicon Valley's high-technology start-ups.

Eric Jackson, who worked with Musk at PayPal, one of Musk's earlier companies, recalled the press sometimes made Musk out to be a playboy. He remembered Musk inviting a reporter to take a picture of him in his Jaguar convertible with his girlfriend and his dog. "But public image notwithstanding, Elon worked incredibly hard and cared a tremendous deal about his company."

Later, when Jackson found himself siding against Musk in a boardroom coup that forced Musk to resign as CEO of PayPal, he was almost apologetic about it: "As much as I disagreed with his business strategies, I respected Elon's grace and continued dedication to the company," he wrote. As he was being ousted from PayPal, Musk "hinted at a humbleness I had not previously detected," he added. One possible reason for Musk's grace under fire was that he still owned 11.7 percent of the company, which gave him the cash to buy his later ventures, including Tesla in 2002 when eBay bought PayPal for $1.5 billion.

So for Musk-watchers, it was probably no surprise that at the end of 2007 he fired Eberhard over the transmission impasse along with twenty-five other people. Eberhard was shocked and sued Musk for slander and for breach of his severance package. Both parties accused each other of lying, but the lawsuit was eventually settled out of court.

In the movie *Revenge of the Electric Car* Musk described his situation in 2008 as "eating glass sandwiches every bloody day." He had invested $100 million in SpaceX and $70 million into Tesla and another $10 million into a third company, called Solar City, which sells solar photovoltaic rooftop arrays to produce renewable energy. Tesla needed more money and SpaceX's first space rockets were crashing, but Musk was tapped out; he seemed to be caught in an impossible straddle. If he saved one company, he would lose the other. "I was essentially living on borrowed money at that point."

Meanwhile supplier demands continued to escalate and so did more trouble with the design of the roadster. "We ended up having to virtually redesign every element of that car. Our crash tests were invalidated. Our car is 30 percent heavier. The load points are different, the body was totally different. In fact, it would have been much better to start with a clean sheet of paper. . . . It was like finding a house that's not quite what you intend and you end up knocking down everything but one wall in the basement, but you're still stuck with the original footprint, so we were stuck with the limitations."

Straubel, who was in the thick of the redesigning effort and later rose to become chief technical officer of the company, eventually resolved the transmission problem by replacing it with electronic controls. He recalls the early birthing days of Tesla as a "kind of total coincidence in a lot of ways," involving people with the same ambitions, but different strategies for bringing a new car to life. "We really all kind of collided together."

It was a collision of vastly different characters. Musk, who styled himself as CEO and "product architect" of Tesla, kept adding improvements to the look and feel of the roadster, from its carbon-fiber body right down to its door latches. Straubel recalled that Cocconi was never concerned with the "niceties," or luxury elements in his bare-bones version of the roadster. "I respect the hell out of that. He's a brilliant guy. He doesn't want to make any energy compromises for comfort of people in a car." Tzero was a good concept, he admits, "but you have to impress passengers who don't even know it's electric. My mom just wants to go from point A to point B."

What finally saved Tesla from crashing, as most new U.S. car companies have done since the 1950s, was a lifeline thrown from overseas. According to Musk the transaction began in October 2007 when he flew to Stuttgart to meet with the head of research and development at Daimler AG, the makers of Mercedes-Benz.

"I said, what could convince you to partner with us?" The answer was that there would be a team of Daimler officials visiting the United States in January 2008 and they would be interested in a proposal for a power train to electrify the company's Smart, a boxy, two-seat urban car.

Musk decided the only way to win a contract from Daimler was to find a Smart and electrify it. He talked to Straubel. The Smart was not available in the United States, but Tesla brought one in from Mexico. "And we adapted a roadster motor and specially made battery pack. When they came to visit in January, they were expecting a PowerPoint presentation. We gave them a car. . . . It had so much power that you could actually pull wheelies in that car," explained Musk.

That produced a research and development contract from Daimler. It later blossomed into a bigger contract to provide the first one thousand electric Smart cars with Li-ion battery packs and chargers. Finally, in May 2009, Daimler followed up by buying a 10 percent ownership in Tesla.

After that came a $465 million loan from the U.S. government and a stock purchase by Toyota. Then Musk negotiated a cut-rate deal for a modern Toyota manufacturing plant in California. After Tesla repaid the government loan early, the stock market began to lift Musk's company out of the financial whirlpool that was swallowing most of the other budding electric car companies in the United States.

The first production model Tesla roadster still hadn't hit the road, and there was a lot of concern over what might happen when it did. "People would ask, what will you do about competition when these big companies realize that electric cars are important? They're just going to steamroll you." Musk explained that, happily, he was now in a position to try to turn his doubters around: "Which of these big companies are you referring to? Would it be, like, Daimler, who is investing in the company, or, like, Toyota, who is investing in the initial public offering?"

Tesla's survival has elicited a certain amount of grudging respect from some of the other people who were bruised in Tesla's wild, sometimes frantic evolution. "I still like Teslas," explained Eberhard. "My wife took ours to a horse show today in Santa Barbara, that's 120 miles round-trip. That's something you couldn't do with a Leaf. She can make it back without recharging."

Cocconi, the original inventor, later sold AC Propulsion to a Chinese real estate investment company and has gone back to his first love, flying high-technology, electric-guided model airplanes. He's become one of the pioneers of a new sport called dynamic soaring. Following a technique adopted from observing birds, he and others fly radio-controlled gliders into different wind currents in the nearby San Gabriel Mountains.

They've found it's possible, like high-tech sailboats, to move much faster than wind speeds by maneuvering their aircraft so that it gains rather than loses momentum from the wind. Speeds of more than four hundred miles per hour are achievable. Cocconi's house and his garage are now filled with his models.

Getting out of the electric car business was for him, he admits, a great relief. What he liked best about it was developing Sunraycer and the early versions of GM's Impact at AeroVironment, Paul MacCready's creative skunkworks in nearby Monrovia, California.

"I enjoyed working with AeroVironment because their culture was working with these one-off weird projects that nobody had ever done before. So they had a whole engineering approach where you could sit down and look at the trade-offs and come off with a reasonably good result on the first iteration."

Running his own company, AC Propulsion, offered a different kind of excitement that Cocconi found far less appealing. He was selling a few relatively expensive electric prototypes to car companies interested in sampling his technology. "That's what paid the bills, barely. I put a lot of my own savings in it over the years, working without salary most of the time." After fifteen years of that, he decided to get out of the business.

Tesla, he said, paid him slightly more than $1 million for the technology transfer and $25,000 to license his patents. But then the royalties on the patents stopped after Tesla said it was relying on its own inventions. AC Propulsion later bought a Tesla roadster and tore it down to discover that the electronics were very similar to what Cocconi had designed. However, changes had been made, and the patents were so loosely written, Cocconi said, that lawyers concluded they were probably unenforceable.

From what he's seen of Tesla's new cars, Cocconi thinks they are too heavy and not very efficient. "With the new batteries you ought to be able to do a car with a four-hundred-mile range very easily." Still, he admits, Tesla's performance is closer to the mark of an ideal car company than others that he can think of. "They were successful at pumping up their stock price and delivering cars, so it's more than I ever managed to do."

FOURTEEN

Shocking Moments

O ne of the many ironies in the electric vehicle business is that the messy, noisy, and litigious birth of the Tesla roadster led directly to the birth of the second successful launch of a new American electric car: the Chevrolet Volt. And the worldview of the father of the Volt, General Motors' vice chairman Bob Lutz, is markedly different from Elon Musk's.

In 2005, when Lutz began to battle within GM for a third try at an electric car, Lutz was seventy-three, a generation older than Musk. Part of Musk's motivation since college had been to develop a market for electric cars to help save the planet from the droughts, torrential rains, rising seas, and killer storms of global warming. Lutz's view was that global warming "was a total crock of shit."

Musk sometimes sounds like a disciple of former Vice President Al Gore, who described in the documentary *An Inconvenient Truth* the dangers that carbon dioxide emissions from cars can cause by trapping more of the sun's heat in the upper atmosphere. In his recent book *Car Guys vs. Bean Counters,* Lutz assures the world that

Gore's views in the movie are "absurd." The oceans aren't rising and people can quit worrying about melting ice and struggling polar bears, he explains. "Hello—they can swim!" As for cars with fossil-fueled internal-combustion engines exacerbating a warming climate: "It's simply not true," concludes Lutz.

But as he prowled the corridors of GM's upper bureaucracy as the company's new vice chairman, he found company executives in shock over the fact that while their first two attempts to launch electric cars, the Impact and the EV1, had been expensive and embarrassing failures, Toyota's Prius now owned the pole position in a race to capture a growing, green segment of the world's car market.

"We stood by, nearly speechless, with envy over the countless billions Toyota reaped in terms of corporate reputation for the measly three hundred million the initial Prius may have cost them," explained Lutz. He blamed the nation's "left leaning" media for overly praising the Prius. Lutz admits GM may have sent the wrong signal by buying the gas-guzzling Hummer while Toyota was demonstrating there were an increasing number of Americans interested in a car that sharply reduced gasoline use. And Lutz does admit that repossessing and crushing the EV1s was a "PR blunder of truly gargantuan proportions."

What Lutz and Musk do share in common, though, is that they're not content with simply wringing their hands over market obstacles. They are both masterful, charismatic salesmen and Lutz quickly set about trying to figure out how GM might move into the passing lane in the sales race against the Prius.

By 2005 the Prius had begun to establish itself as something "car guys" such as Lutz refer to as a halo car—a brand whose attractions and publicity value give added zest to a company's entire lineup of cars. The zippy, stylish Corvette, for example, had done that for GM in the 1950s through the 1980s. (In 2005 Lutz still drove one to work.)

During his meandering career as an auto executive, Lutz had fashioned a few halos himself. While he was an executive vice president at Ford, he helped launch the Ford Explorer and as the head of global product development for Chrysler he championed the muscular Dodge Viper.

Lutz, who had started his career at GM after flying Phantom fighter jets for the Marine Corps, knew that the Corvette had started with a stunning debut as a concept car for an auto show in 1953. He found himself thinking about repeating that feat with an electric halo car, a light, aerodynamic four-seater. He had heard some buzz from California that powerful lithium-ion batteries might give such a car stunning acceleration and a range between refueling of somewhere around two hundred miles.

Lutz had been brought back into GM in 2001 to develop new products for its sagging car lineup. By 2005, Lutz had already canceled a number of what he felt were tepid, "sales proof" concepts that would bomb in the showrooms, as many GM cars recently had. He tried to revitalize GM's design department, pushing away what he called "bean counter" business school types and handing power back to the engineers. Cars, to him, were like people; they did better if they were handsome and reflected power. The previous year he had trotted out a more streamlined, powerful version of the Chevrolet Camaro.

But when he broached the idea of a new electric to GM's automotive strategy board, he was, as he put it, "cruelly shot down." Other board members asked him how could GM launch another electric car while it was busy fighting California's mandate for zero-emission vehicles.

But the vexing question of how to deal with Toyota's growing presence in the U.S. market kept coming up in meetings of GM's strategy board. When it did, Lutz would reoffer his new concept car idea. At one session the company's chairman, Rick Wagoner, asked him wearily: "Bob, we lost over one billion bucks on EV1. How much do you propose we lose this time?" Lutz went back to his drawing board.

Before he had returned to GM, Lutz had served for four years as CEO of Exide Technologies, a large battery manufacturer. He knew enough about Li-ion batteries to be annoying, if not dangerous. GM sent a team of its battery engineers to Lutz's office to spar with him. They kept reciting a mantra of limitations and risks that the battery would pose in a car.

Lutz had almost decided to give up his new quest when a press release arrived on his desk. It was the one Martin Eberhard of Tesla had written to raise funds amid worries that his start-up might not survive. It promised a roadster that could achieve a top speed of 140 miles per gallon and race from zero to sixty in four seconds. It would have a range of two hundred miles and it would do all this with Li-ion batteries.

Lutz took Eberhard's press release with him on his next trip to the boardroom. He posed a question: "How is it that everybody at GM convinces me that this can't be done . . . and here is this outfit in California that nobody has ever heard of, and they are gonna put a car on the market with lithium-ion batteries? . . ."

This time he got grudging permission to explore the idea, but only as a concept. It wasn't a no, Lutz reasoned. "Whatever . . . I ran with it."

But before he ran too far, he had a meeting with Jon Lauckner, a veteran GM engineer who was then the company's vice president for global vehicle development, who talked him out of an all-electric car. The car would be too heavy and have a limited range, Lauckner argued. It could have a lighter battery pack if it were connected to a small gasoline engine that could recharge it, thus assuring an almost unlimited range.

Lauckner pulled out a pad of paper and the two executives sketched out the specifications for what would become the Chevrolet Volt. In April 2006, the executive board gave the car a green light for production. In the late winter of 2007 GM gave the car—still not much more than a concept—a big badda-boom moment at the Detroit Auto Show.

After video projections of the first printing press, the first moon landing, a space shuttle slowly, powerfully rising from the launch-pad, a brief glimpse of Thomas Edison appeared and the hall began to rumble. The projection screen split in two. There were blue lightning bolts and sparks and flashes before Lutz rolled out, sitting in the passenger seat of a prototype Volt.

"Well, here it is," he said after shaking hands with Rick Wagoner. "The Chevrolet Volt, an electrically driven car from General Motors. I am shocked, truly shocked," said Lutz. "A GM electric vehicle is an inconvenient truth."

Lutz explained the car was a "new type of electric vehicle." It resolved the range problem, had room for four to five passengers and baggage. It could climb a hill or provide air-conditioning without draining the battery, and if the driver's commute was less than forty miles, the Volt could be plugged in at home and recharged at night.

A driver who did that would "never need to buy gasoline during the entire life of the vehicle. And you would save five hundred gallons of gasoline and eliminate 4.4 metric tons of carbon dioxide a year from the tailpipe," Lutz continued.

Chris Paine, the director of *Who Killed the Electric Car?* was shocked, too, when Lutz wrote him an e-mail offering to give him an inside look at the Volt project, including access to secret GM testing facilities that he had been barred from in his earlier movie. Paine was already filming Elon Musk's effort to build the Tesla when Lutz popped up on his computer.

"Our deal [with GM] was anything we wanted," recalled Paine, who promised, in return, not to show his second film, *Revenge of the Electric Car,* until GM introduced the commercial version in 2011.

Somehow, Lutz had also worked out the same anything-we-want

deal internally with GM. During 2008, as the U.S. economy came crashing earthward and GM drifted into bankruptcy, the Volt project got what it needed to get the car into production by late 2010. That would be nine months sooner than a typical development schedule.

One reason it could move so fast is that its engineering team assembled for the Volt included engineers who had produced the EV1. Jon Bereisa, the EV1's propulsion expert who had begun to think of electric cars as a "career killer," remembers feeling hopeful after seeing many familiar faces. "The old band is back, but now we had an audience," he recalled. "In the Volt there was no invention required. We already had what we needed. . . . That meant we could do things really fast."

GM had had a long learning curve with the modern electric car. It learned from Sunraycer that lightness and streamlining were crucial. Volt stylists spent five hundred hours in wind tunnels studying how to tweak better streamlining from its body, more than twice the time needed for a production car.

GM had also had the experience of dealings with Andy Frank, a professor of mechanical and aeronautical engineering at the University of California at Davis. Frank had been working on hybrid-electric cars since the early 1970s, when he entered one in a contest for a low-emission "urban car" sponsored by the U.S. Department of Transportation. It was held on GM's sprawling proving grounds in Michigan.

The car with a crudely shaped fiberglass body was powered by lead-acid batteries and a small propane-driven engine that kept the batteries charged. Frank had discovered a way to deal with the electric car's limited range. What he hadn't prepared for was the possibility that the contest might be held in the rain, which it was. Electricity from the batteries arced into the water pooled on the asphalt pavement, causing a fire that frightened the GM test driver, who couldn't get out of the car fast enough. It was the only hybrid-electric in the contest, though, and it won a prize for the most innovative design. "It should have gotten an award for the scariest vehicle," recalled Frank.

He had more success with GM in 1998, when he rolled out a more sophisticated version of his old hybrid and GM gave him an EV1 and a $500,000 contract to install a small gasoline engine and a generator. "We had quite a few GM engineers hovering around our lab at that time," recalled Frank, who is now retired. He and his students produced an EV1 that got eighty miles per gallon and had a range of eighty miles. "Shortly after that they decided to pull all the EV1s back and they started junking them." He said he never heard any more about what happened to his plug-in hybrid version of the EV1.

One of Frank's former students, Mark S. Duvall, is now director of electric car research for the Electric Power Research Institute, an independent group that does research for American electric utilities. He thinks Frank's early designs helped GM's Volt in the same way Alan Cocconi's inventions helped the Tesla roadster. The Volt emerged with a "range extender," a small gasoline engine that recharges the batteries. "Frank was an incubator of the idea. It doesn't necessarily mean he invented it. You can get a lot done if you aren't too concerned about who gets the credit."

In 2007, after GM launched the Volt, its propulsion team came up with a bolt-on battery pack that weighed in at a relatively svelte four hundred pounds. The actual batteries for the Volt still didn't exist, but GM was combing the world's battery manufacturers, some twenty-four in all, to see who could make the exotic batteries operate dependably and safely. The sifting brought it down to two: LG Chem, a South Korean company; and A123 from Massachusetts. The battery testing continued through 2008.

Meanwhile versions of the concept car had already hit the streets, disguised as Chevrolet Malibus. In industry jargon they were the "mule cars" used to allow testing on the open road without revealing new prototypes. Inside they were Volts. Lutz had his first drive in one of them on May 22, 2008.

Andrew Farah, Volt's chief engineer, has vivid memories of that. He was another veteran of the EV1 and had been brought back from Europe to make the development run smoothly. As he explained his job, it was to segment the work so the best, most expert people were working on the element of the car they knew best.

That was not always easy. "You've got to remember that in a big company like GM everyone is looking to do the land grab," Farah said, explaining that warring departments often tried to elbow out rivals for jurisdiction over as much of the car as they could. Farah had also spent three years working for Johnson Controls, a battery manufacturer. "The good thing is that when I came back I knew just enough to tell when the battery guys were lying."

Farah and his team had done their level best to make sure the Volt was ready for Lutz's test drive. "There's lots of film and stuff about Bob Lutz driving the mule car and we're all standing in the background in our sunglasses, hoping to God he doesn't break it."

As the time for Lutz's test drive neared, Farah had his own shocking moment. A colleague walked up and assured him that everything seemed ready, except they had just discovered the Volt wouldn't start. Its electrical system had gone stone-cold dead. "The damn car wouldn't move and we couldn't figure out what had happened!" Farah remembers. At the last minute the engineers discovered that a television technician installing a tiny camera inside the car to film Lutz had accidently bumped the "E-stop" button. This was a safety feature that turned off all of the electricity in the car in an emergency.

The engineers fixed the button just as Lutz arrived to put the car through its paces. Later when he emerged from the car, he was grinning at the engineers, who were grinning back at him, peering through their sunglasses. Then the cameras recorded Lutz as he signed and dated the car's hood with a permanent marker. He wrote: "We are making history today."

In the brutal corporate surgery that followed in 2009, GM amputated the Saturn, Hummer, Pontiac, and Saab brands as part of its failed attempt to avoid bankruptcy, but the Volt rolled on. That summer more mules concealing the Volt hit America's roads as GM engineers began driving the car in subarctic Canada, baking it in Florida's summer heat, and pushing it up 14,000-foot Pikes Peak in Colorado.

But the real pinnacle came for the Volt in November 2010 when production began and the car was introduced to the press at GM's research center in Warren, Michigan. A shiny fleet of white Volts sat outside, waiting for reporters to drive them. "Quiet, isn't it?" said an engineer riding in the backseat as I, one of the journalists invited for the debut, pushed a button and drove the car soundlessly into the street.

But this was not a day to be quiet. GM was going through the aftershock of a wrenching bankruptcy. What it desperately needed was a spark of new life. Inside the center a battery of cameras, politicians, and reporters awaited as Fritz Henderson, the newly named GM chairman, drove a Volt into a large conference room. He got out and stood in front of a large billboard that said RE: INVENTION. Here was the car, according to GM, that could be gasoline-free on average commutes and get the equivalent of 150 miles per gallon on longer drives. Here was a car that might trump the Prius.

Michigan's then governor Jennifer Granholm proclaimed that the arrival of the Volt meant that Michigan would remain the automotive capital of the world, a "place where breakthroughs occur." Not to be outdone, Senator Carl Levin said it wasn't just that GM had been reorganized to create the Volt. "It was being reborn."

The experience with the Volt has since hatched a smaller, all electric car called the Chevrolet Bolt, which is expected to appear in 2017 with a 200-mile range between charges and a price tag of around $30,000. A concept version was unveiled at the Detroit Auto Show in January 2015.

"We are pretty convinced that this is the right vehicle for the market at the right time," said Alan Batey, GM's chief of North American sales and marketing. "We would not be talking about the price and battery range if we weren't able to make it happen."

FIFTEEN

Hit One Out of the Park

By the beginning of 2011, as the first all-battery-powered electric vehicles reached America's showrooms, one thing seemed clear. It had taken a long, difficult struggle to implant a new technology in an auto industry that was huge, rich, growing, and, seemingly, set in its ways. Since 1901, though, when the brash, young, charismatic tinkerer Henry Ford emerged from rural Michigan to anchor the U.S. auto industry in Detroit, improbable innovations have sometimes had a way of disrupting the status quo.

For example, in the late 1980s the exploits and dreams of Hans Tholstrup, an Australian adventurer, inspired GM, then the largest automaker in the world, to invest in Detroit's first new electric car venture, which eventually became the EV1. In the 1990s it was the lofty ambition and determination of a U.S. vice president, Al Gore, to reduce the danger of carbon dioxide and other so-called man-made greenhouse gases known to be causing climate change that led to another improbable shift. That started up as a U.S. government–led crash program to build an eighty-miles-per-gallon family car. Foreign car companies were excluded. While the U.S. effort ultimately fizzled, the exclusion was the impetus that launched Toyota's Prius, the first modern hybrid-electric car.

In the first decade of the twenty-first century it was the continuing struggles of one of the pioneer builders of GM's Sunraycer, Alan Cocconi, to build an electric-powered roadster, the Tzero, that provided the push that led to Tesla, the first all-new U.S. auto company in over a half century. Tesla went on to defy more tradition by showing that its battery-powered sedan could be competitive and make money in the luxury car market.

Finally, it was Tesla's example that led to the second thoughts in GM that put the Chevrolet Volt on the road. In sum, the re-emergence of the electric car resulted from a series of improbable-seeming struggles.

But the longest struggle, the electric drivetrain with the most improbable beginnings, the most expensive development phase and perhaps most disruptive prospect of them all, was none of these. It is a car that is just beginning to find its way into showrooms and into consumers' hands: the fuel cell–powered car.

By 2011, automakers around the world had begun to build prototype vehicles propelled by fuel cells, a space-age technology. Fuel cell cars had already absorbed at least $10 billion in private research and government-funded subsidies. The meandering path of this invention has been so difficult, risky, and expensive from an engineering standpoint that fuel cell cars for automobiles have lingered in the development stage since 1966.

That was when GM rolled out the Electrovan, a converted GMC van that put improbability on wheels. It weighed more than seven thousand pounds, making it twice as heavy as the average van. It had no space to carry freight because the drivetrain, liquid hydrogen and oxygen fuel tanks, and related equipment took up most of the vehicle apart from the driver's compartment. According to some accounts, it took three hours to start and often didn't in cold weather.

The Electrovan's most memorable feat was its speedy exit to the scrapyard. As GM historians later explained, the experiment showed fuel cells were "cost prohibitive." The platinum needed as a catalyst in the fuel cell cost enough to "buy a whole fleet of vans" and there was "absolutely no hydrogen infrastructure" to support such a vehicle at the time.

Despite all this, fuel cell–driven cars remained alluring. Regulators saddled in Washington, California, Asia, and Europe with the mission to reduce greenhouse gas emissions often saw them as the ultimate solution because they produced electricity by combining oxygen and hydrogen. The by-product was water. Here was the possibility of a true zero-emission vehicle.

Beginning in the early 1990s many of the world's automakers had begun to experiment with fuel cells, in large part because their competitors were. Younger engineers saw them as a promising challenge because fuel cell–driven cars, assuming their costs could be lowered from the "prohibitive" range, had the potential to meet the most stringent future regulations and might eventually become simple and cheap enough to outsell cars propelled by gasoline and other fossil fuels.

Equations flashing on hundreds of computer screens around the world showed the possibilities. Fuel cell cars should be cheaper to drive and maintain. They required fewer moving parts than cars driven by a nineteenth-century technology that needed explosions, pistons, cam shafts, and gears to turn their wheels.

Because they carried their own fuel, fuel cell cars might also nose ahead of battery-powered cars because fuel cells were lighter than batteries, yet had the power to deliver as much as three hundred miles of driving range and three-minute fill-up times. This is what most American car drivers are accustomed to. And if excess amounts of electricity generated when the wind is blowing and the sun is shining can be stored and then used for electrolysis to derive hydrogen from water, fuel cells have essentially inexhaustible sources of energy that do not contribute to global warming.

But the pace of development of fuel cells had been glacial, so slow that environmental groups, which had once been enthusiastic about them, had grown cynical. Several concluded that fuel cells were really a mirage perpetuated after the year 2000 election of President George W. Bush to appease American auto companies that really wanted the status quo.

S. David Freeman, an engineer and former head of the Tennessee Valley Authority, and one of the most respected graybeards among environmentalists, asserted fuel cell–driven cars served the same function as the mechanical rabbit in a dog race. They looked very exciting but the dogs (in this case automobile consumers) were destined never to catch one. But this was misleading: by the early 1980s the pieces of another auto industry revolution were already in the public domain. What was needed was a company to arrive with the money, the inventiveness, and the tenacity to put them all together.

That package began to take shape in 1983. But it didn't happen in Detroit, Germany, or in Japan. It grew out of a conversation between two reformed alcoholics at an Alcoholics Anonymous (AA) center in Vancouver, Canada. One of them, Geoffrey Ballard, fifty-one, a geophysicist and former U.S. Army scientist, had spent months listening to a younger man, David McLeod, talk about his failures.

AA support groups are fueled by truth, the stories of the trials and failures of people with drinking problems. McLeod, then in his early thirties, had certainly had his share of them. He came from rural Nanton, Alberta, a town of 11,000 souls where his father nurtured some of them as the minister of the Baptist church.

But the minister was also an aviation buff who left copies of *Scientific American* strewn about the house for the younger McLeod to devour. Minister McLeod's greatest flight of fancy was that David would follow him into religious life. For a short while, David tried, but soon found there were distractions. Liquor was the strongest one. "I guess I was more like the typical Baptist minister's son, you go the other way, which is how I wound up in AA," was the way he would later describe it.

The younger McLeod never went to college. He made his way as a pool hustler, a game that offers survival for people who can think three shots ahead. (He later encouraged his two sons to take up pool "so they would never go hungry.")

He eventually found his way to Vancouver, which had a budding computer industry. New start-ups and new products seemed to pop up overnight and the industry offered McLeod, a quick study and a born salesman, a niche in marketing. He liked the business's rapid-fire stream of change, but he also found he liked the stability. He settled down and, with the help of AA, began to stay sober.

Members at the Vancouver chapter took turns at the podium telling their stories. "AA is honesty in all of our affairs," explained McLeod. "It's all about being real and open to your fellow alcoholics, that's where it starts. . . . The only way to stay sober is that you have to tell the truth. I knew intuitively I had to run my life like that."

A mentor-like relationship began with Ballard, who had listened to many of McLeod's sessions at the podium, where he talked about several failed attempts to start his own business. One night, when McLeod had confessed that his current company had offered him a promotion in Boston, where he didn't want to go, Ballard sat him down and invited him to join Ballard's company, then called Ballard Research.

McLeod knew that Ballard was in the business of developing some kind of high-technology batteries, a venture funded by Amoco, a major oil company. Through the AA sessions he had also heard how Ballard had been through his own failures, including a bankruptcy in a long quest to develop a commercial breakthrough in rechargeable lithium-ion batteries. McLeod confessed he didn't know a thing about batteries.

Ballard told him that didn't matter. Ballard was worried that, like some of his previous sponsors, Amoco would soon lose patience and pull its money out. Ballard wanted McLeod to develop a new, and completely different business for Ballard. The older man wasn't sure what it might be, but he felt that by now McLeod had failed enough to know how to find a good one.

"The measure of the man is whether you can get up and try again. Maybe now is the time to hit one out of the ballpark," he told McLeod. McLeod took the job and he, Ballard, and one of the company's other executives eventually found an opportunity that seemed promising, a request for a proposal by Canada's Department of National Defence for a fuel cell that was similar to one the United States had used to power the Gemini series of space flights in the 1960s.

Ballard's company, which had one of Canada's best electrochemistry labs, was awarded the contract. It was a $500,000 project to develop remote power sources for military communications systems—small potatoes compared with the multimillion-dollar U.S. Army research projects that Ballard had directed in the past—but as a business possibility it was different enough that Ballard bought the idea and entrusted McLeod to help flesh it out.

The first person that McLeod hired was David Watkins, a big, bearlike man with scraggly, long hair who rode up on a motorcycle. What impressed McLeod was Watkins's adventurousness. He had left the slumping economy of St. Johns in New Brunswick and had driven 4,300 miles across Canada on his motorcycle to go to engineering school in Vancouver. Then he'd worked in the oil fields around Calgary and later worked for a company that wanted to make an animal feed supplement out of paper mill sludge. Watkins made it work, but the company discovered that soybeans were cheaper.

When McLeod asked Watkins what he wanted to do in life, his reply was quick and succinct: "I want to build something." That was the right answer for Ballard, who admired Watkins's intensity and made him head of a four-man skunkworks apart from the company's battery development plant in North Vancouver. Their experiments began in a small industrial park in an area largely populated by auto body shops.

Fuel cells were not new. They had been under experimentation since 1839 when William Grove, a Welsh lawyer and physicist, made a discovery. By then the process of electrolysis, using electricity to split water into its constituent elements, oxygen and hydrogen, was known. What Grove found was that in reversing the process, in joining oxygen and hydrogen to make water, the reaction resulted in a small amount of electricity.

It was not enough electricity to compete with batteries, so research was largely shelved until World War II when a British scientist, Francis T. Bacon, began examining fuel cells' potential for a lightweight power source. His concept, elaborated upon by General Electric, was picked by NASA in 1962 to power the two-man Gemini earth-orbiting flights.

The components of fuel cells have the same names as batteries. The cells have an anode, a cathode, and an electrolyte, but the similarities stop there. Batteries can make a small amount of electricity, but are used mainly to store it. Fuel cells can produce a great deal of electricity by modifying oxygen and hydrogen and then combining them in an electrolyte using a catalyst for a reaction that takes the hydrogen molecule apart. When that happens the energy bonds that hold two hydrogen atoms together in a molecule are released, resulting in a stream of moving electrons and a catalytic change that combines part of the former hydrogen molecule with oxygen to make water. The parts of the electrolyte that make this happen consist of a thin polymer membrane and a platinum-coated catalyst.

The device was called a Proton Exchange Membrane (PEM) fuel cell. In 1963 it was attractive to NASA and the Gemini astronauts because it seemed to work and was much lighter than a battery. At the time, NASA was in a major hurry-up mode, driven by President John F. Kennedy's vow to put a man on the moon within a decade.

The Gemini spacecraft, which were enlarged and renamed versions of the older, single-man Mercury space vehicles, were needed to simulate the long moon missions in Earth orbit and for practicing the rendezvous and docking maneuvers that would later be needed to launch and then recover the lunar landing module. What was important and exciting to the astronauts was that the lightness of the PEM fuel cells made it possible for their eight-thousand-pound spacecraft to stay in orbit with enough power and supplies for the crews to be aloft for two weeks. Besides providing electricity, the fuel cells might even help Gemini make its own drinking water.

"Unfortunately, in the mid-sixties the fuel cell was still an experimental device and not only had a short operating life, but the water produced by them turned out to be the color of strong coffee," recalled one of the Gemini's crew members, Michael Collins. The coffee-like water had little puffy objects floating in it that the astronauts dubbed "furries." This made fuel cell water undrinkable, but Gemini carried enough water to satisfy the crews, who accepted the other quirks presented by their fancy new power system.

"Unlike batteries, they had character," recalled Collins, who later compared the six fuel cells Gemini missions carried to sled dogs. "Some were stronger and pulled more than their share of the electrical load; others were malingerers and had to be coddled and rested periodically."

Before each launch, he recalled, crews were given a piece of paper describing the peculiarities of each cell. This was helpful because after two Earth orbits by *Gemini 5,* the instruments showed that pressure in the oxygen tank was dropping sharply. The crew powered off the fuel cells, abandoning part of their training mission, but later found the fuel cells and the oxygen supply had somehow revived.

The astronauts, most of them military pilots, were used to living with or around snafus and had what they felt to be much bigger unknowns to worry about, such as the first major space walks. But Chuck Matthews, the director of the Gemini program, confided to Collins twenty years later that an unfixable fuel cell malfunction was one of his biggest nightmares.

After the Gemini series, work on the PEM fuel cell was discontinued and GE later sold the technology. But before it did, it made a report for Los Alamos National Laboratory on the potential uses for the PEM fuel cell in automobiles.

Twenty years later, McLeod and Watkins began making visits to Los Alamos. In 1984 they found that the GE report, along with GE's plans and detailed accounts of the devices it used to test the fuel cells, were all in the public domain. They also found a mentor in David Huff, who had been appointed by the laboratory to find commercial applications for fuel cells and other technologies that were languishing on the laboratory's shelves.

It was Huff who had been encouraging Canada to try fuel cells for remote communications systems in the Arctic and now he had a Canadian company eager to experiment with them. Huff told Watkins that potential uses for the PEM battery had been overlooked.

Watkins examined the GE plans and found they would require a lot of work to put in a car. NASA had spent millions to make a few stacks of PEM cells. They used expensive, exotic materials such as platinum, niobium, and titanium. For fuel they required tanks of pure oxygen and hydrogen. While they were all the rage in newspaper accounts of space travel and futuristic-sounding plans for clean power production, there seemed to be few prospects for commercial uses for them. The economics looked doubtful.

"These just weren't terrestrial things," explained Watkins, who decided to start out by making one of the cells from GE's drawings.

He had soon put together a single three-by-five-inch PEM cell and was thrilled to see the output was enough electricity to light a small bulb.

It was after midnight, but he roused McLeod, who lived five blocks away from the makeshift laboratory. McLeod soon arrived. "When you know him [Watkins], trust me, you get up," McLeod explained. "If you don't, you're an idiot." It was the first fuel cell that McLeod and Watkins had ever seen and the dim light it produced was shining at them in the quiet darkness of their shacklike laboratory. The moment brought out some of the still-latent elements of the Baptist minister in McLeod. "He made me hold it in my hands. As God is my witness, that was the day my world changed. It was just stunning."

From then on, Watkins felt, it was going to be pure, grind-it-out engineering, finding ways to make the cell cheaper, better, and simpler to operate. The first job he tackled, though, was trying to figure out how to make it run on oxygen drawn from the air, a move that would probably cut power production, but was essential to drive down cost.

Those experiments brought in Danny Epp, a mechanical engineer, who had worked at Ballard's company in Vancouver before taking a leave to work in the oil fields. Now he was back and his assignment was to mill patterns of tiny one-eighth-inch grooves in small plates of solid graphite that would serve as fuel cell walls. Graphite was much cheaper than the niobium used in the Gemini cells, but it was hard to cut and Ballard's budget had no money to buy the necessary machinery or to do the milling.

Epp, however, proved to be an expert scrounger. He found a small Vancouver company with computer-guided milling machines that engraved bowling trophies, award plaques, and other items. The company agreed to give Epp time on its milling machines in exchange for some specialized clamps he made for them that made it easier to engrave various items.

Wally Rippel speaking at the start of the "Great Electric Car Race" in Pasadena, August 26, 1968. *Courtesy Wally Rippel*

Wally Rippel's electrified 1959 VW Bus, just before the start of his winning, cross-country race to Boston. *Courtesy Wally Rippel*

MIT's electric Corvair getting a charge from a power pole along the 3,398 mile route to Pasadena. *Courtesy Children of Leon Loeb and Stephen Horner*

Leon Loeb, manager of the MIT team, takes a rest in the wire-strewn front seat of the Corvair after one of its many breakdowns. *Courtesy Children of Leon Loeb and Stephen Horner*

A skeptical power company lineman looks on as an MIT student uses a hammer to crack chunks of ice used to cool the Corvair's overheating batteries. *Courtesy Children of Leon Loeb and Stephen Horner*

Amory Lovins, an American futurist who inspired environmental groups and California regulators to support the rules that led to the recent commercialization of electric cars.
Copyright © Judy Hills Lovins 2006

Hans Tholstrup, the Australian "adventurer" who organized the "Solar Challenge," the 1987 solar-powered car race across Australia's outback.
Courtesy Hans Tholstrup

Paul MacCready—famed for building the first solar-powered aircraft to cross the English Channel—tests another of his creations: the lightweight frame of Sunraycer, GM's winning entry in the first "Solar Challenge" race across Australia.
Photo courtesy of Alec Brooks

Technicians at work in Australia's outback on GM's Sunraycer, which crossed Australia from north to south in six days—two-and-a-half days ahead of its nearest rival, a Ford entry called "Sunchaser."
Photo courtesy of Alec Brooks

Alan Cocconi preparing the electronics of Sunraycer. His later work led to GM's prototype electric car, the Impact, and also contributed to the Tesla Roadster. *Photo courtesy of Alec Brooks*

Bob Lutz, the father and chief salesman of the Chevrolet Volt, makes a pitch between two of them. *Courtesy General Motors*

Century of progress: A Renault Spark Formula E race car, capable of 140 mph, poses alongside a Krieger Brougham, a French-built electric made in 1904 that managed 14.9 mph. The photo, taken just before the Formula E racers sped through the streets of Buenos Aires in January 2015, is a reminder of an earlier era when electric cars ruled the roads. *Courtesy of FIA Formula E*

Formula E racers take a trial run at Donington Park Race Circuit in England in August 2014, preparing for the first season of global, electric car racing by Formula 1 drivers. The races are designed to attract young buyers to the speed, acceleration, and quiet of electric cars. *Courtesy of FIA Formula E*

Elon Musk, the chairman and product architect of Tesla Motors, poses with the successor to the Tesla Roadster, the Model S sedan. *Courtesy AP Photo/ Richard Drew*

Japanese buyers exploring Toyota's first commercial fuel cell car, the Mirai. *Courtesy Kyodo via AP Images*

Formula E racers snake down a hill at Donington Park Race Circuit in England in August 2014, preparing for the first season of global, electric car racing by Formula 1 drivers. *Courtesy of FIA Formula E*

John "Plasma Boy" Wayland, a pioneer of electric car drag racing and cofounder of the National Electric Drag Racing Association. *Courtesy of John Wayland*

Dr. Geoffrey Ballard, the founder of Ballard Power Systems and the father of the fuel cell–powered electric car, after being named a member of the Order of British Columbia in 2003. *© Province of British Columbia. All rights reserved. Reproduced with permission of the Province of British Columbia*

John Wayland's "White Zombie," an electrified 1972 Datsun with twenty-eight lead-acid storage batteries in the trunk, does a "burnout" on a drag strip in Portland, Oregon. "It's like being shot out of a cannon," explained Wayland. *Courtesy of John Wayland*

"Big Daddy" Don Garlits and his first electric drag racer, the Swamp Rat 37. *Courtesy Lisa Crigar Photography*

Working with the models of fuel cells he had made out of the GE designs, Watkins could see some errors. He suspected that the channels engraved on the fuel cell plates that guided the oxygen and hydrogen into the cell to the polymer membrane were being clogged by accumulating water. Redesigning the pattern to remove the water, Watkins concluded, should result in more fuel going into the reaction and, thus, more power.

In late 1984 the team had a Eureka moment, of sorts, when they assembled a stack of cells from Epp's newly engraved plates and hooked them up to some battery cables, which promptly began to melt. The stack, now drawing oxygen from the surrounding air, had produced four times more power than they expected.

The results at Ballard were interesting enough that people from Los Alamos began to visit them. One visitor was Nicholas Vanderborgh, an electrochemist, who was also visiting GM's labs run by competing divisions in the company that were also working on fuel cells. At the time, Vanderborgh recalled, automakers seemed to think fuel cells were foolish. "GM seemed almost bent on proving it was. They were trying to cram stuff into existing vehicles."

By contrast, he found Ballard's effort to be much smaller, more methodical, and simpler. It was, as he found it, a "low-buck operation." Watkins and the others had low salaries, but had been awarded stock in the Ballard company that, they felt, would pay off when their project succeeded. "If they needed something like a tape recorder, they would have to buy it out of their salaries," noted Vanderborgh.

That wasn't the half of it, according to Epp and Watkins. They had spent enough time in laboratories to know that equipment made to lab standards was customarily ordered from a company called Thermo Fisher Scientific, a Massachusetts company with offices in fifty different countries.

The running joke at Ballard, later renamed Ballard Power Systems, was that the fuel cell team got their materials at "Beaver

Scientific," which was their name for Beaver Lumber, a hardware and materials store just down the street. Sometimes Epp didn't have to go that far. He kept an eye out for useful items in refuse barrels outside other companies in the industrial area.

As their lab work progressed, McLeod and Watkins began to do more networking. They attended meetings at Los Alamos and elsewhere where scientists from companies representing potential users or investors were discussing fuel cells. Geoffrey Ballard, who spent most of his time working on the battery side of the company, stayed behind, but he mentored both men on the right language they needed to approach potential investors and describe their research as it advanced.

Ballard's hands-off management style was helpful in more ways than one, according to McLeod, Epp, and others who worked with Ballard, because he did not suffer fools well and had a tendency to yell at people who disagreed with his theories. "Geoffrey was dangerous, frankly, when standing in front of investors because he would just go off on them," recalled McLeod. "He believed in us when a lot of people didn't, but he didn't know half the time what we were doing."

Sometimes at their technical meetings Watkins and McLeod weren't sure what they were doing, either. At first, they felt awkward and out of place. Accustomed to month-by-month sea changes in the computer business, McLeod had a hard time understanding the leisurely pace of government-sponsored research, especially when it was attached to the military-industrial complex. There was a preoccupation with what seemed to be arcane levels of technical detail. "The first conference we ever went to did not seem to be a serious business because it was all about perpetual funding; everybody in that world was attached to large corporations."

Watkins, who did understand the technical detail, felt it often seemed not to lead anywhere. The repetition frustrated him to the point where he once rose, grabbed the nearest microphone, and sputtered: "What is the problem you are trying to solve?" Then, according to McLeod, the room grew silent.

But the meetings and the networking eventually paid off. There were people in those rooms who understood what the Canadians were trying to do. They gave Watkins tips and provided some new materials.

For example, the polymer membrane at the heart of the GE fuel cell they were working with had come from DuPont and was called Nafion. Watkins learned that there was a thinner, more specialized polymer membrane available from Dow Chemical and he acquired some samples. Membranes had multiple uses in defense research, including some that were still shrouded in secrecy. Some were created for attempts to separate plutonium from nuclear production reactors to make nuclear weapons. Others were used in U.S. Navy subs to provide oxygen through electrolysis.

Watkins continued to make progress with his fuel cell experiments. He'd figured out how to make the reaction work by feeding it with methanol, a relatively cheap source of hydrogen.

His trial-and-error approach continued until one night in October 1986, when he hooked up the thinner Dow membrane and suddenly got an unexpected surge of power. The bolts on the connecting cables got so hot they were turning a bright red. By Watkins's calculations this was the leap in power density that should make fuel cells a commercial possibility for automobiles.

"A eureka moment just knocks off your socks," he recalled. "I sat down and watched that first single cell all night. I was sitting there and thinking that as an engineer you dream about a step change and that you're there and you recognize that that is what you have." Sometimes the moment takes time to sink in, added Watkins. "But I knew when I was looking at this cell that no one else on the planet had seen what we were seeing."

"The Canadians," as McLeod and Watkins were called at Los Alamos, described the results at the next technical meeting. There were some skeptical comments, but Watkins also saw some people in the audience go running out of the room.

Byron McCormick, then the head of fuel cell development at Los Alamos, invited McLeod into his office and gave him the phone number of people at GM to call. "I don't think you appreciate what it is you people have done," he told him. "This is the most significant breakthrough in fuel cells that I've ever seen."

McLeod said the first thing he did was change his flight plans. He hopped on a plane to Ottawa where the Canadian government was continuing to fund the Ballard research. He wanted them to help put a patent on what Watkins had done "because we couldn't afford it."

GM became the first major auto company to visit Ballard, but the meetings did not go well. Nicholas Vanderborgh, the scientist from Los Alamos, attended one of them and witnessed a shouting match between Ballard and the GM executives. According to McLeod, GM looked at the Ballard technology but decided that they could do the same thing themselves, in house. Then McLeod said Ballard might potentially make a deal with Daimler, the big, technology-hungry German manufacturer of Mercedes-Benz.

Someone on the GM side actually laughed. It was at that point, according to McLeod, Geoffrey Ballard exploded and ordered GM off his company's property.

"This is where Geoffrey was very useful," McLeod explained.

SIXTEEN

Running Ahead of the Pack

German engineers began showing up at Ballard's fuel cell skunkworks in the early 1990s. They were from Daimler AG, one of the largest vehicle manufacturers in the world and, perhaps, the most technology-hungry.

The Stuttgart-based company, feeling it was falling behind the United States and Japan in automotive electronics, had opened up a major research department in the 1980s and it sent its engineers and scientists scouting the world for ways to take back the lead in the fast-growing and highly competitive global market. The Daimler visitors carried a certain amount of engineering pride with them, a mind-set that comes from producing Mercedes-Benz, probably the best-known luxury car in the world.

"For Mercedes, one of the brand's images is to be a technology leader. So they could not accept that others could be in the lead," was how one of the new visitors to Vancouver, Andreas Truckenbrodt, later described it. But the Daimler men did not come off as being arrogant, rubbing the Ballard team the wrong way the way GM's representatives had.

Daimler's credentials as a leader in the automobile business go all the way back to the very start, in 1883, when two German inventors, Gottlieb Daimler and Karl Benz, working independently of each other, developed the first internal combustion engines that were light and yet strong enough to propel a car. They both built companies and designed cars. Daimler's were so good that in 1899, after winning a series of the world's first auto races in Nice, France, with a specially built, low-slung, and powerful car Emil Jellinek, the driver, was impressed enough to name it after his daughter, Mercedes.

Mercedes-Benz, the name the two companies took after they were merged in 1926, was built upon a history of defying doubters and dazzling critics. Benz, nearly broke after the early days of his research, watched his investors walk away when they heard he was building something as silly and useless as a horseless carriage. They wanted him to use his engines to power pumps, a solid business that, they felt, was the real future for this noisy, but powerful machine.

Much later Mercedes-Benz built a flashy modern museum in downtown Stuttgart where the first thing visitors see is an empty room containing only one thing: a stuffed horse. There is no explanation except for a small silver plate screwed into its wooden platform bearing an engraved quotation from one of their most illustrious critics, Kaiser Wilhelm II, the last German emperor. He is believed to have said: "I do believe in the horse. The automobile is no more than a transitory phenomenon."

Benz, a cautious but stubborn engineer, learned to maneuver his way around opposition to his startling new technology. In 1895 it seemed to come from all levels of German society. He made a horseless carriage in his rented shop, installed his engine, and took it out for a spin on the backstreets of Mannheim. The local police were so outraged at the explosive racket and speed of his machine that they created the first traffic ordinance for cars: horseless carriages could go no faster than a horse.

This meant that Benz could not test how fast his machine could really go, so he managed to lure a powerful and curious regional government minister to go with him for a ride. On the side, Benz had made a deal with a local milkman to pass him in his horse-drawn milk cart and then jeer at him. They even rehearsed it to get the timing just right.

When the milkman rumbled past and then turned to jeer at them the minister was outraged. "Good heavens, man," he shouted, "are you going to take all day to cover a mile or so?"

Benz meekly replied he was obeying the law.

"Never mind about that," said the minister. "We can't have milk carts passing us; push her along as hard as she will go!"

Benz shot past the milk cart. The law was repealed. Benz was free to go as fast as he wanted on his explosive joyrides in the German countryside where elderly farmers knelt down and made the sign of the cross when he passed and young boys threw stones at him. Suspicious innkeepers took his money but made him park his vehicle in an open field, fearing it would blow up.

In sum, it takes stubbornness, moxie, and guile to introduce the public to a new commercial technology and Karl Benz and the men he trained set the standard. He seemed to have an endless supply.

"They [the engineers from Daimler] were the perfect fit for us," recalled David McLeod, then Ballard's marketing director, who became the official greeter for the visitors. "They were far more sophisticated and they intuitively understood David Watkins." Watkins was the Ballard engineer who had made the breakthrough with the Ballard fuel cell stack.

Ballard executives knew it was a risk talking to Daimler's savvy engineers, so at first the Daimler people could only meet with McLeod, the only nonscientist involved in their fuel cell project. That, at least, would give Ballard some level of protection against the visitors from Stuttgart ferreting out the details of what Watkins had done to make the stack simpler, cheaper, and more powerful than its predecessors.

McLeod was determined not to give anything away. "I said the only way we can continue this discussion is that we'd need to have a joint venture. What you're looking for, we've pretty much done."

The team from Daimler already knew that. It had recently acquired Dornier, a German aerospace company where scientists had told them of the fuel cells used to provide electric power in a spacecraft. Their sense was Ballard's design might be the best one in the world to propel a car.

Daimler, like other automakers, had become concerned that history was repeating itself. Just as Daimler and Benz had replaced the horse, proposals to tighten auto emissions controls around the world, beginning with California's Zero Emission Vehicle mandate, might someday require the replacement of the internal combustion engine.

If that technological revolution were to happen, Daimler wanted to lead it. As the requirements for ever-lower emissions standards grew, based on a fleet average, having a number of ZEVs to sell would help protect sales of the more expensive, heavier, luxury models of the Mercedes-Benz, which was Daimler's bread and butter.

The joint venture with Ballard came together in 1992 and Danny Epp, a mechanical engineer who fabricated parts of the first fuel cells using borrowed machines at a place that made bowling trophies, found himself enjoying the novelty of working with the Germans. They sent teams of manufacturing experts to Vancouver and marveled at the lack of bureaucracy controlling operations at the Ballard lab. "We had teams that went over there. We even took German lessons. We worked quite closely with them," recalled Epp.

Daimler technicians in Germany installed their first Ballard fuel cell stacks in a commercial van called NECAR 1 in 1994 at a research facility in Nabern, a suburb of Stuttgart. The bulky white vehicle soon showed there was much work left to be done. Its top speed was fifty-six miles per hour. It had an eighty-mile range and the van's cargo compartment was crammed with equipment needed to make the vehicle's electric drive system work so there was no room left to carry anything else.

But the Ballard-Daimler venture soon developed a brisk, cash-producing business selling the Ballard fuel cell stacks to other automakers, who followed Daimler's lead and wanted to sample the magic that Watkins had discovered. The list began with Toyota, Honda, and GM. Fuel cell technology was proliferating, which is just what the Daimler people wanted to happen.

Ballard "stands out in the first group of organizations," concluded a study on fuel cells done for the California Air Resources Board in 1998. It had a better business plan than most automotive manufacturers and Daimler's resources behind it, noted the report, which added that Daimler was the only company in a position to strenuously test the Ballard design in a car.

CARB had developed a keen interest in the blossoming enterprise in Vancouver because fuel cells seemed to have the best prospects for eventually meeting California's ambitious and controversial zero-emission mandate. When it came to perfecting the fuel cell, Ballard was even running ahead of Los Alamos National Laboratory, one of the U.S. Department of Energy's major nuclear weapons labs, which had started the spurt of interest in automotive fuel cells in the 1970s. But Los Alamos had invested most of its research money into a different technology, called phosphoric acid fuel cells that, increasingly, didn't seem as well-suited for cars as Ballard's stacks.

In 1996, however, General Motors hatched a plan to put Detroit back out in front. It had been working closely with Los Alamos researchers and in 1986 it hired Byron McCormick, the engineer who headed the laboratory's program. A new director at Los Alamos intended to refocus the lab's main effort back upon making and refurbishing the U.S. arsenal of nuclear weapons and McCormick, who had become increasingly interested in commercial applications for fuel cells, let it be known he was thinking of leaving. He promptly got a call from GM.

First, he became absorbed in the defense-related programs at GM, later switching over to the team that launched the ill-fated EV1. Then one day in 1996, he received a call from Harry J. Pearce, the automaker's newly anointed vice chairman, who asked McCormick to drop by for a chat.

In the upper echelons of the auto business, it is helpful to have people around who can envision the world eight years ahead, because that's about how long it takes to develop a car from scratch. Pearce, the former head of a Bismarck, North Dakota, law firm, also had an engineering degree and a philosophic bent. He was sometimes called upon to play the futurist for GM's board.

When McCormick arrived, Pearce began by dwelling on the fact that there were more than six billion people in the world and when they all became prosperous enough to buy cars, gasoline supplies would likely run out. Then Pearce mused a little further into the future. If all of those six billion people did succeed in gassing up their cars, the resulting pulse of carbon dioxide would probably bring chaos. These heat-trapping emissions would accelerate global warming, which could make life in some parts of the world very difficult.

"I don't know which one of these things is going to rise as a problem, but at the end of the day it's going to make the things we make obsolete," McCormick recalls being told. "Fuel cells," Pearce went on, "are the best thing I've ever heard about how we go forward. We've got to start a program."

McCormick, who had had to scrounge money from a variety of other programs to build the fuel cell effort at Los Alamos and who had managed to hang on during the many ups and downs of the EV1 program, came up with a way to build a separate fuel cell organization with research units in Detroit, a suburb of Rochester, New York, Torrance, California, and another in Germany. It had a big budget and McCormick and Pearce did everything they could to insulate it from the competitive needs of other GM departments and laboratories. Budgetary infighting within the massive company, then still the world's largest automaker, was endemic and McCormick and Pearce knew it would remain a serious threat to their new project.

Further, the emergence of a vehicle that depended on hydrogen fuel would be enormously disruptive to other businesses, beginning with the major oil companies. That would be a headache and GM officials wanted to get a ballpark estimate of the economic clout of the various industries that an emerging era of hydrogen-powered cars might disrupt. McCormick did a back-of-the-envelope calculation. It was somewhere around $4 trillion.

The rejuvenated GM program bought a number of fuel cell stacks from Ballard, but McCormick found relations between the two companies continued to be difficult. "We'd buy a sample of something from them, or we'd buy some test equipment and they'd run a press release saying GM has bought this."

According to McCormick, Ballard, hungry for cash returns from its research, was trying to hype its stock prices by suggesting that GM was on the verge of buying Ballard fuel cell stacks for GM cars. "Finally we got so disgusted with them that we got our lawyers to write them a cease-and-desist letter," he recalled. "Then they put out a release that would say a major automotive company was about to buy their fuel cells." In sum, according to McCormick, "We and they had a troubled relationship."

In the meantime, Daimler was preparing to raise the ante in the fuel cell game. It called in Ferdinand Panik, the former head of its research department, from his post overseeing truck production in

Brazil. Panik was an electrical engineer educated in Berlin and familiar with the cutting edge of automotive technology. But this time he was summoned for his negotiating skills.

A tall, slim, charismatic man with a full head of curly gray hair, Panik had brought the European automakers together for the first time ever in the 1980s to jointly develop a crash program to make their automotive electronics competitive with cars from Japan and the United States. Daimler's new mission for Panik was to make fuel cell–powered cars happen. The first step would be for him to bring together the world's major automakers to push governments hard enough to develop a radically different fuel system that could deliver some form of hydrogen fuel for cars.

The logic went something like this: mass production has always been the magic of the auto industry. Starting with Henry Ford, it made the internal combustion automobile cheap enough to attract a large number of buyers. To accomplish that with these radically different, space-age cars, there had to be a counterpart of the gasoline station, a large, visible network of retail outlets that could reliably deliver some form of hydrogen fuel.

For that, Panik had to lure in major oil companies and get them and the automakers to develop the tanks, the pumps, and global market standards for making and retailing hydrogen. Daimler emphasized that no one company had the political clout or the money to make all of this happen. Panik sat down in a small room at Nabern and worked out a plan to bring automakers together. First he felt Daimler needed what he called an "anchor," a major presence in the fuel cell business to convince Daimler's competitors that he was serious. For that he flew out to visit Ballard in Vancouver.

McLeod, Ballard's marketing director, was thrilled. "From a management point of view, you'd be surprised he was a Mercedes guy. He was a hell of a salesman, kind of wonderfully crazy. He knew what the game was and made a lot of money at it."

After looking at Ballard's fuel cell technology, Panik put some of Daimler's money on the table, offering $250 million Canadian for 20 percent of Ballard's stock. He wanted to create a joint venture with a major American and a Japanese automaker. The most logical choice was GM, which had been negotiating with Ballard and buying its fuel cell stacks to experiment with, but Byron McCormick, now the negotiator for GM, reiterated the company's long-standing position that, despite the use of Ballard's stacks, GM had the engineering skills to go it alone.

Panik's next choice for a joint venture partner was Honda, which was also experimenting with Ballard's fuel cell stacks. "The idea was to get them to look at it, decide whether they wanted it, and then, maybe, join the club," explained Panik. But Honda, though intent on beating its archrival Toyota—which had also begun working with Ballard's fuel cell stacks—was also leery of a joint venture with Daimler. "We negotiated almost three years, but the feeling was not good from both sides because Honda wanted to do it more or less by themselves," Panik recalled.

Panik had much better luck with his next negotiating target, which was the California Air Resources Board. All the automakers who sold substantial numbers of vehicles in the state's huge auto market were paying very close attention to CARB because if they didn't meet the requirements of the mandate, they couldn't sell cars in the state. California was important; its residents were buying sixty thousand new cars every year.

And CARB was paying close attention to Daimler. In 1998 a panel of fuel cell experts hired by CARB to evaluate automotive fuel cells found there had been "impressive advances" in development in the short span of five years and that Daimler's joint venture with Ballard "was a milestone that signaled automobile manufacturers involvement on the necessary scale."

Noting that Ford was also involved, the report went on to say "it seems quite likely that these efforts will succeed" and that the

Ballard-Daimler-Ford partnership planned to produce "commercial quantities" of fuel cell vehicles as early as 2004. It was a plan that CARB's experts declared was "credible."

This was an alarm bell that got the attention of the auto industry, the oil industry, and the financial markets. The race was on and one horse was already shooting out of the gate! For his discussions with CARB, Panik had invited others to join him and he quickly found willing partners lining up. There were GM, Toyota, Ford, Honda, Ballard, and major oil companies including Texaco, Shell, and BP.

As the leader, Panik told CARB that there might be a technology that was superior to batteries in its ability to make a car that could find commercial acceptance and reach the zero-emission level. The automakers wanted to develop prototypes to prove it, but they wanted credit from CARB for making the effort. On Earth Day, April 20, 1999, the group founded the California Fuel Cell Partnership with CARB as a member of its board.

Big Oil and Big Auto involve companies that spend billions to reach their objectives and don't do things by halves. The members voted to erect a large new building near downtown Sacramento where industry members could keep close contact with California's regulators and key politicians. The building included an automotive laboratory where automakers could work on their demonstration vehicles in adjacent work bays.

"This was a good negotiation," Panik recalled. The pieces for his ambitious plan for a kind of mega-lobby, a fusion of the automakers and oil companies that could negotiate terms for a standardized, global hydrogen fuel delivery system, looked as though they were coming together.

It was certainly a good negotiation for Ballard. Its stock, which had been stumbling along at $9 a share, shot into the stratosphere, hitting $188 within a few months. The three denizens of Ballard's fuel cell skunkworks, McLeod, Watkins, and Epp, who had been paid mostly in stock, "all became moderately well off," explained Epp.

By 1990 Ballard had become a different company, now with robust resources and two major automakers as partners. It was a bittersweet moment for Geoffrey Ballard, the main founder and former chairman of the board, who had resigned for health reasons in late 1997. He felt estranged from the company that he'd built as a research unit. Now it was firmly in the hands of business types who were tightly focused on the stock price and not about to take the kind of risks Ballard had. In the coming years McLeod, Epp, and Watkins would also leave.

Before Ballard died in August 2008, he continued to rail at his skeptics, calling them "pistonheads." In 1999 *Time* magazine called him a "Hero of the Planet," and Ballard crowed in an interview that he had finally won over his skeptics. Science colleagues who were once "embarrassed to be seen with me at professional symposia," he said, were now inviting him to give speeches.

Speak he did, telling college audiences to "Dare to be in a hurry to change things for the better." *Time* noted that "If Ballard, a trim sixty-six-year-old with an unflinching gaze, sounds cocky it may be because he has finally won respect at the end of a long and winding career." But *Time* failed to note that Ballard, by then a multimillionaire, had always sounded cocky, even in his darkest days of failure and near-bankruptcy.

So in one sense, nothing had changed. Ballard went on to tell *Time* magazine that by 2010 "the internal combustion engine will go the way of the horse. It will be a curiosity to my grandchildren."

Needless to say, that hasn't happened, but Byron McCormick, who sometimes crossed swords with Ballard as a negotiator for GM, thinks Ballard deserves credit for taking the first step toward this monumental objective by selling the first workable samples of fuel cells to auto manufacturers. "People could say, oh, my gosh, you could sort of get it in a car and it does sort of work. Yeah, he did start the process."

SEVENTEEN

Into the Valley of Death

There were countless ways that the multibillion-dollar companies of Big Oil and Big Auto could get bogged down in the complexities of planning a global support system for a radically new automobile, so the members of California's new Fuel Cell Partnership came up with a rule that would give them a simple solution, or no solution at all: their decisions had to be unanimous.

That presented the first problem for Dr. Panik, the partnership's chairman of the board in 2001. There was considerable enthusiasm among the board's members for hydrogen-fueled vehicles, but major disagreements over where the hydrogen would come from. Most of Daimler's experiments had been done by extracting hydrogen from methanol, a toxic liquid fuel.

Daimler's theory was that a liquid fuel would provide the easiest fit with consumers' ingrained habit of refueling at the neighborhood gas station. In theory, a methanol pump could be positioned alongside the gasoline pumps so drivers could roll in and fill up. The process would take about five minutes.

Daimler, like many of the automakers, had studied the dismal showing of GM's EV1 and wanted to avoid both range anxiety and the eight-hour recharge times. At least in the beginning of the partnership, that was what Big Oil wanted, too. They were not in the business of making and selling electricity.

So Panik believed there was the potential for a consensus. Although Daimler builds a spectrum of automobiles, including hybrids and electrics, he was sure then and is still sure now that fuel cells will eventually dominate. "Fuel cell vehicles are the choice when zero emissions and a potential for broad market coverage are required."

But while Daimler and others were bullish about methanol, there were other paths to get to hydrogen. GM and Exxon were involved in a joint experiment to make refueling fuel cell cars even more familiar to consumers. They showed board members a small pickup truck. You drove into the gasoline station, filled it up with gasoline, and equipment in the truck, called a reformer, converted the gasoline into hydrogen.

Catherine Dunwoody, a biochemist borrowed from the CARB zero-emission mandate program to be executive director of the Fuel Cell Partnership, remembers looking at the truck and feeling distinctly underwhelmed. "It basically took up the whole back of the vehicle."

While the theory of deriving hydrogen from an existing liquid fuel was initially popular, board members grew increasingly doubtful that a reformer could ever be made small and cheap enough to work in a commercial car. Reformers required energy to operate, sapping some of the fuel cell's touted advantage in energy efficiency. Moreover, because they used methane, a fossil fuel, as a hydrogen source that made them noncompliant with the zero-emission mandate.

Meanwhile, lawyers from the oil companies began to worry about the liability aspects of refining and selling large quantities of methanol, a form of alcohol that some people might be tempted to drink. It attacks the central nervous system and can result in blindness, coma, and death. Gasoline stations already had a serious problem with gasoline additives leaking into underground aquifers. Adding methanol tanks would invite more than just a few additional headaches.

"The more we looked at it [methanol], I think we all kind of agreed that would be a bad way to go, there were just too many environmental issues," explained Byron McCormick, who represented GM on the partnership's board. He was beginning to worry that deciding to reform gasoline to get the hydrogen would rule out attractive future possibilities of using electricity from solar and wind power to split hydrogen out of water using electrolysis.

This had been the desired endgame of Harry Pearce, McCormick's mentor on GM's board. It was the dream of regulators and some environmental groups because it had the potential of clearing the air of much of the smog from the transportation sector and protecting the atmosphere from its substantial climate-changing greenhouse gas emissions. To McCormick, the evolving discussions at the partnership seemed kind of circular. "We'd be down to, well, let's use a petroleum product and petroleum was one of the problems we were trying to solve," he recalled.

So in late 2001 the auto companies, racing to bring fuel cell vehicles to market, agreed to make a giant, collective U-turn. They rejected the idea of filling up with a liquid fuel and switched to a simpler and more farsighted concept. Drivers would pull into gas stations and fill up a specially designed tank with compressed hydrogen. The oil companies saw they could get this business and indicated they would go along with it.

As chairman of the board, Dr. Panik, who had pressed Daimler's case for using methanol, supported the shift. The endgame for him was getting the combined political and economic power represented by the board members lined up behind a single approach for what he felt would be the car of the future. "We had to make a joint decision. It wasn't possible if one was going for one way and another was going for a different one. The group decided that with all the accumulated experience we had that hydrogen might be the best."

By the end of 2001, planners in Washington were applauding the shift. The incoming George W. Bush administration was sensitive to the U.S. auto industry's interest in fuel cell vehicles and began laying plans to replace the earlier Clinton administration's push for a hybrid-electric Supercar with a program for Freedomcar, which would rely on fuel cells.

California and Washington seemed headed toward what experts call the "hydrogen economy" that would eventually rely on stored hydrogen as an energy carrier. It had the potential of sharply reducing uses of oil, coal, and other more troublesome forms of fuel.

But that meant that Dr. Panik's group had to quickly pivot to the next problem, one they had helped expose: there was almost no experience with using hydrogen as a retail fuel for automobiles. This meant further delays because special delivery pumps and hydrogen tanks had to be designed and standardized for cars. Firemen and other first responders had to be trained to deal with hydrogen safety problems.

Jokes began to spread among environmental groups. Hydrogen was the fuel of the future and always would be because automakers and gasoline companies liked the idea of a future policy that remained glued to the distant horizon. They made their profits from the status quo.

Here was the classic nightmare for marketers. What if you spent millions of dollars developing and advertising a dog food and the dogs didn't like it?

CARB organized a series of focus groups around California to measure how serious this problem might be. What they found was not comforting. In general, the public felt fuel cell cars might be "small and not functional, lacking in power, unsafe, unattractive, too expensive to make up for the fuel economy improvement, and too early in development."

Buying a car to improve the environment "was either very low on the list or absent altogether." Men wanted cars with more space, power, reliability, fuel economy, and safety. Women prized low cost, fuel economy, style, amenities, and safety. The only hopeful sign was that if fuel cell vehicles performed as well as conventional cars, future buyers might be persuaded to spend a little more to drive one away.

In 2007 CARB decided to send outside experts around the world to take a second look at the progress of automakers. They found that the cost of storing hydrogen on vehicles had emerged as one of their major concerns. Although research money was now pouring into this area "hydrogen storage technologies have advanced relatively little in recent years." The report also warned that the cost of delivering hydrogen to gas stations might make the proposed fuel of tomorrow much more expensive than gasoline.

The news became still more dismal in the following year when GM's bankruptcy forced the shutdown of three of its four fuel cell research facilities. While some of its engineers transferred to a remaining unit in Michigan, "many left the company," according to McCormick, who also chose that year to retire. But before he left, GM, Toyota, and Daimler had passed a milestone: an historic agreement on the standards for a global hydrogen fueling system.

The automakers had seen battery-electric vehicles launched with conflicting refueling systems. One carmaker's plug would not fit into a competitor's charging station. "We all did not want to have that happen with fuel cells," McCormick explained.

The GM fuel cell research and development program has since been reconstituted and McCormick, who was involved in both Ballard's and GM's research efforts, remains hopeful. He asserts that the fuel cell car is now basically unstoppable, although a period of low-volume sales for fuel cell cars may linger for some time, which means that automakers will lose money in every sale.

"That's the valley of death and everyone is looking at it right now and trying to figure out how to work their way through it." He believes the popularity of fuel cell cars will continue to grow in "an ad hoc way," although the market will continue to be scary in the early years. Among companies there will be winners and losers. New companies could emerge, he believes. "But I think that the companies who have thought this through are going to come out of it early and are going to come out really well."

Automakers have made a great deal of money introducing new technology over the years, but unlike other businesses, it often requires patience to do it, explains Christian Mohrdieck, a physicist who replaced Dr. Panik at the California Fuel Cell Partnership and at Daimler's Nabern, Germany, facility, where the company has a whole warehouse filled with different experimental models of its fuel cell cars. They represent a $1.5 billion investment over the last two decades, Mohrdieck points out. The result is that Daimler is now road testing a fleet of more than two hundred fuel cell vehicles, which it believes to be the largest in the world. "We don't need any more cars for the demonstration phase, we can learn enough from these," he explains.

However, what Daimler needs to learn more about is the changing economics and how to adjust to current market conditions for the car, which have evolved since the more bullish days of Dr. Panik. Daimler's earlier plan was to lead the global launch of fuel cell cars by introducing its first commercial models in 2015. Now the company has pushed that date back to 2017.

It has had to navigate a variety of bumps in the road. Ballard's high-flying stock that resulted from the partnership with Daimler created problems for the big German carmaker. "We had no controlling interest. This was one of the issues because the other shareholders wanted to see very short-term profits. But the automotive fuel cell profit will take more time," Mohrdieck explains. That forced Daimler to renegotiate its contracts with Ballard four times until it achieved a controlling interest in the Ballard operations that made the fuel cells.

While the Canadian company was very good on the technology side, they were not an automotive company. It was more difficult for them to manage the long, disciplined grind to work out mass-production standards needed to meet regulatory targets and begin to recover its costs.

Costs come in two varieties, Mohrdieck notes. First there are variable costs, which is what it takes in labor and materials to put a given car together. Then there are the research and development costs, that lead up to mass production. For a while Daimler and most automakers will be in the "valley of death" with regard to both.

Over the next decade, he expects his company will begin to see profits because the results of the risky gamble that Dr. Panik took to create the global hydrogen fuel standard look better as time goes on. California shows no sign of weakening. Germany, having abandoned nuclear power, is in the process of switching over to more aggressive renewable fuel targets. Sometimes the electricity flowing in from solar and wind power units now outstrips the need of Germany's electric grid for electricity, which means that either this electricity will be wasted or that it must be used for electrolysis to make hydrogen, which can be stored. There are signs that the European Union, Japan, and China may soon follow suit.

But in 2008 came another bump: Ford managed to survive the economic crash without going into bankruptcy, but it suddenly had to withdraw from some of the fuel cell research it had been conducting jointly with Daimler.

Daimler's development effort rolled on. Ford eventually rejoined it and then Nissan, which preferred to launch its fuel cell car in 2017, became a partner as well. A collaborative effort for a finished commercial product was necessary, Mohrdieck pointed out, because it cut costs. Neither Daimler nor its partners wanted to spend the resources or use their engineers to produce three different fuel cell drivetrains, although the resulting cars will look different and carry three different brand names.

Other major automotive manufacturers have made similar decisions. General Motors has formed an alliance with Honda, and Toyota—which began selling its fuel cell car, the Mirai, in late 2014 in Japan—has a joint arrangement with BMW. Volkswagen has partnered with Ballard.

Robert Bienenfeld, a senior manager of energy and environment strategy for American Honda Motor, explained that his company has gone through the same struggles as Daimler, starting with fuel cells purchased from Ballard, graduating from methanol fuel, and then developing higher energy densities and a miniaturized Honda-built fuel cell stack in 2005. He describes the joint venture with GM as a "marriage of strength to strength" because the two companies own more patents on fuel cell technology than anyone else.

Honda is preparing to launch its first commercial fuel cell car in 2016. Honda's calculations show that internal combustion engines will become more expensive as regulators raise miles-per-gallon standards, and fuel cell cars will become more competitive. Honda's focus groups show that people liked driving its earlier experimental versions. "They see this as a vehicle that's exciting. It feels like driving the future to them," said Bienenfeld.

He admits "there is still a lot that has to go right with technology and consumer acceptance. Honda is not the company that goes out and brags there will be 25,000 vehicles by 2025. We stick to our knitting. Success is not assured for anything. We're nervous every time we bring out a new product."

The new alliances and the approaching launch dates have changed the way the California Fuel Cell Partnership works in its spacious office building near downtown Sacramento. It still offers separate bays where technicians might work on demonstration vehicles, but today many of them are not used. Individual automakers began moving back to the greater security of their California headquarters. "They didn't want their competitors working in the bay next to them," explained Catherine Dunwoody, the executive director. By comparison, the early days of the partnership were a kind of *Brigadoon*, a place where harmony often reigned and the partners were able to operate within a consensus. "The leadership of Dr. Panik was instrumental in what happened and what followed," she recalls.

The most recent bump in this road came when all the major oil companies, which had been members of the California partnership since its formation, dropped out, a series of quiet departures that was completed in 2011. That leaves the road ahead, as far as filling stations that sell hydrogen, looking rather empty.

For Mohrdieck, this was yet another reason why Daimler should delay its launch. In 2014 there were fifteen hydrogen stations in all of Germany, a miniscule amount. The United States also had fifteen up and running that year. At least hundreds are needed. Germany, the United States, Japan, and California have all mounted crash programs to try and fill the hydrogen supply void.

The walkout of the oil companies was doubly frustrating to Mohrdieck because it is the one element of the business plan that the automakers can't control. He doesn't understand the oil companies' desire to sit on the sidelines in California while the fuel cell cars—a whole new market for a fuel product—emerges. His sense is that they didn't want to send the wrong signal to their shareholders. He hopes they will show more activity because in the approaching zero-emission vehicle market selling batteries won't be a business for them. In Germany the outlook is more hopeful because three oil companies have teamed up with hydrogen providers and automakers to develop a nationwide hydrogen delivery system.

Dr. Panik, now a business consultant and a professor in a technical school near Stuttgart where his students experiment with fuel cells, also admits that he feels frustrated. He recalls that part of his mission in developing the fuel cell partnership was to keep Daimler firmly in the lead. In the automobile business, he explains, "the image in being the leader is so important."

EIGHTEEN

The Chickens Come First

On June 10, 2014, Timothy Bush signed a lease for the first commercially available fuel cell car in the United States. It was a white, four-door Hyundai hatchback and Bush got it for $2,999 down and $499 a month. It came with a promise of a three-year supply of free hydrogen fuel and free maintenance at three participating Hyundai dealerships in the Los Angeles area.

Bush was ecstatic. He had a zero-emission vehicle that could go 265 miles between refuelings, which would take three to five minutes. "I'm really excited to be able to pack up the kids and the dog and surfboards in the back and go to the beach or head up the local mountains, which we can totally do in this car," he told a reporter from Reuters at a small ceremony held by a Hyundai dealer in Tustin, California, a suburb of Los Angeles.

At the time there were only nine hydrogen stations in Southern California. There were a few more around San Francisco, but Bush's newly leased car lacked the 415 range to reach them. And he'd better not linger with his family and his dog in the state's popular tourism destinations like Palm Springs, Napa Valley, or Lake Tahoe, either, because they didn't have any.

Under the plans laid out by the California Fuel Cell Partnership, this was not supposed to happen. Recognizing that the emergence of hydrogen-fueled cars presented "a classic chicken-and-egg dilemma," the partnership recommended that in order to sell the cars more hydrogen-equipped retail stations had to come first. Why? Because the group's research showed that Californians, whose lifestyle probably depends more on car travel than residents of any other state, won't divert from their daily travels more than six minutes to find refueling.

But detailed state and federal planning for more hydrogen stations had started only a year previously and now the "chickens" were beginning to roll out. Just how refueling large numbers of them would be handled was a matter that would be dealt with later, perhaps much later.

Competing automakers, who had known about Hyundai's ambitions to launch first for some time, were perplexed by the timing (most automakers want to be first to deliver a startlingly new product) and by the acute lack of retail refueling outlets. But they were also upset by Hyundai's price: $499 and free fuel for three years was almost a giveaway for the first models of a car that industry experts generally agreed must have cost manufacturers somewhere between $90,000 and $100,000 to produce.

In May 2014, Ed LaRocque, national marketing manager for Toyota's fuel cell car, which was coming later in the year, said the Hyundai lease price was a "line in the sand" for his company, the world's largest automaker. "We don't have our price yet. We know it's critical," he told questioners at a symposium on electric cars.

"Marketing and reality are sometimes not consistent," remarked Christian Mohrdieck, the head of Daimler's fuel cell program. "I would wait and see how many cars they [Hyundai] would really put on the market." Daimler, which plans to launch its fuel cell car in 2017, doesn't have a price yet, either. The drums of the marketers for companies planning to deliver the pioneering new cars began pounding at the world's auto shows as early as 2013, although their initial rollouts of fuel cell vehicles may not be completed until the end of the decade.

Toyota's campaign was kicked off by none other than Takeshi Uchiyamada, the father of the company's trailblazing Prius. He took aim at growing competition from Tesla and Chevrolet's Volt. "The electric vehicle is not a viable replacement for most conventional cars. We need something entirely new."

At the Consumer Electronics Show in Las Vegas in 2014, the sales pitches grew louder and, seemingly, more confident. "Fuel cell vehicles will be in our future and in much greater numbers than anyone expected," announced Bob Carter, the senior vice president in charge of automotive operations for Toyota in the United States. He noted that Toyota's investment in fuel cells over the last twenty years has been "massive," but the resulting cost reductions have been "staggering" when compared with battery electric vehicles. So much so that Toyota had asked its headquarters in Japan to ship more fuel cell vehicles to the United States. "This will be a very special vehicle and we believe we can bring it in at a very reasonable price for a lot of people."

Toyota took another shot at Elon Musk, the cofounder and chief designer of Tesla who had told cheering employees at a new service center for his battery electric vehicles in Germany late in 2013 that "the fuel cell is so bullshit." Hydrogen fuel, he added, "is kind of dangerous. It is suitable for the upper stage of rockets, but not for cars."

Koei Saga, Toyota's chief development specialist in Japan, responded by calling most current generation battery electric vehicles "loss makers." "Tesla is a rare case," he explained to a reporter from *Der Spiegel,* the German weekly news magazine. "They are targeting rich people and you have many rich people in California." But Teslas weren't suitable for the mass market, he added.

Honda, also planning an early launch, got involved in some of the hype. "This is like a marathon," said Stephen Ellis, Honda's manager of fuel cell marketing, to the *Los Angeles Times*. "You can't run in it if you don't commit to it, train for it, and then show up at the starting line."

It certainly was shaping up to be a race, but what mystified a reporter for *Asahi Shimbun,* Japan's second largest national newspaper, was that a crucial element was still missing. Japan had prepared only a few hydrogen filling stations to operate in four major cities. "The current number of stations in operation is far too small to facilitate the practical use of FCV's [fuel cell vehicles]," the reporter noted.

Finally, on June 25, 2014, Toyota stepped out to draw its own line in the sand. It said it would sell its first production fuel cell Toyota, called the FCV, for roughly $7 million yen, or about $68,600, making it slightly cheaper than the Tesla Model S.

Mitsuhisa Kato, an executive vice president of Toyota Motor, explained to a packed press conference in Tokyo that the company could bring the price that low by sharing some of the parts in the Prius's electric drivetrain, which are in mass production. He noted that, globally, his company has sold more than six million of the hybrid-electric cars.

"Toyota regards hydrogen as core technology to be applied to many vehicles," he added, touting the FCV as an eventual solution to global warming and growing pollution levels in increasingly crowded cities. Fuel cell cars, he said, would create "a sustainable mobility society."

Where would the hydrogen come from? Chihiro Tobe, director of the hydrogen and fuel cell promotion office of Japan's powerful Ministry of Economy, Trade, and Industry, took Kato's place at the podium to announce that the Japanese government had just completed a three-decade "road map" to make hydrogen the fuel of the future for both cars and for energy storage on electricity grids. "We want to capture the world technology."

"Cars and stations have to progress hand in hand. . . . [they] have to move in tandem," Tobe explained, assuring reporters that the Japanese government would support the early spread of hydrogen filling stations and suggesting that it might also provide a financial incentive to Japanese buyers of FCVs to build demand for hydrogen.

How much would the support be? A month later Japan's prime minister filled in that blank. He announced the country would offer at least 2 million yen ($19,700) to subsidize fuel cell vehicles. "This is the car of a new era because it doesn't emit any carbon dioxide and it's environmentally friendly," Shinzo Abe told reporters. "The government needs to support this."

The matter of how to support a hydrogen fuel system hasn't been fully decided in the United States, but how to run such a system is not a mystery. Between 2005 and September 2011, the U.S. Department of Energy staged what it called a "learning demonstration" involving the testing and refueling of 183 demonstration models of fuel cell cars. It set up twenty-five hydrogen refueling stations for the cars, which ran a total of 3.6 million miles and used 152,000 kilograms of hydrogen.

The car companies involved were Daimler, GM, Hyundai, Kia, and Ford. The fuel companies included BP, Shell, Chevron, and Air Products. The companies were organized into teams and operated in five regions of the United States. The results showed rapid improvements in the durability of the test vehicles with the third generation getting double the performance of the first.

Only a third of the vehicles' maintenance problems involved the fuel cell stacks, and the vehicles "had a very strong safety record" with only two minor hydrogen leaks during the last four years. During the tests the hydrogen-fueled cars were involved in four crashes, but safety mechanisms on the cars prevented any hydrogen leakage.

While there was one serious hydrogen fire at a filling station and some "near misses," according to DOE's final report, the largest single problem at the refueling station involved the rather mundane machinery needed to compress the hydrogen before pumping it into the cars. Spare parts for the compressors were hard to get and so were enough skilled technicians who knew how to fix them. After the testing and all of the learning experiences, though, most of the refueling stations were later shut down, according to the report, because there was, as yet, very little demand for hydrogen for vehicles.

Car companies have since taken the testing a bit further. Toyota's engineers fired rifle bullets at the cars' new high-pressure hydrogen gas tanks. "The smaller-caliber bullets would just bounce off the tank," explained Matt McClory, one of the principle engineers involved. "It took a fifty-caliber armor-piercing bullet to penetrate the tank, and it then just left a hole and the gas leaked out."

Automakers knew that the public's perception of hydrogen used as a fuel was negative and that it had to be overcome before cars rolled out of the showrooms. Hyundai set one of its cars on fire and a temperature-activated hydrogen venting system opened and avoided the possibility of explosion. Fuel cell cars have met crash safety tests, and car salesmen are preparing to disabuse people of what Hyundai calls the "*Hindenburg* perception," lingering public fears relating to the 1937 disastrous fire on board a hydrogen-filled German zeppelin. Mike O'Brien, Hyundai's vice president of product and corporate planning, predicts that "only miles on the road and people in the seats of these vehicles will overcome those perceptions."

Another current perception that may have to be overcome is that the most well-heeled and experienced companies in the United States to prepare existing gas stations with hydrogen fuel pumps are the major oil companies. While some of them are still involved in preparing hydrogen fuel stations in Europe and Japan, the major oil companies in California, the first American beachhead for fuel cell cars, have left the business to others.

The oil companies seem to have decided that the much-touted "hydrogen economy" might be a disguised threat to their business. California had a regulation, the Clean Fuels Outlet rule, that required oil companies to help prepare stations to handle hydrogen, but oil companies opposed it. Then the California Fuel Cell Partnership participated in a coalition that included the oil companies that convinced the state legislature to intervene in September 2013 and prolong a tax on cars, boat registrations, and new tires that will yield $20 million in annual funding, enough for 101 hydrogen-equipped stations in the state by 2023.

That is not enough for more than a token fuel cell vehicle launch, according to the partnership, which recently received a report at an executive meeting that enthusiasm on the business side was still lacking. While California offers grants of up to $1.5 million to equip a station, recent state funding offers have been undersubscribed and developers who have received awards are taking a "long time" to open new stations. "Discussions with potential investors show that uncertainty remains high, confidence remains low that a large-scale market for fuel cell cars will emerge," the report states. It estimates that as many as 250 hydrogen stations will be required before a commercial market for fuel cell stations will emerge.

Catherine Dunwoody, executive director of the partnership, said the oil companies were needed to help broaden public support for the state-sponsored grants. One part of the new law that drew their support was that it removed their regulatory obligation under the Clean Fuels Outlet rule, which they were preparing to fight. "Nobody wanted to get it hung up in court," she explained.

The oil companies "are kind of sitting on the sidelines waiting for the market to develop," explained Steve Szymanski, the business development manager for Proton OnSite, one of a number of smaller companies that are trying to help California fill the hydrogen supply void. Szymanski's company sells electrolyzers that use electricity to split water into oxygen and hydrogen. They are a variant of the same technology used in fuel cell stacks to make electricity, only they reverse the process. "There are a lot of entrepreneurs out there and they see this state money getting into it. They're getting much more active in trying to start and sustain a business. It's an interesting situation."

Proton OnSite's current customer base includes the U.S. Navy, whose submarines use electrolysis to make oxygen for its submarines, and laboratories that would rather make hydrogen on site as needed, rather than buy large shipments and store it. Based in Wallingford, Connecticut, Proton OnSite is building a larger version of its current electrolyzer to sell to hydrogen fueling stations. The first new California hydrogen-equipped gas stations will probably truck in hydrogen made by big suppliers that extract it from relatively cheap natural gas or other hydrogen-rich fossil fuels, he thinks.

But the state of California has a regulation to limit the resulting greenhouse gas emissions by requiring 33 percent of the hydrogen coming into the new fuel cell auto market to come from renewable energy sources. That's where Proton's new electrolyzer will find a market, Szymanski hopes.

Unlike Europe, where many gas stations are owned by major oil companies, in the Untied States the majors have tended to pull away from the retail business, leaving many gas stations locally owned. A number of owners have signed up to participate in California's hydrogen fuel station effort.

As Szymanski sees the market developing, station owners can buy renewable energy credits to assure they have a suitable supply of "green" electricity, which comes from wind turbines, hydroelectric dams, and the state's fast-growing inventory of solar arrays. They can use it to run a Proton electrolyzer, or other available brands, to make and store hydrogen. "You don't need the oil companies of the world to participate in this," Szymanski asserted.

The United States, which is currently enjoying a shale oil boom, has nothing like Japan's hydrogen fuel road map into the future, but California's new law at least gives budding hydrogen entrepreneurs a pathway into the corner gas station. All they have to figure out is the chicken-and-egg problem. "Everybody is trying to guess how many cars are going to show up and when," says Szymanski.

NINETEEN

Crossing Points

The most recent update of the risks and challenges posed by global climate change was issued in March 2014 by the Intergovernmental Panel on Climate Change (IPCC), a body of experts that was set up in 1988 by the United Nations to give world governments regular reports on what the evolving science tells us about climate change and its potential impacts.

The report was the most serious and least equivocal warning yet that the world we live in is about to undergo changes. Coming weather extremes will make life as we know it a memory of past comforts. Our experience will seem otherworldly to our children—left to battle with record droughts and rainfall, more powerful storms and more acidic oceans. The steady intrusion of sea level rise from melting polar ice caps will require huge shifts and expenses for those who live in coastal cities. There will be "large risks to global and regional food security and the combination of high temperatures and humidity compromising normal human activities including growing food or working outdoors in some areas for parts of the year."

The threat was the warming of Earth's atmosphere and the cause was greenhouse gas emissions, the rising concentration of man-made gases beginning with carbon dioxide that are trapping more of the sun's heat in the atmosphere. The report listed a number of industrial sectors that have contributed to it and went on to explain that the largest of them and the one that will be the least easy for governments to reduce is the transportation sector.

For the world's richest governments and for most automakers, this threat has been emerging as a large red warning light in the middle of a busy intersection: a message that business-as-usual is no longer prudent, sustainable, or even humane. The troublemakers are the 10 percent of the globe's population that account for 80 percent of the globe's passenger miles traveled "with much of the world's population hardly traveling at all." And when the world's economies and food supplies begin shrinking because of more severe storms, rising sea levels, and the myriad other instabilities the IPCC now unequivocally predicts, the burden will fall first and hardest on the people whose lifestyles have almost nothing to do with the causes of the problem.

"So what?" some might ask. Life is unfair. It is, but it will become still more unfair if governments and companies don't do what they can to mitigate the problem. Recent U.N. conferences called to work out strategies to curb these emissions have become gridlocked because developing nations—which far outnumber industrial nations—are outraged and often demand more assistance than industrial nations can politically muster.

In climate change politics there are tipping points, just as in climate change science, where scientists worry about changes in the ocean currents or the more rapidly melting of polar ice caps that may suddenly emerge to make matters much worse. Unless industrial nations don't quickly mass produce cars that reduce greenhouse gas emissions, the billions of people in India and China who are reaching the economic prosperity to own a car are in a position to compound the globe's emission problems.

They could be a tipping point if they imitate the U.S. experience with cars since 1970. According to the University of Michigan's Transportation Research Institute, the market's behavior quickly undermined efforts by government policy makers to reduce fuel use by making cars more energy efficient.

While carmakers, driven by government regulations, improved the overall fuel efficiency of cars by 40 percent, car owners managed to move the needle the other way by driving 155 percent more vehicle miles and driving with fewer passengers, usually just the driver. The result was that emissions shot upward because 53 percent more fuel was burned.

That experience, hopefully, won't be the model for China. It has already overtaken the United States as the world's largest car market and still has plenty of room to grow. Only forty-four out of every thousand residents own a car compared with 423 per one thousand in the United States, according to the World Bank. What China's wannabe drivers need is a different model along with more energy-efficient cars.

But for that to happen, according to the IPCC, public behavior will have to change. At the moment few consumers will pay more for a new car because they see it has more society-wide benefits, according to the IPCC. Or, as one wag recently put it: "Everybody thinks that everybody else should be driving a green car." The decisions made in buying new cars determine the characteristics of used cars, which make up the bulk of the globe's car fleet. The result is "there may be a five-year or longer lag before cleaner technologies reach secondhand vehicle markets in large quantities, particularly through imports to many developing countries."

There are some signs that the public is beginning to learn. In the United States, where 65 percent of transportation emissions come from cars, there have already been some examples showing that our personal driving binge will carry a heavier price tag when the future predicted by climate scientists fully arrives. In the state of Vermont, where the massive flooding and scouring effects of Hurricane Irene in 2011 cost almost $200 million in damages, state officials say they can't afford to rebuild the entire system of roads and bridges because storm-proofing it will be too expensive.

The expense that has daunted them may just be for starters as sea levels rise and powerful storm surges destroy bridges and drown roads on the nation's long coastlines. For example, in the Gulf Coast region 2,400 miles of major highway are projected to be inundated within this century. The cost of rapidly melting permafrost on highways and roads in the state of Alaska are expected to run into the billions.

Where will the money for that come from? A recent study suggests a change in habits might soften the economic blows. While many Americans have become accustomed to gridlock, it estimates that the growing costs of highway congestion in loss of productivity, waste of fuel, and so on, is at $100 billion. Of that, weather-caused delays caused 15 percent of the costs, and that percentage is likely to rise.

There is some data that shows that the old business model for selling cars is beginning to change around the world. Globally, more people are moving into large cities where they use fewer cars. In the United States the lure of city life and the rising prices of cars and gasoline may be driving young people away from car ownership. In 1984, 83 percent of nineteen-year-olds had a driver's license. By 2010 the percentage had dropped to 69.5 percent.

But the facts on the ground show that the nation that Henry Ford helped design with cheap, affordable personal transportation is still wedded to gridlock. Sprawl is still the defining characteristic of most U.S. cities, and the nation's public ground transportation systems, once the envy of the world, aren't anymore.

Henry Ford might be pleased with current market behavior—America's most popular vehicle for the past thirty years is the Ford 150 pickup truck—but were he analyzing future market signs today, he might see a different market evolving, one where America's reliance upon the automobile could continue unabated. If he saw that there was money to be made and jobs to proliferate by designing a family of near-zero-emission vehicles that were cheaper to run and maintain than existing gasoline-powered vehicles, Ford would be in it. Remember, he was a visionary as well as a charismatic salesman. He made Detroit the world's motor city and workers on Ford's assembly lines made salaries that created worldwide envy.

"It is all about economics," explains George Muntean, the chief engineer and director of transportation programs at Pacific Northwest National Laboratory (PNNL). The PNNL grew out of the nation's nuclear weapons program in the 1940s and later went on to invent the technology that led to compact discs, which revolutionized the data storage and entertainment industries.

Dr. Muntean, a mechanical engineer and mathematician, leads a team that is looking at the future of both fuel cell and battery-driven cars. His endgame is to find a way to make these vehicles cost-competitive with cars with internal combustion engines. He doesn't think the final answer will be government subsidies that artificially drive down the costs of alternative technology cars. "This is not something that the government can make universally happen. It's beyond its financial capability," he asserts. But he does see the trend moving toward more powerful, efficient batteries and fuel cell stacks that are getting cheaper. Meanwhile he sees evidence that gasoline and other fossil fuels will gradually become more and more expensive. "The crossing point is out there in the future. I'm sure of that. The real question is when do these curves cross? That's the one that's very elusive."

For example, Dr. Muntean sees battery technology in the United States advancing by about 2 percent every year. "You're not going to see leaps and bounds. That may not be fast enough to satisfy public expectations. But ten or fifteen years from now you will be amazed at how much better they are." He worries that European companies, such as Daimler, and Japanese automakers have more pressure and support from their governments to innovate, and enjoy greater public tolerance when they do.

Shifting politics in the United States make long-term development projects more difficult to launch and harder to sustain. The Clinton administration pushed hybrids, for example. Then the George W. Bush administration switched support to fuel cells. Barack Obama's incoming agenda focused heavily on battery-powered electric vehicles and only recently shifted its attention to more support for fuel cells.

That left a support system of public charging stations for electric vehicles still incomplete, especially in major cities. "Some level of public charging infrastructure is required to overcome range anxiety," noted one coalition of electric vehicle supporters, "but the question of how much and where it should go is still open for debate."

Next year a new administration will arrive, probably with a different approach. If it's a Republican administration, the new president will have to wrestle to form a consensus with the powerful right wing of the party, where there is strong support—some of it financed by fossil fuel industries—to take an agnostic position on whether man-made greenhouse gas emissions are a problem.

But recent polling data from the Pew Research Center shows that a majority of younger Republicans—those who are likely to feel the brunt of climate change impacts during their lifetimes—are opposed to a do-nothing attitude about climate change. They feel it is already underway. Eighty-three percent of these Republicans say the

United States "should do whatever it takes to protect the environment."

If another Democrat emerges, he or she may be able to fuse support for a carbon tax, supported by many economists and even a few right-wing think tanks as the simplest and cheapest policy. If greenhouse gases portend a more difficult and expensive future, putting a price on these emissions might bring on the quickest and most adaptive responses from industry. The proceeds from the tax should boost U.S. research, support necessary retooling by U.S. automakers, and replace current federal incentives—supported by general tax revenues—that give buyers a cheaper price for low-emission vehicles. Hopefully this approach would stimulate a national mass market for low-emission vehicles and the American jobs that will come with them more quickly.

Referring to the U.S. network of national labs, which helped launch both the battery and fuel cell car initiatives, Dr. Muntean says the long-range tradition of the labs is to follow the science and not the politics. Old programs become hard to kill and new programs, such as the fuel cell research that led to automotive uses, are sometimes hatched out of funds for existing programs. "Our role is to try to be the rudder and try to sustain longer term programs. We try very hard to keep all the horses in the race."

He is sure a second Henry Ford moment will happen with electric vehicles, but it won't happen in the labs and there's no certainty it will happen in the United States. "If industry sees a way to make money, they'll find a way to make money." Governments, he thinks, will have to wait and let the market solve the chicken-and-egg problem dealing with the support systems, such as the fueling stations needed to support the winner.

Some industry veterans who have been involved since the early stages of the car wars, the competitions and clashes that have led to the current state of the electric car market, are not sure about that. Ken Baker, former head of research for General Motors and former head of GM's early electrification ventures including the EV1, says the battlefield has changed. "When I was in the fight it was to beat Ford and Chrysler and Toyota. Now it's a global competition. We're looking at a global stage. We were once viewed as being the place where the new technology comes from. Now most of the technology is coming from Southeast Asia. We need to know how to build something that other people can't build more cheaply. Look at the machine tool industry in the United States. It's been devastated."

Baker, now a technology broker in Scottsdale, Arizona, thinks an economic revitalization is needed in the United States. "The only way we're going to get out of the economic morass that we're in is innovation."

What needs to happen for both fuel cells and battery-powered electric vehicles, he believes, is that they have to become cheaper for mass acceptance, and the infrastructure that supports them is part of that. It has to be fleshed out. He sees a "solid ten years ahead" before these things happen.

In the United States, as the political consensus between the two political parties has become more tenuous and divergent, he worries that planning for such long time frames may no longer be possible because strategic goals last longer than a given administration. China and Japan both have economic planning agencies, such as Japan's METI, with decade-long planning horizons and funding schemes.

"They've looked at how do I make this an entire system, not just a car," explains Baker. "Those kinds of big research agendas are really scary to me. I'd almost be willing to say, let's pick a focus and just sustain it. Make it a big focus, such as electrification of our transportation system or reducing the vulnerability of the electric grid." Baker adds, "It could be important to the strength of the country from a point of pride, as well as from the performance perspective."

As for China, it is certainly not waiting for the United States to settle on a marketing strategy. Plagued by health-threatening smog problems, and the world's highest carbon-dioxide emission levels, it is plunging ahead, making its own ambitious plans for selling and supporting what it calls "new energy" cars.

In July 2014 its State Council, or cabinet, announced that buyers of hybrids, fully electric, and fuel cell cars would not have to pay the nation's 10 percent sales tax on the price of the vehicles. The tax waiver, which applies to foreign imports as well as domestic-built vehicles, comes on top of a government incentive system that can discount as much as $18,400 from the price of a car.

The government's target is having five million new alternative energy vehicles on the streets by 2020. In 2014 there were less than seventy thousand in use, and among China's biggest problems was a lack of electric charging stations in a nation where few buyers have a garage where they can do their own charging.

Another issue for the government was that first-time buyers of China's domestic cars preferred flashier, cheaper gasoline-driven models. Just to make sure China's automakers got the message, China's Automotive Technology and Research Center let it be known that it is preparing a new policy that would allow other Chinese manufacturers to enter the market for "new energy" cars and compete with China's familiar auto brands.

In announcing the sales tax waiver as the first of what are expected to be more forthcoming government incentives, the State Council said: "For achieving industrial development and environmental protection, this is a win-win."

One result has been a stream of mini electric cars entering the market, targeted at young couples such as the two-seater ZD brand's H1 model, which sells for just under $7,000 once all the subsides have been factored in. Lin Xing, a prospective buyer from Guangdong province, told a *Wall Street Journal* reporter that he was won over by the idea of using it as a second family car to run errands.

"It's so cute. My wife will really like it."

TWENTY

Dealing

In the late spring of 2014, auto sales figures showed the number of plug-in electric vehicles on U.S. roads had suddenly doubled in one year, reaching 211,097.

There were lots of other signs that a new market was beginning to emerge. In just May of that year 52,227 hybrid-electric cars rolled out of showrooms and into the hands of new buyers. The plug-in electric vehicle market, analysts noted, was becoming a fixture, but it was still in its infancy. The vehicles were little known and poorly understood by the public and at least a dozen new models had yet to be introduced.

This meant different things to different people. John Gartner, an automotive analyst for Navigant Research, felt confident enough to predict a continuing high growth rate that would put 3.5 million electric vehicles on the road by 2023.

Critics of electric cars pointed to one of the electric vehicles' most powerful champions, President Barack Obama, who reemphasized one of his earlier campaign goals in his 2011 State of the Union speech, saying that one million electric cars would be on the highways by 2015. Those in the ephemeral business of weighing and hyping expectations raised the question four years later. Was this shortfall not a marketing disaster?

The more down-to-earth auto analysts for *Consumer Reports* didn't think so, but they did sense that something might be wrong. They had just given the icon of the new industry, Tesla Motors, their highest rating ever for its new Model S. They knew that word of mouth, cheaper and far more potent than flashy advertising, was pushing up the sales figures. So what was missing?

To find out, *Consumer Reports* sent nineteen of what it calls its "secret shoppers" to eighty-five auto dealers in four states. They made their rounds posing as car buyers between December 2013 and March 2014. These shoppers focused on basic sales elements that electric vehicle buyers would need to know. What were the federal tax incentives? How much did the car's plug-in battery cost; how long would it last and was it covered by warranties? What would it cost to charge an electric vehicle at home and what charging equipment would be needed?

At thirty-five of the eighty-five dealerships, the salesmen told them: Nah, they really didn't want to get involved with an electric. What they really wanted was one of those snappy new gasoline-powered cars to be found in abundance on their lots.

The shoppers had already checked out the lots and found most dealers had only one or two plug-in cars in stock. Why was that? "The most common answer given by twenty-one dealerships was that these cars were very popular or sold out. The next most common answer was 'lack of consumer interest' and 'nobody buys them.'" They also found that "Toyota salespeople, especially, were more likely to discourage the sale of plug-in models and less likely to give accurate or specific answers to basic questions about electric cars or to say they didn't know."

Overall, sales people at Chevrolet, Ford, and Nissan dealers seemed to be the best informed, though there were exceptions. A sales manager at Manhattan Ford in New York City, a rare Ford dealership owned by Ford, first denied there was a Ford Focus EV. When he found there was one, he told the would-be buyer that it couldn't be leased. Both answers were wrong.

Fuel cost savings are one of the biggest selling points of electric cars, but "only 19 percent of the dealers visited could give even a ballpark estimate of what it cost to charge a car," recalled Eric Everts, who organized the survey for *Consumer Reports*. And less than 40 percent of sales people had useful information about the warranty that covered the cars' pricey batteries.

When they didn't have the answers, some salesmen reverted to a time-honored strategy: they made them up. A Nissan salesman in California assured one shopper that charging a car at home would not increase the buyer's electricity bill, explaining that charging an electric car took less electricity than a hair dryer. A Chevrolet salesman in California told a customer not to worry about battery life because the range of the Chevy Volt actually increased over time. A Toyota salesman didn't know the cost of a battery for a plug-in car, but suggested it would need replacing "every couple of years."

Although *Consumer Reports* didn't evaluate them, some basic economic differences between electric and conventional cars may also have contributed to the poor showing they found in the showrooms. Because electric cars are new and complex, it takes more time to sell one, and sales commissions are often higher for many gasoline-powered models. Some salesmen probably felt tempted to pitch the gas-burners.

Elon Musk of Tesla has built a distrust of dealers into his business plan. He doesn't sell his cars through dealers. He asserts that they have a fundamental conflict of interest in selling electric vehicles. "They make most of their profit from service, but electric cars require much less service than gasoline cars." Electric cars, he noted, "require no oil, no spark plugs or fuel filter changes, no tune-ups, and no smog checks."

"Overcharging people for unneeded servicing (often not even fixing the original problem) is rampant within the industry," Musk asserted in one of his recent blog posts. Car dealers have struck back at Tesla, prodding some state legislatures to use franchise laws to ban direct sales to customers via Tesla's boutique-style salesrooms, which are patterned after Apple stores. Musk argues that the laws, passed in the early days of the car business to prevent major automakers from abusing their dealers, "are being twisted to an unjust purpose" in blocking Tesla's option not to use dealers in the first place.

"He needs to stop and take a breath," replied Jim Appleton, who heads the New Jersey Coalition of Automobile Retailers. "If you're an Internet billionaire, maybe you think the world revolves around you and the world springs from your laptop. Well, I got news for him. This is not a new law. Tesla is operating illegally, and as of April 1, they will be out of business unless they decide to open a franchise."

Tesla has succeeded in working out compromises with dealers in some states, including New Jersey, but the question raised by the collision of interests and conflicts over state laws governing how to market a substantially different car could be headed to the Supreme Court. However, the legal side may be only one aspect of the dealers' dilemma with selling (or not selling) a brand-new product.

"We're dealing here with human nature," explained Rob Healy, the EV infrastructure manager for North American BMW Group, which has been working since 2008 to prepare its dealers for the arrival of the BMW i3, an electric car with a lightweight carbon-fiber body that is designed mainly for city driving. BMW's training for the 2014 U.S. launch of the i3 included sessions for sales managers and salespeople as well as more in-depth training for mechanics that work on the car's high-voltage battery. For people who have worked on cars with internal combustion engines for their whole careers, confronting them with a brand-new technology can be, well, a wrench. At a recent conference on electric cars, Healy was sitting at the podium listening to a discussion and at the same time answering e-mails from his dealers who had been trained for months. The main question, he explained, began with "Why do we have to do this?"

Salespeople have to apply extra effort to electric sales in order to understand the buyers' situations because BMW expects 90 percent of the i3 customers to be charging at home. That pushes the salesman into conversations about the economics of home charging systems as well as the installation of different kinds of chargers and the costs and benefits of solar power at home. To simplify sales, BMW contracts some of this out. It has a partnership with Solar City, a company that installs solar power arrays, for example, that gives buyers discounts for hooking up with solar-generated electricity.

Autowatts, a Denver-based start-up, is based on the premise that dealers are missing a fundamental opportunity about selling electric cars. The sales proposition for them could be richer than for conventional cars because they can help sell customers on a lifetime supply of fuel for the car in addition to the car—an added multithousand-dollar benefit that they can't get with the gasoline guzzlers that they have sitting nose-to-nose on their lots.

The opportunity that Autowatts sees comes after the buyer has already agreed to buy a plug-in electric and is arranging the financing or the lease payment with the dealer's financial expert. The expert is pecking away at a computer equipped with a patented software package from Autowatts that knows the precise answers to all the questions posed by the "secret shoppers" from *Consumer Reports* and quite a few more.

"The dealers are not well-equipped with facts because a sale like this is different for every single person," explained Alex Tiller, a former product developer for Fidelity Investments who has been testing this phase of the sale, working with dealers in Hawaii, where EV sales are booming.

This phase of the sale would begin with the sales manager reviewing an offer to buy or lease a plug-in electric car. Looking at the paperwork, the sales manager tells the prospective car buyer frankly that "when you take your car home and plug it into the wall, your power bill is going to go up." The question then becomes whether the buyer is willing to pay more to assure the increase in electric bill will stay low for the life of the car.

"Here's the thing. This is a really easy sale," predicts Tiller, who notes that the buyer has already agreed to buy the car and is, like the great majority of electric car buyers, college-educated, usually a homeowner, and a good credit risk. They are not tire-kickers because they have usually scoped out electric cars on the Internet and know that electricity is a cheaper fuel than gasoline, but they don't know exactly how much.

It's a complicated question because electricity prices differ in every state and depend on charging equipment needed at the home and often incentives offered by local utilities. But a few keystrokes on the computer will give them the correct answer. It will likely be an impressive savings because national average electricity prices have been running near the cost of 75 cents for the equivalent of the energy in a gallon of gasoline. But the sales pitch isn't over yet. The average monthly fuel cost could be even lower with an Autowatts package that includes a solar array tailored to fit the buyer's driving habits and the peculiarities of his or her home.

Does it have a northern or southern exposure? How big is the roof? Is there a big nearby tree shading the roof? A few more keystrokes and usually a cheaper monthly fuel cost appears on the screen. All the buyer has to do is sign a loan for a $10,000 to $15,000 rooftop solar system.

If a buyer's eyebrows are raised at this, he or she is assured, as Tiller explains, that the cost of the fuel for their car would have to be paid anyway. "It doesn't matter because you were going to consume that fuel and buy it from somebody, here you're buying it from yourself and saving money."

Just sign on the dotted line and Autowatts will throw in a faster, $1,500 home charging system for free. And it will also slip an extra commission to the car salesman who already sold or leased the car. As for the dealer, it gets an additional product to sell along with the car.

"The driver gets the opportunity to drive on sunshine. There's a lot of appeal around that. That's soon going to be the number-one thing," Tiller predicts. He's developing a nationwide network of solar installers and lenders that will finance the EV-tailored installations. The network and the software will allow Autowatts to expand from the dealers it works with in Hawaii and go national by 2016.

If the influx of the unfamiliar battery-powered electric cars, the opportunity to help sell their fuel, and the looming arrivals of the even more exotic fuel cell electric cars weren't enough excitement for car dealers, there will be a second learning experience for buyers and sellers beginning in 2016, when approximately 100,000 battery-electrics begin showing up on their used car lots.

The possibilities for confusion and flimflam could rise exponentially, but the handful of experts that have begun to explore this market see moderating factors as well as legitimate opportunities to make money. For one thing, highly favorable experiences of current electric car owners, they predict, will help attract a larger number of curious tire-kickers along with the cheaper prices.

Norman Hajjar, managing director of a company called PlugIn-sights, has begun to survey veteran electric car owners whose car leases will soon expire or who plan to sell their cars. Ninety-six percent of them, he says, plan to buy or lease a new electric car.

Driver satisfaction with electrics, he says, is way above average automotive statistics. "Tesla's is beyond anything I've ever seen." The resulting strong, sometimes even passionate word-of-mouth support for these used cars will attract a new influx of buyers that is far beyond the small number of sellers—which he pegs at 1.9 percent—that plan to switch back to conventional cars.

He calculates that driver satisfaction for the Tesla Model S is in the 94 to 99 percent range. The Chevrolet Volt ranked between 79 and 85 percent and the Nissan Leaf ranked third, between 49.8 and 66.8 percent. While the Leaf appeared to be falling in approval, Hajjar pointed out that its satisfaction rating still ranks higher than those for most conventional cars, including the highly rated Toyota Lexus.

One of the seminal questions buyers of used electric cars will have is how long will their used, expensive batteries last? Dirk Spiers, the head of an Oklahoma City company called ATC New Technologies, has worked with General Motors, Subaru, and the U.S. Department of Energy's national laboratories on how batteries age and how they might be repaired, rebuilt, and reused.

ATC's parent company, ATC Drivetrain, has been rebuilding automobile transmissions and engines for years. It sees rebuilding both hybrid and plug-in electric vehicle batteries as a natural extension of ATC's "remanufacturing" business and a sizable future market.

These batteries are huge, sometimes taking up the entire under-side of a car, and they can cost between $10,000 and $40,000 to re-place, but they are new and no one really knows how long they will last. Some laboratory simulations of battery wear-and-tear suggest they might outlast the life of the car and may then have a second life as backup electric storage systems for utilities, homes, and businesses.

Like the secret shoppers of *Consumer Reports,* Spiers hangs around showrooms and has watched salesmen steer putative EV buyers to conventional cars.

"I am standing next to a Toyota dealer showing the electric version of the Toyota RAV4 to excited customers. Then the subject turned to price and a potential buyer says, 'Ouch, that is a lot more expensive compared to the non-EV model.' And the dealer says, yes it is. That was it. I was aghast. These people were now driving an SUV and spending close to $5,000 on gasoline a year. Because electricity is cheaper than gasoline, the electrified RAV4 could save them around three-quarters of that annually." Spiers thinks that EV sales figures will eventually force car dealers to reeducate their sales staffs on the selling points of EVs because "this is money left on the table."

His company is working with carmakers to develop refurbished battery packs, covered by a warranty and perhaps bearing the automaker's brand "so the customer knows it is done properly." Because regular advances are being made by battery researchers and battery prices are dropping, he thinks the replacement batteries could be better than the originals.

Also, the prospect of warranty-covered battery replacements could help spur business on the used car lots and there are probably a lot of other sales innovations that will make both new and used EVs moneymakers for dealers. "We're all pioneers here. We're all trying to figure this out," Spiers explained. "It's still very early days in this business."

TWENTY-ONE

Innovation

In the summer of 2012, Gregory A. Ballard, the newly reelected mayor of Indianapolis, was mulling over an idea.

A retired Marine colonel and staunch Republican who had built a record of balanced budgets and programs to rebuild his city's aging infrastructure, Ballard was thinking about doing something radical. The notion had spun out of his experiences in the Gulf War.

He had been the operations officer for a battalion of young Marines preparing for battle in the, bleak, cold, rock-strewn desert of Kuwait in early 1991 during the final days leading up to the war. Although the history books say the war lasted only a hundred hours, it lasted considerably longer than that for some Marines. Ballard's men had been under nightly Iraqi artillery attacks for two weeks before it started. He had seen men preparing to brave the unknown, wearing bulky rubber chemical warfare suits. They carried small medical packs containing syringes they were trained to inject as a blocking agent to stop the effects of nerve gas in case the next incoming warheads contained some. Some reports said Saddam Hussein was prepared to use the weapons if U.S. forces tried to push him out of oil-rich Kuwait.

In the end, that didn't happen. The worst that Ballard's unit was hit with were dense clouds of sooty, greasy smoke from Kuwait's oil fields, located just to the north. Before they fled, Hussein's engineers had spun open the valves and used explosives to set the emerging gushers of crude oil on fire.

"I lived in that for three days," Ballard recalled. "When I tell people that, it's hard for them to imagine. It was black, it was right where you were, on the ground. We had to eat in that and brush our teeth. It was just odd. War does strange things to people."

It was an experience he continued to dwell upon after he retired. As electric car technology began to mature, Ballard began to realize that with a little push the scenario of the oil-drenched battlefield he carried in his mind might well become history.

As he prepared for his second term as mayor, he was thinking about how the times and technology had changed. When that happens it sometimes creates opportunities for innovation and Ballard saw one that he, as the ultimate manager of the city's fleet of around six hundred vehicles, had standing right in front of him.

The mayor picked up the phone and called a friend, Paul Mitchell, the head of an Indianapolis nonprofit that had been working since 2009 with Indiana business groups to raise awareness, about the potential for electric vehicles in the state. His group had helped install eighty electric charging stations around Indianapolis and another two hundred were on the way.

"Paul, I want to do something big," Ballard told Mitchell. "Can we realistically save money if I transfer the entire city fleet over to electric drive cars? If we can, I want to do it right away."

Ballard's thinking up to that point had gone something like this: If the U.S. vehicle market, which uses something like 40 percent of the nation's oil, switched over to electric fuel, the long-standing U.S. dependency on imported oil would end. "When that happens there would be no need to maintain the status quo and say 'Okay, we'll get through this oil price spike again and we'll just send these guys to war again.' We don't have to do that anymore."

If Indianapolis and several other cities began to switch their vehicle fleets over to electrics, more people would see them on a daily basis. Once taxpayers saw convincing evidence that they were reliable and cheaper to drive and maintain, they might be more tempted to own one.

Hoosiers have played a role in U.S. automotive production and marketing since 1909 when an enterprising Indianapolis auto parts manufacturer, Carl G. Fisher, opened the Indianapolis Motor Speedway. Innovations over the years at the racetrack had changed the way cars braked and shifted gears. They resulted in safety and engineering features that found their way into the family cars. GM, Ford, and Chrysler, along with their suppliers, paid close attention to racing developments and established subsidiaries in Central Indiana. GM affiliates in Indiana had gone on to develop the drive-train for GM's EV1, the first modern electric car, and leaders in that team had later formed Bright Automotive, a company that had promised thousands of jobs in pioneering an electric truck industry, based around a hybrid-electric van called the Bright Idea.

Here was a theme that Mayor Ballard felt he could harmonize with. Five years previously his idea of a city fleet replaced by hybrid-electrics and plug-in battery powered vehicles would have been impossible, but now some of these cars were staring at him from the showrooms and others were coming.

The city and Mitchell worked out the math. At a time when gasoline was selling for $3.70 a gallon, the equivalent in electrical energy was running about 75 cents. Indianapolis had 525 nonpolice pursuit vehicles in its fleet. If they were replaced with electric cars, the cheaper fuel and maintenance costs would save Indianapolis taxpayers around $6 million over the lifetime of the vehicles.

The numbers grew more exciting if Indianapolis could find a way to replace its hulking, gas-guzzling fleet of Ford Crown Victoria police cars that were running day and night. They averaged ten to twelve miles per gallon. If the city could substitute hybrid-electrics that could get over forty miles per gallon, that would save $6 million every year. Then, if Indianapolis replaced its fleet of snow plows, trash trucks, and fire engines with vehicles that ran on compressed natural gas, that would save still more money because compressed natural gas cost $1.50 less than a gallon of gasoline.

"Everyone wins. Taxpayers save money. Natural gas is an abundant domestic energy source, which helps our economy, and it's another way to reduce our demand for imported oil," Ballard explained to the Greater Indianapolis Progress Committee on December 12, 2012, the day he had signed an executive order converting city vehicles to "post-oil technology" by 2025.

"This choice will save lives. It will save taxpayer dollars," the mayor concluded. "I ask that other cities, states, and companies follow in our footsteps and that the federal government rise to the occasion," he told the group. Ballard has since signed an agreement with the mayor of Sacramento, California, to work together on the conversion of their car fleets and he says he is working with a half dozen other cities to explore potential fleet deals with auto manufacturers.

He has kept his approach upbeat, focusing on money savings, economic revival, and national security: issues that resonate with Hoosiers. Much has been made of the ingrained hopefulness of Midwesterners. "If you build it, he will come," was the theme that the movie *Field of Dreams,* set in nearby Iowa, was based upon.

Some signs of that hopefulness even persisted in 2008 after the crash of the economy and the influx of foreign cars had shut down much of central Indiana's once-sturdy presence in the auto business. Over 25,000 GM jobs had been lost in Anderson, Indiana, alone as auto-related companies shut down or relocated to places such as Mexico.

But that freed up a supply of skilled autoworkers, engineers, and empty office and factory space in the hard-hit town, giving John Waters, a former GM engineer, an opportunity to implement an idea he'd been thinking about for a long time. He launched his company, Bright Automotive, in 2008 along with other former GM engineers who had worked on the EV1 development team. It was a company equipped with what Waters called a "Silicon Valley attitude and industrial Rust Belt experience."

Waters's idea was a variant of EV1. Instead of an electric car, he believed there was a larger, more valuable market for a lightweight plug-in, hybrid-electric van. The van—called the Bright Idea—was designed to weigh only 65 percent as much as the average van and, using breakthrough aerodynamics, was able to get up to one hundred miles per gallon, more than five times the mileage of typical gasoline-powered commercial vans.

Bright Automotive planned to be producing fifty thousand Bright Ideas a year by 2015. The stock market crash in the fall of 2008 made it temporarily impossible to raise money by selling stock, but Bright had attracted over $100 million in commitments from institutional investors. It was also negotiating with the Obama administration's Department of Energy to lend Bright some $450 million more from its Advanced Technology Vehicles Manufacturing (ATVM) program, which Congress had authorized in 2007 to provide up to $25 billion in government-backed loans for more fuel-efficient vehicles.

Google liked the aluminum van. So did Alcoa, the aluminum company, and Johnson Controls, the biggest U.S. battery maker. Amory Lovins, the early guru of electric vehicle technology, helped Waters design the vehicle at his Rocky Mountain Institute. Potential fleet customers such as Coca Cola also participated in the van's design.

In 2010 General Motors agreed to invest $5 million, promising spare parts and design help to build the vehicle as inexpensively as possible. Even the political atmosphere seemed to be improving. In 2010 Indiana's governor, Mitch Daniels, set out to make Indiana "the electric vehicle state."

Bright moved ahead, hiring more than sixty people and developing a sales plan that would guarantee to cut fuel costs of fleet owners by $4,000 to $5,000 a year if they replaced their vans with the Bright Idea. Bright had more than $30 million worth of advance orders, including strong enthusiasm from the U.S. Postal Service, which has the largest fleet of vans in the United States.

But then the structure of hope and promise that had kept Bright's innovations afloat sank. A Freemont, California, company called Solyndra, which made tubular, thin film solar cells, went into bankruptcy on September 1, 2011, taking $535 million in U.S. Department of Energy loans with it. The collapse made front-page headlines.

Solyndra had nothing to do with the auto business, but Republicans went on the attack, bashing all of the Energy Department's "green" loan programs. When that happened Bright Automotive's long conversation with DOE's Loan Program Office came to an abrupt end.

In 2010 Bright had agreed to raise more capital and reduce its loan request to $314 million. When DOE asked it to form a partnership with a major automaker, it brought in the loan from General Motors. Michael M. Brylawski, a Bright executive vice president and cofounder, said it had met many conditions set by DOE.

Waters and Brylawski recall a conversation where a DOE official promised to "move heaven and earth" to complete the loan if the partnership with a major automaker happened. But after Solyndra, Brylawski said, "It was clear they were not going to give out any loans."

In a letter to the *Chicago Tribune* on February 5, 2012, Mike Donoughe, chief operating officer of Bright, made a final plea, responding to a line that President Obama had just put in his annual

State of the Union address: "My message to business leaders is simple: Ask yourselves what you can do to bring jobs back to this country, and your country will do everything we can to help you succeed."

"Here is what we are prepared to do," Donoughe wrote. Bright's hybrid-electric van would be developed in Michigan, engineered in Anderson, Indiana, and assembled in an AM General plant in Indiana that once built the now-defunct GM Hummer. Bright was preparing to renovate the plant. The venture would create 2,500 manufacturing jobs "and will be 100 percent U.S. based." Donoughe noted that DOE had been looking at Bright's loan application since December 2008, when their application was deemed to be "substantially complete" by the agency.

But DOE continued to look. The upshot was that on February 28, 2012, Bright's cash flow stopped. Bright's investors withdrew its loan application and sent the company's sixty-three employees home. The Bright Idea would shine no more.

"They [the DOE] hired over a dozen consulting groups and spent likely over $10 million reviewing our application, never able to make a decision. They never turned us down, for the record. We had to withdraw," explained Brylawski.

While the Obama administration wanted automotive jobs to return to the United States, Brylawski is not sure the government is equipped to help with the "capital-heavy" needs of industries. "They don't have the management, technical, or financial expertise to effectively grant the loans."

The U.S. Government Accountability Office reached the same conclusion. After talking to other U.S. auto manufacturers and other applicants for the DOE loans, GAO investigators found that the process had become so long and burdensome that "the costs of participating outweigh the benefits of participating to their companies." GAO concluded that unless DOE could show new market demand for their loans, Congress should consider shutting the program down.

It also found that a risk management division the loan office set up in February 2012, the month that Bright Automotive died, took almost two more years to assemble a staff, probably making DOE lenders even more risk-averse. Since then DOE has been trying to reorganize it. After defending the loan program to a House committee, noting that it had made successful loans to Tesla Motors and Ford Motor, Secretary Ernest Moniz told reporters: "Maybe I'm worried that the arguments will change, that we're not taking enough risk."

The idea of a more fuel efficient hybrid-electric truck isn't dead, it just got pushed into the future, out of Indiana and, perhaps, out of the country. Tesla and at least two Japanese automakers have announced they're working on plans. So is VIA Motors, a private start-up company in Salt Lake City.

VIA went to Bob Lutz, the father of the Chevrolet Volt. Lutz, by then retired, helped VIA make an innovative deal with GM. It allows VIA to buy top-selling Chevy Silverado pickup trucks off the assembly line where they are made in Silao, Mexico. VIA has built an adjacent facility there that turns them into plug-in electric hybrids, like the Volt.

The current process is slow; it takes eight hours to electrify a truck, but when VIA is done, it has a pickup truck that the company says can get up to a hundred miles per gallon. The price is higher than the conventional truck, admits Dave West, the chief marketing officer for VIA, but for companies and government entities such as Indianapolis and the U.S. Department of Defense that are beginning to buy vehicles based on their life-cycle costs they can be considerably cheaper.

VIA says the trucks will last twice as long, have more torque, and may come with a free charger. Lutz, who later became chairman of the VIA board, says the auto industry "started at the wrong end" with passenger cars. By turning a full-size truck or an SUV, which gets maybe ten to twelve miles per gallon in city driving, into a hybrid "now you're really saving money and saving a scarce natural resource and reducing carbon dioxide emissions drastically."

According to West, VIA's spokesman, Texas's Republican governor Rick Perry recently saw one of its trucks and gave it his highest accolade: "Goddamn, you've finally built a vehicle for Texas."

Perry, who like many Republican governors has ambitions to run for president, is just one of the political puzzle pieces confronting Mayor Ballard of Indianapolis as he presses his campaign to get more cities to buy electric cars. Perry could move the needle in favor of electric cars. But then there is Indiana's latest Republican governor, Mike Pence. His view could move the needle in the opposite direction.

Pence recently sent a letter to the state's Republican delegation, urging them to defund President Obama's proposal to limit carbon dioxide emissions from existing coal-fired power plants. Indiana, he pointed out, has a three-hundred-year supply of coal.

A recent poll conducted by one of the world's largest survey research organizations, the United Kingdom–based Ipsos MORI, interviewed people in twenty nations around the globe. The results show how contrarian the United States has become on the issue of climate change. When asked if they agreed with most scientists that climate change is the result of human activity, only 54 percent of U.S. respondents said yes, ranking them at the bottom of the list. China ranked first with 93 percent seeing the human connection. Americans also came in dead last on a second question, whether people saw the world heading toward environmental disaster unless human behavior changed quickly. Forty-three percent disagreed.

Bowing in the direction of Republican conservatives, Mayor Ballard says he never mentions the term when he is touting the benefits of more electric vehicles. Ballard's main issues are saving money and bolstering U.S. national security.

"Climate change? Well, I don't go in that direction. I'm trying to get my side [Republicans] to get there," he explained, noting that many Democrats already support electric cars.

TWENTY-TWO

Room at the Top

In late June 2014, a revolutionary event took place at the second oldest auto race in the United States. A tiny, electric i-MiEV made by Mitsubishi, the cheapest plug-in electric car sold in America, came within a heartbeat of winning the Pikes Peak International Hill Climb, probably the toughest auto race in the nation.

Since 1916, drivers and cars have been severely tested by the 12.42-mile event, also known as the Race to the Clouds, based in Colorado Springs, Colorado. It roars from the 9,390-foot mark on Pikes Peak up to the summit at 14,115 feet.

For the last thirty years this has been uphill warfare pitting specially built cars with monstrous engines twisting and blasting their way through the 156 turns to the top. But this year the small, lightweight i-MiEV did it in nine minutes and eight seconds, just three seconds behind the winner, Norma M20 RD, a specially built, 450 horsepower French race car.

While Mitsubishi could not break out the champagne, the likelihood is that electrics will soon own this race because at 14,000 feet an internal combustion engine loses about 30 percent of its power. Some of the oxygen it needs to get the explosive force out of gasoline is missing at that altitude. But electric engines don't breathe oxygen, which is why there were eight electric cars competing in 2014, a record for the event. Together, they sent an ominous, disruptive message to the traditional trendsetters in this race.

For almost thirty years, they have usually been purpose-built cars, like the Norma, with huge engines, racing in the "unlimited" class. The Pikes Peak all-time record holder in 2014 was an 875-horsepower mid-engine Peugeot, a behemoth that had gunned up the Peak in the previous year in eight minutes and thirteen seconds.

Monster cars, which can cost millions of dollars to develop, are now far beyond the reach or even the imaginations of most motorsports fans, who have made vehicle racing the most popular sport in the world, but the basic i-MiEV that shook up the 2014 race is close to a Walter Mitty dream. Its motors came off the Mitsubishi production line. The car, normally equipped with one electric motor and one gear, can cost as little as $15,495 in the United States, once federal incentives are factored in. Alex Fedorak, public relations manager for Mitsubishi Motors North America, admits the company's engineers built a special body and did some tweaking.

They crammed in a few more lithium-ion batteries, added three more small electric motors, and fiddled with the car's software. Now, he says, Mitsubishi is beginning to smell the roses. "This is our third year. We've really closed the gap. I've been telling everyone we've put a stake in the ground in the mountain."

While Pikes Peak is a great testing ground for technology and was dominated for decades by American cars and drivers, starting in the 1980s the race evolved into a more appealing target for European and Japanese racing teams. They have held the overall speed records almost every year since.

In 2014 U.S. television crews didn't bother to show up. However "the race has a huge following in Asia," Fedorak pointed out. It may be that for Americans, over the years, the Pikes Peak race has become like the air at the top of the mountain. It is too rarified with cars that most people can't relate to and technology they would never hope to see in the family car.

That is what has happened to another American motor sport, professional drag racing, which evolved out of hot rods. "Big Daddy" Don Garlits is one of the more celebrated dragsters and founders of the sport who made the transition. He won his first major victory in 1955 and went on to win seventeen world championships. One of his "Swamp Rat" dragsters is in the Smithsonian Museum.

Now eighty-three, wearing two powerful hearing aids after six decades of hearing the throaty roar and experiencing the eight-G force delivered by some of the biggest internal combustion car engines on the planet, Garlits is busy working on Swamp Rat number 37. It has an electric motor.

Big Daddy discovered electrics quite literally by accident. Darrell Gwynn, one of his toughest competitors, was severely injured in an exhibition race in England during the 1990s. He was paralyzed from the waist down, one arm was severed and the other was crippled, but four years ago Gwynn and Big Daddy hit the speedways again.

They had commissioned two small electric cars without much more power than a golf cart, and the two legends staged match races against each other for an entire season. Both men had been champions of what the sport calls "Top Fuel" dragsters, big, specially built cars that can hit three hundred miles per hour from a standing start in a quarter mile.

The electrics barely went thirty miles per hour. "That's all he [Gwynn] could control," explained Garlits, but the races were a hit with fans and raised money for Gwynn's foundation, which supports spinal cord injury victims. They sold the cars at the end of the season and gave the money to charity, but then Garlits found himself going back to the cars' designer.

If he built a real electric dragster, what could it hit at the end of a quarter mile? Garlits wanted to know. The expert figured it might get to two hundred miles per hour. Big Daddy, who had first crossed the two hundred miles per hour threshold a half century earlier, hired him to build one. At the time the record for electrics was 150 miles per hour. Garlits intended to beat it.

But, as Garlits explained in an interview, going faster wasn't the real reason for what became Swamp Rat 37. He hopes that the car will rejuvenate the sport.

His first reason has to do with the cost of entry. While it began with hot-rodders, professional drag racing is dominated by a few very rich team owners because top fuel dragsters are extremely expensive. According to Garlits, the cars accelerate so fast their engines have to be rebuilt after every run. That can cost $50,000 a pop.

Electrics, with far fewer moving parts, don't have that problem. Garlits figures he can get the cost of a run down to 7 cents, about the cost of the electricity. Plus the initial cost of electrics would be a lot cheaper, perhaps less than $100,000, and that would lure in more sponsors and more teams to compete, he hopes.

Then there's safety. While top fuel dragsters can hit three hundred miles per hour, Garlits says: "We're not interested in that. These cars won't ever go over 250 miles per hour because drag strips were mostly built in the 1960s. They can't handle three hundred miles." Plus, noise restrictions near major cities are shutting drag strips down.

Finally, there's showmanship. The cars that hit three hundred miles per hour do it in 3.7 seconds. "The spectator is cheated out of the excitement of a race. Three point seven seconds is not a race, it's just a score. So we want the battery cars to run around 250 miles per hour." The slower races will prolong the competition and generate more crowd reaction.

Television generally shuns drag racing because it takes too long for the behemoth three hunred miles per hour cars to be ready to run again. "We want something that's live on TV and a sport that will be something that the general public can support and can happen almost anywhere . . . and it won't bother the neighbors.

"Don't get me wrong," Garlits emphasized, "I love internal combustion engines, they're my life." But times are different, he pointed out. "I believe tomorrow the Environmental Protection Agency could say to the NHRA [the National Hot Rod Association, which sanctions races] you can't run top fuel dragsters anymore, they're too nasty, they put too much stuff in the environment . . . it would only take a felt tip pen running across a piece of paper and then what would they do?"

In April 2014, a crowd assembled at a drag strip near Bradenton, Florida, to watch Big Daddy do his burnout, locking the brakes and spinning Swamp Rat 37's tires on the cement to get them sticky enough to compete. The light went green. A quarter mile later he shot past the timer at 184 miles per hour, making an angry, high-pitched whine. It was a pretty good start, enough for a record, but for Big Daddy that wasn't enough. He is still gunning for two hundred miles per hour.

Georgio Rizzoni loves the sound of internal combustion engines, the bigger the better. "Look, I'm a Formula One fan," he explains, referring to the most popular form of auto racing in Europe. "It's difficult for an Italian not to get interested in motorsports. In motorsports the sound of a vehicle is a very important part."

He reminisced about how the Paris-based International Automobile Federation—known to most as FIA, the acronym for its

French name—has made rules reducing the size of its engines over the last two decades for safety reasons, among other concerns. There was the throbbing vibrato of the Ferrari's huge V-12 engine, but then engines were downsized to V-10s and now the FIA limits racers to a V-6. "People are complaining that it's the wrong sound, that it sounds kind of tinny and small."

Twenty years ago, when this downsizing was just starting, Rizzoni was way ahead of the game. As an engineering professor at Ohio State University and director of its Center for Automotive Research, he prepares students to design, build, and test cars of the future.

Rizzoni was having them build and race electric cars in the 1990s, financed by a Cleveland-based utility. They were part of a class called Lightnings, modeled after Indianapolis-style racers, and they ran against college teams from twenty other universities. His teams won all three national championships held with the cars, which were very heavy because they were loaded with lead-acid batteries.

While electrics can easily compete in short hill climbs and drag races, road and track racing becomes more difficult the farther they go because batteries have less energy density than gasoline and have to be recharged.

"Our teams used to do pit stops where they could replace the battery packs, which weighed 1,200 pounds, in seventeen seconds," he recalled. The college races went on from 1994 to 2000 without any safety incidents, but neither the FIA nor any potential private sponsors showed any interest, so the races stopped in 2001.

Rizzoni and his students went on to two other projects. One was working with Ford Motor Company to build a fuel cell racing car called the 999, named after the racer that made Henry Ford famous. (Ford's involvement ended in 2008 when it disbanded its fuel cell research as a result of the economic collapse.)

But the OSU electric car team rolled on with another project called the Buckeye Bullet. Rizzoni's team of undergraduates and grad students took the engine out of a fuel cell–powered bus, built by Ballard Power Systems, and put it in a car shaped like a missile. It was three feet high and thirty feet long and it was designed to see if an electric car could approach the world's speed record for an internal combustion engine car, about 450 miles per hour.

In trial runs on the Bonneville Salt Flats, the Buckeye Bullet has reached 315 miles per hour. That drew the attention of a Monaco-based electric car producer, Venturi Automobiles, which is sponsoring a new OSU effort called the Venturi Buckeye Bullet 3, aiming to break four hundred miles per hour. That would set a new world record for electric cars, one that is very close to the upper limit of internal combustion engines, a technology that has taken more than a hundred years to reach. "That would put our vehicle in a very small group of eight to ten vehicles in the world," said Rizzoni. "That's a huge success."

The effort has pushed his students to work on a list of unsolved problems, most of which have to do with keeping an electric car under control and its systems working under enormous stress. To describe Rizzoni as being competitive would be an understatement. "This is such an intense and demanding project that the individuals who come out of this program are exceptional and the industry has to fight to hire them when they graduate," he explained. It still troubles him, though, that aside from a little tire tread noise, the high-pitched whine of the gears, and the swoosh of the car knifing through what amounts to a four-hundred-mile-per-hour wind, the Buckeye doesn't have any signature sound.

His students don't have the nostalgia for the roar of classic racing cars that their professor does, but they have suggested a solution. Bursting with the electric equivalent of almost three thousand horsepower and an array of computers, the Venturi Bullet can easily carry a set of amplifiers on board. One of its computers could be programmed to project any sound he wants.

In 2008, Azhar Hussein, a British businessman and motorcycle enthusiast, found what he regarded as a great opportunity on the Isle of Man, located just off the British coast. For die-hard motorcycle fans, the Isle amounts to racing Valhalla. Since it started in 1907 its annual Tourist Trophy, or TT Race, has accumulated a list of 242 dead racing heroes and bystanders to prove it. Its track is a 37.5-mile loop that goes down narrow country lanes and winds up hairpin turns on two mountains. For one week each year the Isle's population (85,000) doubles as two-wheeled racing enthusiasts gather from all over the world to watch. The race lost some of its luster in the 1980s when Paris-based International Motorcycling Federation (FIM) withdrew its sponsorship because it considered the course had become too dangerous as speeds of so-called superbikes approached 150 miles per hour.

What Hussein, who was there for an unrelated business deal, sensed was that the deafening roar and the noxious fumes of the bikes created an appealing window for an electric bike race. That would mean that for one day of race week tourists could enjoy a race without the fumes and with little noise.

"None of this had been done before," recalled Hussein. He had visited China and Korea and knew that manufacturers there were producing millions of smaller electric bikes and considering making larger ones. But the idea of an electric superbike, he found, was initially regarded on the Isle of Man as heresy.

"They were very hard core, very skeptical. They had radio shows about what a joke this was. On top of that I was an off islander." Hussein was called a con man and became the target of racist remarks because his parents are Pakistanis, but he persisted, offering to put up some money to sponsor the race. He also found a crucial ally in John Shimmin, who was then the Isle's minister of the environment.

"The thing that really excited me was the technology," recalled Shimmin. "I wanted to push solutions to the problems of the internal combustion engine." At first the pair thought they were stuck. "We had challenges from the petrol heads, the purists who thought these were just golf buggies going to race around their hallowed course."

But Shimmin and Hussein gradually found political traction, pressing their case that an electric bike race would attract more tourists and clean technology companies to the island, particularly big motorcycle producers and automakers who saw green vehicles—especially sporty ones—as one of the keys to their increasingly government-regulated future.

These bikes were definitely not golf buggies. The rules of racing were changed for the first race in 2009. Instead of going six laps around the Isle of Man course, which is the traditional race, electric bikes were limited to one. The winner turned in a respectable average just under eighty-eight miles per hour that year. Five years later the winner for this race, now called the TT Zero, posted a record 117 miles per hour average, just eleven miles per hour under the record average for an internal combustion superbike.

Because the annual speed gains of the electric bikes have increased much faster than the average gains of the conventional racers, Hussein now predicts that in three or four years, electrics will begin winning it. In the nearest U.S. equivalent of the Isle of Man, the motorcycle events in the annual race up Pikes Peak, they've already done it. A California-made electric bike, the Lightning, beat all comers in 2014 with a record climb of just over ten minutes.

A new industry is being born. The brand names of the dozen or so start-up companies making racing bikes may not be familiar to the general public—they include the Lightning, Brammo, Zero, and MotoCzysz—but then there is Mugen Shinden, whose last name translates into Japanese as the God of Electricity. It was founded by Hirotoshi Honda, the son of Honda's founder and now the largest shareholder of Honda.

In 2014 it was Mugen Shinden, driven by the seventeen-time racing champion on the Isle of Man John McGuinness, that turned in the new record racing average for electric bikes. The connections between the team and Honda are now so close that *Motorcyclist* magazine says that the bike could "quickly morph into the Honda Shinden."

Not everybody in motorcycle racing is happy with the assault of the electrics upon their sport. Robert Rasor, director of international affairs for the American Motorcycle Association, was one of the early enthusiasts for testing the electric bikes in the Isle of Man race and helped Hussein establish the event. "There is not a lot of grass roots involvement," he explained. "In some circles people are not interested in electric bikes." Part of it, he thinks, has to do with the sound. "It's interesting when people go by you approaching 170 miles per hour and all it makes is a hum."

But this appears to be a generational difference, similar to one that's been showing up in electric car racing. "Motorcycles are known for their noise, but my generation thinks it's nice that they're quiet," explained Brendan Kelly, then a senior engineering student at Ohio State University and business manager of its electric bike racing team. His team's bike, the Buckeye Current, demonstrated how the lowering cost of racing can attract more competitors by coming in third at the Isle of Man's 2014 race. The Current came in just behind the two bikes entered by Mugen Shinden.

An offshoot of the university's Automotive Research Center, which is also trying to set a new speed record for electric cars, the team behind the Current sees their mission as helping to create a new market for motorbikes. Kelly believes as more people begin to move back into large cities, younger professionals will be drawn to electric bikes for their commute. "Electrics are about as efficient a form of transportation as you can get," he says. Then there is the thrill of driving one. "Being able to go that fast without making a lot of noise is amazing."

It's been eight years since Azhar Hussein first sniffed the opportunity in the Isle of Man's exhaust-tainted air for electric motorcycles to compete in the West. Now one of the grand daddies of the industry, Harley-Davidson, is beginning to smell it, too.

In June 2014, Harley launched Project LiveWire, a tour of its dealerships in thirty cities. It wants to show off its first electric motorcycle with a few handmade prototypes and a simulator to give potential customers a feel for the ride. There were no immediate plans to sell the bike, according to the company. Rather, it described the move as a probe to get customer feedback.

But the company went on to predict that LiveWire would deliver a jolt. As the Harley advertising team put it: "The bike offers a visceral riding experience with tire-shredding acceleration and an unmistakable new sound."

A new race, this time for market share, had begun. "The sound is a distinct part of the thrill," explained Mark-Hans Richer, Harley's chief marketing officer. "Think fighter jet on an aircraft carrier. Project LiveWire's unique sound was designed to differentiate it from internal combustion and other electric motorcycles on the market."

TWENTY-THREE

Win on Sunday; Sell on Monday

The most ambitious battle plan for the future of electric cars began in early 2012 with a blank sheet of paper and signs of unrest within the world's most prestigious and technology-wise racing league, Europe's Formula One.

There were signs of unusual strain among racing teams, engineers, and the galaxy of car companies, their suppliers and advertisers, who depend on the 450 million viewers who watch Formula One cars racing around the world every year. The audiences were beginning to shrink. Formula One's regulators were locked in an endless battle with race car designers, who kept finding exotic new ways to skirt safety-oriented rules and increase engine power every year.

All of that was running up the costs of racing, dropping its income and reducing the last vestiges of any similarity between the cars that people bought and drove on the street and the sleek, roaring, seemingly gravity- (and rule-) defying cars they saw racing on TV.

After the economic shocks of 2008, big automakers that had supported the racing for years began to leave, claiming they could no longer justify the expense of Formula One racing. Honda temporarily left in 2009, followed by BMW and Toyota.

Formula One, like its closest U.S. kin, Indianapolis-style racing, is a sport that was created by wealthy amateurs and car companies who could test their technology during races and burnish their brands when their cars and their drivers won. The business model for many years was "win on Sunday, sell on Monday" and legendary brands like Mercedes-Benz and Ferrari were built upon that.

But the difference between the finely balanced, jewel-like Formula One car engine, which gets its power by developing 15,000 revolutions per minute, is almost light-years away from the car in your garage that can only spin up to about a third of that. And the gap between track and reality continues to widen every year.

Big car companies must take long-term views of the future. It takes eight years to design and produce a new model and there are signs that the coming decades will require cars that would almost seem to come from another planet rather than the cars racing in Formula One events. Carmakers could see regulators in California, Washington, China, Japan, South Korea, and Europe being increasingly drawn into the fight against global climate change, calling for cars in future decades that produce few, if any, carbon dioxide emissions.

Electric cars easily fit with the governments' long-term plans. The gassers that thrill millions on Sundays in Formula One races do not. Moreover, racing officials and teams had begun to closely watch the rapid progress of electric motorcycles at the Isle of Man, Pikes Peak, and other racing venues as they began to challenge the top speeds of veteran racers on bikes with internal combustion engines.

To be sure, crowds and TV audiences still love the noise of Formula One race cars and idolize some of their fastest drivers. But would they still do that if, in the near future, the racing rules allowed electrics to race directly against the gassers and the electrics began to win? Noise can certainly be exciting, but ultimately racing appeals to more primal instincts: few sports fans will worship a loser for long.

It was to fend off disturbing questions like this that an entirely new league of professional racing was born. It is called Formula E and its focus is racing electric cars. Its leader is Alejandro Agag, a forty-four-year-old Spanish businessman and former member of Europe's Parliament who had briefly owned Campos Racing GP2, a Spanish team that competed in the minor leagues of Europe's road racing.

Agag's idea is probably the most ambitious global marketing plan for new cars in automotive history. It has three main objectives: it would field ten racing teams, and hold races in major cities all over the world, generating excitement aimed at attracting younger, more environmentally sensitive fans.

The competitions would serve as a test bed for longer-lived batteries and more efficient electric engines that would give electric cars a longer range and a wider popularity, bringing their prices down. And the lightning-like acceleration of the cars and skills of the drivers would attract advertisers and introduce millions of young, first-time buyers to a new breed of car that was, as Agag likes to put it, "sexy."

Agag has tried to game out all the possibilities of his new sport. Electric vehicles are only as clean as the source of their electricity, which might be a problem in many cities, beginning with Beijing, where the predominant power source is coal. So he's contracted with a British company to supply generators for the races that are powered by a diesel-like fuel that is made from algae.

But the most audacious part of Agag's plan is his endgame. "If we can get a battery that can store four to five times the amount of energy, that's it," he told an audience of electric car supporters in

Indianapolis recently. "New technology will make combustion technology obsolete."

Agag's plan found a ready audience and came together in eighteen months. The new league was approved by the International Automobile Federation and won enthusiastic supporters among leaders in both Formula One and Indianapolis-style racing. One of the first teams to form was Team China Racing, representing the largest car market in the world. Yu Liu, chairman of the team, called Formula E "the perfect platform." He said, "Our presence in the championship will encourage millions of Chinese fans to follow the series."

To emphasize the fact that Formula E racers will create no emissions and little noise, Agag planned to stage the races on Grand Prix–style road racecourses on the streets of major cities. Mayors began to line up for them. Beijing, whose polluted air is probably the world's worst, volunteered to host the first race.

Miami, Florida, was right behind it. Helping to organize the race there is Andretti Sports Marketing, an affiliate of one of the U.S. Formula E teams. It traditionally focuses on Indianapolis-style racing. Hector Scarano, a spokesman for the team, said it is excited to be among the pioneers in EV racing and involved in "technologies we believe will have direct impact on road-going EV vehicles in the future."

One of the features the Andretti team found attractive was the use of social media. Fans can watch the race on their iPhones and then vote for their favorite drivers. The feature is called Fanboost. The three drivers voted most popular before the next race will have the option of pushing a button that gives them a power boost equivalent to ninety more horsepower for 2.5 seconds during the race.

Ho-Pin Tung, the first Chinese driver to test it during a practice run, said it will give drivers an extra option to pass other cars on long straightaways. "It's a significant difference and you notice it a lot. It's going to be a very important feature for the race, both to overtake and defend."

In Long Beach, California, another race site, Southern California Edison, the Los Angeles area's electric utility, is in one of several business groups volunteering to help support the event. While the utility has sponsored campaigns promoting energy efficiency and reducing carbon dioxide emissions, Edward Kjaer, the utility's sponsor of transportation electrification, is sure Formula E offers a "more memorable way" to send those messages.

"People are going to be shocked at what an electric vehicle can do. These things will do 150 miles per hour in a heartbeat," he said. Kjaer, who has spent years trying to help Southern Californians slowly become aware of electric vehicles, counts Agag as one of his heroes.

"I see him as an early version of Elon Musk. He has a purity of concept and a passionate vision. This thing is well funded. Huge brands are involved." Planners for Long Beach, as in Miami, intended to make the electric car race the centerpiece of a day-long celebration of things that contribute to a cleaner environment. "The majority will be families and kids," Kjaer predicted.

Agag did manage to load up on brands while he was out recruiting cities and teams for his league. They include Tag Heur, BMW, the Edison Electric Institute, DHL, Michelin, Qualcomm, Audi, and Renault. Most of them see big future returns in the racing and its impact on electric car sales.

Qualcomm is a San Diego–based conglomerate that specializes in wireless communications. One of its recent acquisitions was a New Zealand–based company called Halo, which has a wireless electric vehicle charging system. It is used in New Zealand to charge electric buses that stop over a special pad, buried under the pavement under their routes that gives their batteries frequent electrical charges.

For cars that follow a particular route, it eliminates the need to carry heavy batteries. For the 2014–15 Formula E racing season, the pads will only be used by race pace cars, but in future years, as the technology is perfected, it will allow electric cars to be lighter, race longer, and recharge during pit stops, much like conventional racers.

Anthony Thompson, marketing director of Qualcomm, explains that the pad buried under the street is connected to underground power lines. They are surrounded by a coil that puts up a powerful magnetic field and the car that rolls over it will have a receiver that draws power from it. He believes store owners will want to install them to attract customers with electric cars. Parking over them, he explains, will be like putting a cell phone in a cradle for an electric charge. "The vehicle of the future is electric and wireless. It does not need to be tethered," he asserts.

Eventually, he hopes, the technology will lead to dynamic charging where cars driving on a highway can draw power from it without stopping. He's excited by the prospect, which will take years to fully develop and market, but in the meantime he's pleased with Formula E's power to attract attention. "One way to do it is to drive really fast around cities and that gets people excited. Formula E will bring a new generation to the table."

Because of battery-powered energy limitations, in the first year of racing Formula E teams will compete with two cars. The races will last one hour and the driver for each team will have a pit stop in mid-race where he or she will jump into a second car and take off while the first car recharges.

The first-year racing cars will all be the same model, put together by Renault and a variety of other Formula One car design and engineering firms. It is called the Spark, and Ho-Pin Tung and some of the other drivers who have tested them say they are slower than Formula One cars, but seem to grip the road better and may go faster into turns. The relative quiet also reduces drivers' tension and gives them more time to think.

By inviting more innovation, Formula E may also take some of the pressure away from Formula One. In its latest effort to limit higher speeds, it is forcing racers to practice energy efficiency. In 2014 they could only consume a standard weight of gasoline for the race, or risk running out of gas.

Audi got around the limitation by perfecting a hybrid. Its 510 horsepower Audi R18 e-Tron captures electrical energy from the car's braking and stores it on a flywheel that can be used to give the gasoline engine an extra boost when it needs it. Audi used it to win the twenty-four-hour endurance race at Le Mans in 2014, where its driver was able to run faster without running out of gas.

While drivers of electric hybrids, such as the Toyota Prius, enjoy such "regenerative braking" every day, the innovation and the rule that provoked it provided a further shock to die-hard Formula One veterans. Asked about the small engine rules, Flavio Briatore, a former leader of a Formula One team, complained: "The audience is clearly enjoying it a lot less, because there are cars that do not make much noise." But the rule about husbanding gasoline consumption was what really set him off. He grumbled about "drivers who are doing their accounting in the car rather than being gladiators."

The second racing year, starting in the fall of 2015, will be the real coming out party for the upstart Formula E. Then, it has announced, it will open up to major innovation, allowing teams to introduce their own cars, either by joining with specific automakers, or collaborating with specialized race car designers to put together cars that comply with Formula E rules and leave the competition behind.

This could be the league's most fruitful moment because some groundbreaking innovations are waiting to be showcased and tested. One of them comes from a team of researchers from Stanford University including Steven Chu, former U.S. Secretary of

Energy and a former Nobel Prize winner. They announced in July 2014 that they had reached the "holy grail" of lithium-ion battery design: a storage device that could boost the range of electric cars to three hundred miles.

Finally, many of Formula E's new leaders fit the model of the early, more business-oriented days of auto racing. They are wealthy amateurs, like actor Leonardo DiCaprio, and they do seem more intent on the older tradition of the sport: cars that can win on Sunday and roll into the showrooms shortly thereafter.

"The future of our planet depends on our ability to embrace fuel-efficient, clean-energy vehicles," asserts DiCaprio, joint owner of a team run by Venturi Automobiles of Monaco, the same company that is working to set a new world speed record for electric cars.

TWENTY-FOUR

Shifting into High

The history of electric cars has always been driven by racing imagery. One reason is because it has been an effective way of attracting peoples' attention to new technology that they might have felt was too difficult to understand or unimportant to the conduct of their daily lives.

Working behind the imagery and often manipulating it are the real forces at work, automakers and governments. Regulators want to impose rules that change public behavior, clear the air, and ultimately weaken the looming scourge of climate change. Automakers, working in an expanding, global market are betting billions of dollars on development programs that will deliver the right goods eight years from now and protect their market share (while trying to grab some from their competitors).

In the end it will be consumers who wave the checkered flag. They will vote with their wallets and bank loans and maybe their votes, but it is too early to tell what sort of car will be doing the victory lap. That moment is still years away.

But it is no longer business as usual. Look back ten or even five years ago and it is hard to imagine the head of a U.S. auto company predicting that the mainstay of the business for over a century—the internal combustion engine—is economically doomed.

Elon Musk recently did that, remarking to a group of financial analysts that pending advances in batteries will make electric-powered vehicles cheaper to buy and accentuate their lower fuel and repair costs. This aspect of the race is "heading to a place of no contest with respect to gasoline," he noted. "But we're trying to make it go there as fast as possible," he explained. "Time is important here. The sooner this can be done, the sooner we can reduce carbon output and reduce the probability of a catastrophe."

The chairman of Tesla Motors was clearly trying to support his company's high-flying stock and sell more Teslas, but the catastrophe he mentioned is not mere imagery. Polls show that most scientists and more people are coming to the conclusion that climate change with more powerful storms, more persistent droughts, rising oceans, and roller-coaster temperature swings is coming. And carbon dioxide emissions from automobiles are among the larger causes of it.

This is the part of human contribution that could vastly accelerate. The International Energy Agency estimates that there are now 900 million light-duty cars and trucks on the planet. By 2050, a little more than a generation from now, it calculates there could be as many as 2 billion.

The agency recently described three scenarios that might happen as a result. The most optimistic of them holds that if 70 percent of auto vehicles for sale by 2035 are either hybrid-electric or pure electric vehicles, then mankind may avert a situation where the climate grows much worse.

Can automakers and car buyers shift that fast? There have been some promising developments lately. One of them, alluded to by

Musk, has been research at Stanford University and elsewhere that suggests more powerful, lighter, and cheaper lithium-ion batteries may be closer than we think.

Another development, again from Stanford research, suggests that Musk might be running on the wrong track. Researchers have found a cheap, nonemitting technology that can use electrolysis to split hydrogen from water. Until now that has required large amounts of electricity and an expensive catalyst, such as platinum. The researchers did it with an ordinary AAA battery.

"This is the first time anyone has used nonprecious metal catalysts to split water at a voltage that low. It is quite remarkable," explained Hongjie Dai, a professor of chemistry at Stanford. It is a breakthrough that could make cars driven by fuel cells far cheaper and cleaner to operate than the current models now being introduced into the market.

So where do we go from here? One possibility is that we don't. We ignore the new technological advances and science's warnings about climate change and drift along, retaining our old habits. That may seem appealing, but the results could be ugly. A new study produced by the nonprofit Institute for Transportation and Development Policy at the University of California at Davis estimates what will happen if the exploding economies of China and India follow the current U.S. example.

Anyone who has walked the streets of those countries has learned that as incomes have risen, owning a private car has become a palpable dream. Auto racing is already the most popular sport in India and political pressures have led to the Golden Quadrilateral project, a network of four- and six-lane freeways that will connect India's major cities.

What will happen if the lure of the open road puts more Indians into cars with internal combustion engines? Assuming this nation of 1.27 billion people can avoid frequent gridlocks, the University of California Davis study predicts that India's annual carbon dioxide emissions from urban transportation could jump from seventy megatons today to 540 megatons by 2040.

That will bring it closer to the United States, currently the world leader, producing 672 megatons of carbon dioxide emissions from urban transportation. China, also working on its network of freeways, could beat everyone in this rush to a dubious achievement. China's annual carbon dioxide transportation output could rise from 190 megatons today to 1,100 megatons by 2050. One outcome could send greenhouse gases soaring into a range that the world's climate scientists say could lead to catastrophic weather changes, impose huge burdens on economies, endanger public health, and restrict a growing population's access to food.

This process is already under way, explained Michael Replogle, managing director for the University of California Davis study. "Transportation, driven by rapid growth in car use, has been the fastest-growing source of carbon dioxide in the world."

While drifting along is often appealing to some politicians and companies, Replogle's study predicts that as a policy it will quickly founder because it may be harmful. The added emissions will accelerate the impacts of climate change and swiftly expose the simple fact that, as more and more people around the world move into major cities, there will be no more room or breathing space for all of these additional cars.

So the study's answer is called the High Shift scenario, which calls for governments to invest more in urban rail and clean bus transport, particularly to a system called Bus Rapid Transport, which provides dedicated lanes and subway-like stations and schedules for buses, and removing investments from road construction, parking garages, and other facilities that lure people to drive downtown. This could save more than $100 trillion in private and public spending and result in healthier cities with more walking and bike riding, according to the study.

Is it doable? In Hong Kong, an island city of 7.1 million people, 90 percent of commuters already travel by bus. That would be a stretch for New York and particularly for Los Angeles where, if you're an oddball and walk the streets, you find people take a peculiar pride in their freeways.

I was once standing in a crowd of tourists on the rooftop of the J. Paul Getty Museum in Los Angeles. It was rush hour, but it wasn't rushing. Some of us in the crowd were struck by the vision of six lanes of cars, miles of them, idling almost stock-still in the gathering twilight on the San Diego Freeway. The tour guide remarked that it was an almost daily occurrence. But then, sensing our interest, she came up with a way to connect it to some of the beautiful artworks she'd just shown us in the museum. Gesturing toward the headlights pointing in our direction and the brake lights extending south into downtown L.A., she said: "Oh, yes, isn't that wonderful? We call those our rubies and our diamonds!"

To further help Los Angeles and other cities, the planners at University of California, Davis, have come up with an adjunct to their High Shift strategy called the Global Fuel Economy Initiative. It calls for government regulators to require fuel use by cars to be cut by half, worldwide, by 2030.

The results combined with the High Shift initiative would cut expected urban transportation's carbon dioxide emissions by 55 percent from what they might be in 2050. It would even make them 10 percent lower than today's emissions.

Is this even imaginable? It is now. We are probably the first generation to be given the tools to do it. Both lithium-ion batteries and fuel cells are based on gifts to us from an earlier generation. They were breakthroughs achieved by researchers during the Cold War, men working on weapons-related projects designed to meet the awesome challenges of their age.

There are hundreds of pioneers of the modern electric car, but few have made an impact that has been as far-reaching as that of

Dr. John Goodenough, a University of Texas physicist. In the 1970s, when he first achieved a workable version of the lithium-ion battery (meaning one that delivered useable amounts of power and did not explode), he was working at Oxford University in England under a $20,000 U.S. Air Force grant to work on energy storage. After he developed his battery further in his Texas lab, Dr. Goodenough found that an engineer from Japan, whom he had trained, had taken the idea home. Goodenough sued NTT, the big Japanese telecommunications company, claiming it had infringed on his patent.

NTT later settled the dispute, brought before a court in Texas, for $30 million, while admitting that it had done no wrong. Lithium-ion batteries were first commercialized in Japan, which continues to dominate the development of this multibillion-dollar market.

In an interview, Goodenough explained that lawyers took most of the winnings from his lawsuit. "The inventor never really gets much. I'm very happy to have worked on a society-transformative problem."

Two other men also rank as prime movers. The modern fuel cell was invented by two General Electric scientists, Thomas Grubb and Leonard Niedrach, in the early 1960s. They were working for the U.S. Navy at the time when they developed a membrane that made the fuel cell generate electricity.

At the time the U.S. was racing to land a man on the moon and the fuel cell was used to power the Gemini spacecraft that led up to the Apollo launches. In the 1970s the Navy reconfigured the invention to produce oxygen on its submarines, including the "boomers" that carry intercontinental ballistic missiles under the seas.

GE later sold the technology, failing to find commercial uses for it, but because the work was done for NASA, the fuel cell's designs were in the public domain. David Watkins, the engineer for a Canadian company, Ballard Power Systems, found them in the 1980s and corrected some design flaws to make them produce more electricity.

Then he went on to adapt them for commercial use in a car that multiple automakers are beginning to put on the road. Watkins insists the glory should go to the original inventors. "I stood on those guys' shoulders. They did this first. They deserve the respect for this. We wouldn't be here if GE hadn't done what they did."

The questions that remain for us are whether the next generations can stand on our shoulders, maintain an auto industry that is globally competitive, end the manipulative dominance of foreign oil producers, and help the world stave off the threats of climate change using the breakthroughs that are just beginning to roll into the marketplace. If we can seize this huge opportunity, our children and their children will undoubtedly thank us.

ACKNOWLEDGMENTS

I first began thinking about this book in the late 1990s when Washington, D.C., was abuzz with stories about the Clinton administration's proposed Supercar, a project that then vice president Al Gore was promoting as one solution to the problem of climate change.

When I wrote about it as a reporter for *The Wall Street Journal*'s Washington, D.C., bureau, the stories drew skepticism from the *Journal*'s Detroit Bureau. I learned that the real "car guys" in Motor City were sure electric cars had no future.

That was hopeful. If there was a story here, I had it all to myself. A few years later, when I mentioned it to my agent, Ron Goldfarb, he ran out and bought shares in Tesla, a then almost unknown California company. After the shares went ballistic, he began pestering me to write this book.

I owe a big debt of gratitude to the pioneers of the resurgence of the electric car in the United States, Wally Rippel, the late Leon Loeb, Alec Brooks, and Alan Cocconi, who had the patience to help me sort out the war stories from fact and gave me a strong sense of how hard it was and yet how exciting it could be to challenge the orthodoxy that reigned in one of the world's largest industries.

There were General Motors veterans, including Howard Wilson, Jon Bereisa, Don Runkle, and Byron McCormick, who helped me peer into the inner workings of GM's automotive research units so I could trace the sometimes stumbling, but continuing journey of this huge company into what amounted to a new world.

I had valuable help on the promise of electric vehicles from Amory Lovins, a futurist who had enormous influence on environmental groups, politicians, government researchers, and regulators. Stanley Young and others at California's Air Resources Board showed me how one state agency has, at times, exerted a gravity-like pull on the world's automakers. Past and present American hot-rodders, including John Wayland and Don Garlits, showed me that this isn't just about future power plays, this is a technology you can have fun with right now.

Martha Voss of Toyota and Christian Mohrdieck and Ferdinand Panik of Daimler helped me peer through the windows of their formidable companies. And David McLeod, the former marketing director of Ballard Research, helped me see the Canadian connection to the saga of fuel cell cars, a story that's just beginning to play on the stages of the automotive world.

Brian Wynne, Genevieve Cullen, and Jeremy Burne at the Electric Drive and Transmission Association in Washington, D.C., provided connections to dozens of companies involved with electric cars and the strategies to sell them, beginning with Formula E racing.

I give thanks to Kevin Braun and Michael Witt, the owners of E&E Publishing LLC, who lured me out of retirement to edit ClimateWire, an Internet publication that gives me a daily education in the looming challenges of climate change, and to Andrew Holmes of E&E's technical staff, who helped me sort out the pictorial side of the book.

Last, but certainly not least, there is my wife, Deborah, who spent many hours proofreading, and Gary Milhollin, a close friend, lawyer, and engineer, who gave me advice that simplified the organization of the book. Finally, thanks to my editor at St. Martin's Press, Rob Kirkpatrick, and Jennifer Letwack, his assistant. They put on the wheels that made *Car Wars* go.

ENDNOTES

Preface

xi. "Keep silent forever" (*Volta: Science and Culture in the Age of Enlightenment,* Guiliano Pancaldi Princeton, NJ: Princeton University Press [2003] 86).

xi. "He had invented the first storage battery" (Ibid., 222).

xii. ". . . they gave it an award for appearance" ("Bottled Energy: Electrical Engineering and the Evolution of Chemical Energy Storage" Richard H. Schallenberg Philadelphia: American Philosophical Society [1982] 257).

xiii. "There is this sense of incompleteness about it" (*History of the Electric Automobile, Battery-Only Powered Cars,* Ernest H. Wakefield, Warrendale, Pa: Society of Automotive Engineers, [1994] 49).

xiii. "A delicate woman can practically live in her car and never tire" (*Taking Charge; The Electric Automobile in America,* Michael Brian Schiffer, Washington, D.C.: Smithsonian Books [1994] 121).

xiv. ". . . worse to take care of than a hospital full of sick dogs" (Ibid., 64).

xv. "Dynamic and attractive, [Henry] Ford exuded a self-confidence" (*Henry Ford,* Vincent Caruso New York: Oxford University Press [2013] 14).

xv. "You have it—the self-contained unit carrying its own fuel" (Ibid., 30).

xv. ". . . pouring drops of gasoline into a sputtering engine's intake" (Ibid., 43).

xvi. "Boy, I'll never do that again" (Ibid, 36).

xvii. "I never really thought much of racing" (Ibid., 35).

xvii. ". . . shot into a crowd of onlookers, killing two and injuring eight" (Schiffer, *Taking Charge,* 84).

1. The Great Electric Car Race

3. ". . . glass-smooth acceleration" (Interview with Wally Rippel, October 2013).

3. "I didn't know what I didn't know" (Ibid.).

5. "Back in those days we had a lot of time on our hands" (Interview with Leon Loeb, August 2013).

5. "The damn thing never did work" (Ibid.).

6. "Boy, was it jerky" (Ibid.).

8. "At that time battery electrochemistry was witchcraft" (Ibid.).

8. "It was at this point when spirits were as low as the battery charge" ("Diary of a Race," *Machine Design* magazine [Sept. 26, 1986]: 24).

9. "You know, I think this is over for us" ("Cambridge or Bust/Pasadena or Bust," *Caltech Engineering and Science* magazine [October 1968]: 13).

2. "Whatever Happens Will Happen!"

10. "Look, we're going to Boston!" (Rippel interview).

11. "It was a lesson that I'll never forget" (Ibid.).

11. "A tremendous current surge resulted" (Ibid.).

12. "The long haul from the Midwest to the California line went quite smoothly" ("Across the U.S. with MIT's Electric Car," Leon S. Loeb, *Popular Mechanics* [November 1968]: 52j).

13. "It was enough to scare someone out of driving an electric car" ("Cambridge or Bust," *Caltech Engineering and Science* magazine, 15).

14. "There wasn't an MIT cheering section there" (Loeb interview).

14. "He said Wally, if we can improve our average speed by 8 percent and cut down our charging time by 6 percent we'll win this" (Rippel interview).

14. ". . . shook their heads in disbelief" ("Diary of a Race," *Machine Design*, 31)

14. ". . . which almost cost Caltech the race" (Ibid.).

15. "I said we don't have a way of getting it there" (Loeb interview).

3. The "Adventurer"

16. "They did push back the darkness a little" ("The Great Electric Car Race," Ron Wakefield and Karl Ludvigsen, *Road and Track* magazine [December 1968]: 51).

17. "If you succeed," he told Tholstrup, "we'll give you the gas" ("9,147 miles in an outboard," *Christian Science Monitor* [Oct. 22, 1970]: 6).

18. "It's keeping Australia on your left" (*The Observer*, Gladstone, Australia [March 27, 2009]: 7).

18. "I said we're supposed to jump the motorbikes, not just run them over" (Tholstrup interview, August 2013).

19. "A stuntman performing under the name of Lawrence Legend" (*Canberra Times* [Jan. 5, 2003]: section A, 5).

19. "I didn't think the world was treating the oil situation with the respect it deserved" (Tholstrup interview).

19. "I figured if he could fly on the stuff, we could drive on it" (Ibid.).

20. "It was as if the 'whole world had burst into a smile'" (*Sunracing*, Richard and Melissa King, Amherst, Mass.: Human Resource Development Press, [1993], 7).

20. "I naively thought that people would say yes" (Ibid.).

21. "These sorts of activities are new" (*Sydney Morning Herald* [April 1, 1987]: 18).

21. "We were running an education event, a brain sport" (Tholstrup interview).
22. "This was just a perfect deal so I promoted it on that basis" (Interview with Harold Wilson, July 11, 2013).
23. "He [Stempel] was basically a very enthusiastic guy, so he bought into it right away" (Ibid.).
23. "Hey, I know a guy back here that really wants to be in this race" (Ibid.).
23. "He's six one and weighs 220 pounds" (Interview with Chester Kyle, August 12, 2013).
23. "... calculating machine with idiosyncrasies" (*More with Less; Paul MacCready and the Dream of Efficient Flight,* Paul Ciotti, San Francisco: Encounter Books, [2002], 105).
24. "Flying laundry bag" (Ibid. p. 106).

4. Charging Toward the Night

28. "I said that I'm really not interested in cars, I prefer airplanes" (Interview with Alan Cocconi, July 10, 2013).
28. "Alan has this instinct for sniffing out the trouble spots" (Rippel interview).
29. "I sort of liked the physics and engineering aspects of it" (Ibid.).
28. "He talked me into it" (Cocconi interview).
29. "There were some pretty heated arguments there" (Ibid.).
30. "This is exactly what we wanted to happen" ("Driven to Extremes," *Los Angeles Times* [Oct. 25, 1987]: N-18).
30. "Is there anyone in that thing?" (*Sunraycer,* Bill Tuckey, Hornsby, Australia: Chevron Publishing Group Pty. [1989], 63).
31. "... the big question at GM was if we enter this, we can't afford not to win" (Interview with J. Bruce McCristal, July 27, 2013).
31. "It [Sunraycer] turned up in virtually every newspaper in the country" (Ibid.).
32. "The Japanese didn't have a clue about motor efficiency" (Kyle interview).
33. "He's way out ahead! Wow . . . he's just flying" (*Sunraycer,* Tuckey, 82).
35. "Paul [MacCready] proved that what we had set out to do could be done" (Tholstrup interview).
35. "It's good to be here" (*The Advertiser/Sunday Mail,* Adelaide, Australia [Dec. 3, 1987]: p. 1).

5. The Dream

37. "... a solar-powered car might be 'five to seven years away'" ("Solar Power Rolls On," *Christian Science Monitor* [Nov. 13, 1987]: 1).
38. "What we have learned makes practical battery and hybrid-powered vehicles more feasible" (*Sunraycer,* Tuckey, 244).
38. "This was just the start of a twenty-five-month public relations campaign" (Ibid., 225).

39. "I read this and I still say, wow, that was one hell of a deal" (McCristal interview).

39. "We never put a number on it" (Ibid.).

39. "What we learn from Sunraycer may be useful" (*Sunraycer,* Tuckey, 9).

39. "Sunraycer had gotten all the public relations boost that GM could possibly want" (*The Car That Could; The Inside Story of GM's Revolutionary Electric Vehicle,* Michael Shnayerson [New York: Random House, 1996], 19).

40. "I said let's work our way from the inside out" (Brooks interview).

41. "Most engineers would still be working on the 1971 Chevrolet" (*The Car That Could,* Shnayerson, 24).

41. "I said okay, my job is done" (Cocconi interview).

42. "And he left them standing in the driveway" (Brooks interview).

42. "I had to fight with other GM divisions to make sure Alan came to work for me" (Interview with Jon Bereisa, July 2013).

43. "Alan built that [the electronic drive system] to move the wheels" (Ibid.).

43. "I have all the goddamn money and none of you has any recourse" (*The Car That Could,* Shnayerson, 45).

44. "So, with GM making these statements" (Interview with Analisa Bevan, September 2013).

44. "All of a sudden I had half the company trying to fight the mandate" (Bereisa interview).

44. "They would figure that car companies had no choice but to buy this stuff" (Ibid.).

45. "We'll be there by 1998" (*New Straits Times* [Nov. 12, 1993]: 2).

6. Who Makes the Rules?

47. "The ZEV mandate may be the single most important event in the history of transportation since Henry Ford." (*Future Drive; Electric Vehicles and Sustainable Transportation,* Daniel Sperling, Washington, D.C.,: Island Press [1995], 2).

47. "He [Lovins] single-handedly converted them from loathing the auto industry to engaging with it" (Interview with Stewart Brand, November 2012).

48. "Amory breezed in in his usual way" ("Entering a Climate-changed World with Chutzpah and Bananas—Amory Lovins," John J. Fialka, *ClimateWire* [Jan. 24, 2013]: 1).

48. "He [Lovins] has a way of talking about the future as if it was aimed in his direction" (Ibid.).

48. "I've heard that before" (*Advanced Light Vehicle Concepts,* Amory B. Lovins, Snowmass Co. : Rocky Mountain Institute [July 9, 1991] 2).

49. "Today's car efficiency isn't like a three-hundred-pound man who's lost a hundred and fifty pounds and can't lose much more" (Ibid., 12).

49. ". . . hope none of your competitors is faster" (Ibid., 16).

50. "One year we were sort of sitting around having a beer" (Interview with Don Runkle, August 2013).

50. "It was the concept car that I'm most proud of" (Ibid.).

51. "You get the green beans and movie stars to fall for these things, but you run through those people pretty quickly" (Ibid.).

51. "Joel is known for blowing things up" (Ibid.).

52. ". . . open up the concept and got a lot of people fighting about it" (Lovins interview).

52. "That's not Amory. That's not what he does" (Interview with James Woolsey, November 2013).

52. "Amory provides the right sort of inspiration, he pokes you in the ribs" (Runkle interview).

53. "Emissions are something that people can't grasp. You've got to have some regulations" (Ibid.).

53. "In the coming two years we plan to ask new car buyers did you know about EV's? Did you buy one? Why not, and things like that" (Bevan interview).

7. Quest for a Better Battery

55. "The fact that it worked was enough" (*The Battery; How Portable Power Sparked a Technological Revolution* Henry Schlesinger, New York: Harper, [2011], 50).

55. "Davy released and identified pure lithium, a light, highly reactive metal that seemed to have no earthly value" (Ibid., 58).

56. "I have no idea, but no doubt you'll find some way to tax it" (Ibid., 75).

56. ". . . French engineer, Gaston Planté, took the time—thirty years—to reflect upon this odd technological trail" (Ibid., 144).

57. "No, I didn't fail. I discovered 24,999 ways that the storage battery does not work" (*The Battery,* Schlesinger, 174).

57. "Nobody cared how it worked or how to make it any better" (Interview with Ted J. Miller, October 2013).

57. "Because the battery is an electrochemical-thermal device" (Miller interview).

58. "Technology capable of meeting the CARB mandate did not exist" ("Effectiveness of the United States Advanced Battery Consortium as a Government-Industry Partnership, National Research Council [1998]: 2).

59. "After picking a car by drawing lots, President George H. W. Bush jumped in the minivan" (*The Car That Could,* Shnayerson, 90).

59. "I learned on my own and at my own pace, faster than I could get it in school" (Interview with Stanford R. Ovshinsky, November 2006).

60. "When you bought Ovshinsky, you got two Ovshinskys" (Ibid.).

8. Supercar

65. "We never wanted to be a hobby shop, working on things that nobody wanted" ("EPA-influenced Vehicles Get Set to Hit Road," *Wall Street Journal* [August 22, 2006]: A-4).

66. "In March, 1994, GM's board tentatively agreed to revive the Impact, but . . . to keep the renewed effort secret" (The full story of the clandestine

revival of the GM Impact can be found in *The Car That Could,* Shnayerson, 181–214).

67. "They wanted a car that got eighty miles per gallon, so Alan says to them well this car already does it" (Interview with Tom Gage, July 2013).

68. "Many carmakers bought one or two samples from us and that was a way for us to survive" (Cocconi interview).

68. "It had a surprising effect; suddenly all the things we had done in research, Toyota was putting into production" (Miller interview).

68. "This is not a concept car. This is not a conversion" (*The Car That Could,* Shnayerson, 256–57).

69. "This is truly a mountaintop moment for America" ("Death of the Supercar; How Politics and Self-Interest Kept A Family Car that Got 80 MPG Off America's Roads," Sam Roe, *South Florida Sun-Sentinel* [Feb. 3, 2003]: 1F).

70. "We definitely think hydraulic hybrid has merit" (Interview with Nick Twork, August 2006).

70. "You can't imagine the grieving we did when Ford left" ("EPA-Influenced Vehicles Get Set to Hit Road," John J. Fialka, *Wall Street Journal* [August 22, 2006]: A-4).

71. "There is a good chance of that happening if people look at the UPS truck sitting next to them at a stoplight" (Ibid.).

9. Crash Program

72. "And then it only went for five hundred meters [547 yards] . . . We didn't know which system was wrong" (Interview with Takeshi Uchiyamada).

73. "What we finally produced was a completely different concept from the auto show prototype" (Ibid.).

74. "I don't want to build just another economy car. We have to rethink development" (*Clean Car Wars; How Honda and Toyota are Winning the Battle of the Eco-Friendly Autos,* Yozo Hasagawa, Singapore: John Wiley & Sons [2008], 34).

75. "But that's outrageous" (*The Prius That Shook the World: How Toyota Developed the World's First Mass-Producton Hybrid Vehicle,* Hideshi Itazaki, The Nikkan Kogyo Shimbun [1999], 72–73).

75. " . . . major pressure, the most intense I had ever experienced" (Uchiyamada in a speech given to the Economic Club of Washington, D.C., October 2013).

75. "It would probably be accurate to say we reviewed PNGV goals and considered them in our [Prius] development process" (Interview with David Hermance, 2006).

77. "Otherwise 'We will miss becoming the first company to launch a hybrid vehicle. Toyota has been second too long'" (*The Prius That Shook the World,* Itazaki, 116).

77. "You can achieve the impossible when you really have to" (*Clean Car Wars,* Hasagawa, 42).

78. "... the battery's operation was 'based on chemical reactions, many aspects of which were still unknown'" (*The Prius That Shook the World,* Itazaki, 166).

78. "Mr. Chief Engineer, you are distracting us by appearing so late at night." (Ibid., 164).

79. "Every time they thought they had the problem figured out, the module would break and explode like a firework" (Ibid., 229).

80. "You shouldn't drive the car in this condition" (Ibid., 270).

10. Doing Less with More

82. "I loved his [MacCready's] whole thing about doing more with less" (Interview with Chris Paine, July 26, 2013).

83. "The acceleration just blew my mind. I thought, wow, this is so fun" (Ibid.).

84. "EV1 was ordained inside GM as a poster child for failure" (Bareisa interview).

85. "Bob Lutz, a later vice chairman of GM, put the total value of the car at $250,000" (*Charlie Rose Show* [Nov., 9, 1011]: "Interview of Bob Lutz about his book *Car Guys vs. Bean Counters: The Battle for the Soul of American Business.* (http://www.charlierose.com/view/interview/11986). Remark occurs at 19:34).

85. "However the value of the car used in the calculations for the lease was $33, 995" ("Driving the Future," Tony Quiroga, *Car and Driver* [August 2009]: 52).

85. "In the early days GM took such great care of us" (Paine interview).

86. "They said here, we have this nice Saturn. Take that" (Ibid.).

88. "I thought my dad was just being an old hippie and I thought this was some goofy little golf cart he was buying" ("Executive Producer Dean Devlin Discusses *Who Killed the Electric Car?*" Rebecca Murray, About .com Hollywood Movies, http://movies.about.com/od/documentaries /a/electriccr06266.html).

89. "Some of the audiences seemed to Rippel to be 'left of center'" (Rippel interview).

89. "A GM spokesman, Dave Barthmuss, made one last attempt to buttress GM's stance on the EV1" ("Who Ignored the Facts About the Electric Car?" Dave Barthmuss's blog, released on July 13, 2006. It can be found at http://www.gm/company/onlygm/fastlane_blog.html#EV1).

89. "It didn't affect profitability, but it did affect image" (*Motor Trend* [June 2006]: 94).

11. Selling

90. "It was an 'odd-looking little bundle left on our doorstep back in 1997'" (Remarks delivered by Bob Carter, Toyota U.S.A. senior vice president for automotive operations, at the 2013 Toyota Hybrid Vehicle World Tour, the first of a series of symposiums to explain the growth and changing nature of hybrids and the hybrid market, in Ypsilanti, MI, August 2013).

90. "We weren't sure about this Prius thing" (Ibid.).

91. "In fact they were suspicious of it" (Ibid.).

91. "It was going to be hard to determine who would want one and how to reach them" (Interview with Geri Yoza, August 2013).

92. "That one customer sold that first year probably 80 percent of the Pi-ruses we sold in the two dealerships" (Bob Carter remarks).

93. "At that time everyone said in the United States no one cares about gaso-line and no one thinks about the environment" (Remarks by Satoshi Ogiso at Toyota Hybrid Vehicle World Tour, Ypsilanti, MI, August 2013).

94. "So many top executives said to me, Ogizo-san, what are you doing? What we should be doing is reducing the costs" (Ibid.).

94. ". . . saw Larry David have a meltdown" (www.youtube.com/watch?v =kY4IMAM-j3U).

94. ". . . *South Park,* Comedy Central's animated cartoon show for adults, topped that by writing a small car called a Toyonda Pious into one of their scripts" (http://en.wikipedia.org/wiki/Smug_Alert!).

95. ". . . great from a marketing perspective because it creates an opportunity for conversations to take place in the home" ("Would You Like Fries with That Monopoly Game?" Stuart Elliot, *New York Times* Business Sec-tion, Sept. 12, 2006).

95. "It is a time-honored tradition at Honda to beat Toyota at whatever the biggest Japanese automaker was attempting" (*Clean Car Wars,* Hasagawa. An elaboration can be found on 67–76).

96. "Our main technology was in a way more elegant than Prius because we got about 80 percent of the benefits at two-thirds of the cost" (Interview with Robert Bienenfeld, October 2013).

96. "Tom and Ray Magliozi of NPR's popular *Car Talk* radio show summed up what they saw as the difference" (*Electric and Hybrid Cars: A History*, by Curtis D. Anderson and Judy Anderson, Jefferson, N.C.: McFarland & Co. [2010], 230).

97. "There were times when driving a Prius in Santa Monica was the only thing to do" (Ibid.).

97. "The Japanese government paid for 100 percent of the development of the battery and hybrid system that went into the Toyota Prius" (A more complete account of Press's remark and the aftermath can be found on a *Businessweek* blog post, "Chrysler's Jim Press and Toyota Differ on Prius Narrative," by David Kilely, http://www. Businessweek.com/autos /archives/2008/04/Chryslers_jim_p1.html, April 2, 2008).

98. "And the United States sometimes spends a considerable amount of money to help American carmakers be more competitive" (See "Results of U.S.-Industry Partnership to Develop a New Generation of Vehi-cles," RCED-00-81, March 30, 2000, by the U.S. Government Ac-countability Office, which puts the U.S. commitment to the six-year program at $250 million per year.).

98. "The success of the Prius, after being locked out of the U.S. PNGV program, 'is something we've all puzzled over'" (Interview with Dr. John Newman, November 2013).

98. "There's a mental approach. Some of these companies just say by God they're going to do it" (Ibid.).

98. "In DOE [the U.S. Department of Energy] if you have an inkling something would work in the next fifty years, the attitude is, we don't want to hear about it" (Ibid.).

99. "I can't go beyond that" (Carter, Toyota symposium).

99. "After ten years, the Prius still feels like what comes next" ("Toyota's Prius: Performance Is All That Matters," Dan Neil, *Wall Street Journal* [Nov. 2, 2013]: D-11).

12. The EV GRIN

100. The initial story that gave rise to this chapter is: "Those Muscle Cars on the Drag Strip Are Really Electric," by John J. Fialka. It appeared on page A-1 of the *Wall Street Journal* on August 1, 2007. All the quotations in this chapter are taken from interviews with the author.

13. A Difficult Birth

108. "The more I looked at it, I came to believe that this problem of global warming was real" (Interview with Martin Eberhard, July 11, 2013).

108. "All the electric car manufacturers had pulled out. You couldn't get anything" (Ibid.).

109. "They had laid everybody off except for six or seven people and they weren't paying salaries to anybody" (Ibid.).

109. "And then a weird thing happened. They basically kicked me out of the office" (Ibid.).

110. "In a battery you are basically trying to take two very reactive materials and get them to react slowly" (Interview with Robert P. Hamlen, Nov. 21, 2013).

110. "Finally the fire chief comes to me and said, if we have to come again, we're going to charge you for the chemicals" (Ibid.).

110. "We said this is a good $50 million business. They said, hell, that's too small, let's get rid of it" (Ibid.).

110. "The difference here is that you had a Japanese company willing to invest long-term and most Americans in the battery business were not" (Interview with M. Stanley Whittingham, Nov. 18, 2013).

110. "I have always been happy to receive good people who are funded by a home laboratory to which they will return" ("Interview of John B. Goodenough (J.B.G.), March 2001, by Bernadette Bensaude-Vincent (B.B-V.) and Arne Hessenbruch (A.H.) http://authors.library.caltech .edu/5456/1/hrst.mit.edu/hrs/materials/public/Goodenough /Goodenough_Interview.htm, p. 14).

111. "But they weren't sure they wanted to talk to me about it" (Eberhard interview).

111. "It demonstrated what you could do with an electric motor if you weren't trying to make a cheap car, but a fast car" (Ibid.).

113. "I have two brilliant children, but Elon's a genius" ("Triumph of His Will," Tom Junod, *Esquire* [Dec. 1, 2012]: 138).

112. "I'm not a car guy for car's sake. I think electric cars are important for the future of the world" (Interview with Elon Musk, Oct. 18, 2013).

113. "I pushed Cocconi. He is a strange cat. It's, like, hard to determine what his motivations are. But, for sure, the idea of going into production with anything is not Al's idea of a good time" (Ibid.).

114. "Their designs were very primitive. It was very old school, so we wound up not using much of their stuff" (Eberhard interview).

114. "In the early days it was quite difficult for us to hire people that had any automotive experience" (Ibid.).

115. "The guy from Siemens described it very clearly: 'You guys are going to buy a few thousand of these things. Our typical customer buys a few hundred thousand of these things'" (Ibid.).

115. "But public image notwithstanding, Elon worked incredibly hard and cared a tremendous deal about his company" (*The PayPal Wars; Battles with eBay, the Media, the Mafia, and the Rest of Planet Earth,* Eric M. Jackson [Los Angeles: World Ahead Publishing, 2004], 111).

115. "As much as I disagreed with his business strategies, I respected Elon's grace and continued dedication to the company" (Ibid., 163).

116. "I was essentially living on borrowed money at that point" (Musk interview).

116. "We ended up having to virtually redesign every element of that car" (Ibid.).

117. "We really all kind of collided together" (Interview with J. B. Straubel, Nov. 15, 2013).

117. "I respect the hell out of that. He's a brilliant guy. He doesn't want to make any energy compromises for comfort of people in a car" (Ibid.).

117. "I said what could convince you to partner with us?" (Musk interview).

117. "When they came to visit in January, they were expecting a PowerPoint presentation. We gave them a car" (Ibid.).

118. "People would ask, what will you do about competition when these big companies realize that electric cars are important?" (Ibid.).

118. "I still like Teslas" (Eberhard interview).

119. "I enjoyed working with AeroVironment because their culture was working with these one-off weird projects that nobody had ever done before" (Cocconi interview).

119. "That's what paid the bills, barely" (Ibid.).

120. "With the new batteries you ought to be able to do a car with a four-hundred-mile range very easily" (Ibid.).

14. Shocking Moments

121. ". . . was a total crock of shit" (*Detroit City Is the Place to Be: the Afterlife of an American Metropolis,* Mark Binelli, New York: Metropolitan Books, Henry Hold and Company [2012], 150).

121. "Lutz assures the world that Gore's views are 'absurd'" (*Car Guys vs. Bean Counters: The Battle for the Soul of American Business,* Bob Lutz New York: Portfolio/Penguin [2011], 35).

122. "We stood by, nearly speechless, with envy over the countless billions Toyota reaped" (Ibid., 147. Toyota has never revealed what it cost to develop the Prius; however, its U.S. executives say the car has earned profits since 2003.) .

122. ". . . crushing the EV1s was a 'PR blunder of truly gargantuan proportions'" (Ibid., 148).

123. ". . . he was, as he put it, 'cruelly shot down'" (Ibid., 150).

123. "Bob, we lost over one billion bucks on EV1. How much do you propose we lose this time?" (Ibid., 152).

124. "How is it that everybody at GM convinces me that this can't be done . . . and here is this outfit in California that nobody has ever heard of, and they are gonna put a car on the market with lithium-ion batteries?" (*Bottled Lightning: Superbatteries, Electric Cars and the New Lithium Economy,* Seth Fletcher New York: Hill and Wang [2011], 66).

124. "Whatever . . . I ran with it" (*Car Guys vs. Bean Counters,* Lutz, 153).

125. "'Well here it is,' he said, after shaking hands with Rick Wagoner" (*Bottled Lightning,* Fletcher, 73).

125. "A driver who did that would 'never need to buy gasoline during the entire life of the vehicle. . . . '" Ibid.

125. "Our deal [with GM] was anything we wanted" (Chris Paine interview).

126. "The old band is back, but now we had an audience" (Jon Bereisa interview).

127. "It should have gotten an award for the scariest vehicle" (Interview with Andrew Frank, August 13, 2013).

127. "We had quite a few GM engineers hovering around our lab at that time" (Ibid.).

127. "Frank was an incubator of the idea. It doesn't necessarily mean he invented it" (Interview with Mark S. Duvall, August 2013).

128. "You've got to remember that in a big company like GM everyone is looking to do the land grab" (Interview with Andrew Farah, Oct. 3, 2013).

128. "The damn car wouldn't move and we couldn't figure out what had happened" (Ibid.).

129. "We are making history today" (*Chevrolet Volt: Charging Into the Future,* by Larry Edsall Minneapolis: MBI Publishing, [2010], 125).

130. "We are pretty convinced that this is the right vehicle for the market at the right time" ("Charging Ahead in Detroit," *New York Times,* January 14, p. B-3).

15. Hitting One Out of the Park

133. "As GM historians later explained, the experiment was 'cost prohibitive'" (http://history.gmheritagecenter.com/wiki/index.php/1966_GM_Electrovan).

134. " . . . fuel cell–driven cars served the same function as the mechanical rabbit in a dog race." (Freeman's remarks were captured in *Who Killed the Electric Car?*, 2006).

135. "I guess I was more like the typical Baptist minister's son" (Interview with David McLeod, April 2014).

135. He later encouraged his two sons to take up pool "so they would never go hungry" (Ibid.).

135. "AA is honesty in all of our affairs" (Ibid.).

136. "The measure of the man is whether you can get up and try again" (*Powering the Future: The Ballard Fuel Cell and the Race to Change the World,* Tom Koppel Toronto: John Wiley & Sons Canada, [1999], 74).

138. "Unfortunately, in the mid-sixties the fuel cell was still an experimental device" (*Liftoff: The Story of America's Adventure in Space,* Michael Collins [New York: Grove Press, 1988], 75).

138. "The coffee-like water had little puffy objects floating in it that the astronauts dubbed 'furries'" (Ibid.).

138. "Unlike batteries, they had character" (Ibid.).

139. "But Chuck Matthews, the director of the Gemini program, confided . . . that an unfixable fuel cell malfunction was one of his biggest nightmares" (Ibid.).

139. "These just weren't terrestrial things" (Interview with David Watkins, April 9, 2014).

140. "When you know him [Watkins], trust me, you get up" (McLeod Interview).

141. "GM seemed almost bent on proving it was. They were trying to cram stuff into existing vehicles" (Interview with Nicholas Vanderborgh, March 18, 2014).

141. "If they needed something like a tape recorder, they would have to buy it out of their salaries" (Ibid.).

142. "Geoffrey was dangerous, frankly, when standing in front of investors because he would just go off on them" (McLeod interview).

142. "The first conference we ever went to did not seem to be a serious business because it was all about perpetual funding" (Ibid.).

143. "What is the problem you are trying to solve?" (Ibid.).

143. "A eureka moment just knocks off your socks" (Watkins interview).

144. "I don't think you appreciate what it is you people have done" (*Powering the Future.* Koppel, 94).

144. "He wanted them to help put a patent on what Watkins had done 'because we couldn't afford it'" (McLeod interview).

144. "This is where Geoffrey was very useful" (Ibid.).

16. Running Ahead of the Pack

145. "For Mercedes, one of the brand's images is to be a technology leader" (Interview with Andreas Truckenbrodt, March 22, 2014).

147. "Good heavens man," he shouted, "are you going to take all day to cover a mile or so?" (The tale of Karl Benz, the milkman, and the minister can be found in: *The Invention of the Automobile (Karl Benz and Gottlieb Daimler),* John L. Nixon, London Country Life, [1936], 81–82.

147. "They were the perfect fit for us" (McLeod interview).

148. "We had teams that went over there. We even took German lessons" (Epps interview).

149. Ballard "stands out in the first group of organizations" ("Status and Prospects of Fuel Cells as Automobile Engines," published by the California Air Resources Board [July 1998] III–73).

150. "I don't know which one of these things is going to rise as a problem" (Interview with Byron McCormick, April 28, 2014).

152. "From a management point of view, you'd be surprised he was a Mercedes guy" (McLeod interview).

153. "The idea was to get them to look at it, decide whether they wanted it, and then, maybe, join the club" (Interview with Dr. Ferdinand Panik, May 28, 2014).

153. "We negotiated almost three years, but the feeling was not good from both sides because Honda wanted to do it more or less by themselves" (Ibid.).

153. "Daimler's joint venture with Ballard 'was a milestone that signaled automobile manufacturers involvement on the necessary scale'" ("Status and Prospects of Fuel Cells as Automobile Engines," iii–75).

153. ". . . it seems quite likely that these efforts will succeed" (Ibid., iii–48).

154. "The Ballard-Daimler-Ford partnership planned to produce 'commercial quantities' of fuel cell vehicles as early as 2004" (Ibid., iii–74).

154. "That was a good negotiation" (Panik interview).

154. "The three denizens of Ballard's fuel cell skunkworks, McLeod, Watkins, and Danny Epps, who had been paid mostly in stock, 'all became moderately well off'" (Epps interview).

155. "Before Ballard died in August, 2008, he continued to rail at his skeptics, calling them 'pistonheads'" ("Listen, Detroit: You'll Get a Charge Out of This," *Time* magazine [February 22, 1999]: 80).

155. "Science colleagues who were once 'embarrassed to be seen with me at professional symposia'" (Ibid.).

155. "If Ballard, a trim sixty-six-year-old with an unflinching gaze, sounds cocky it may be because he has finally won respect at the end of a long and winding career" (Ibid.).

156. "People could say, oh, my gosh, you could sort of get it in a car and it does sort of work. Yeah, he did start the process" (McCormick interview).

17. Into the Valley of Death

158. "It basically took up the whole back of the vehicle" (Interview with Catherine Dunwoody, June 18, 2014).

159. "The more we looked at it [methanol], I think we all kind of agreed that would be a bad way to go, there were just too many environmental issues" (McCormick interview).

159. "We'd be down to, well, let's use a petroleum product and petroleum was one of the problems we were trying to solve" (Ibid.).

160. "We had to make a joint decision. It wasn't possible if one was going for one way and another was going for a different one" (Panik interview).

160. "... the public felt fuel cell cars might be 'small and not functional, lacking in power, unsafe, unattractive, too expensive'" ("California Hydrogen Highway Network, Year End Progress Report to the Legislature," prepared by the California Air Resources Board [December 2006]: 19).

161. "... hydrogen storage technologies have advanced relatively little in recent years." ("Status and Prospects for Zero Emission Vehicle Technology," California Air Resources Board [April 13, 2007]: 5).

162. "That's the valley of death and everyone is looking at it right now and trying to figure out how to work their way through it" (McCormick interview).

162. "We don't need any more cars for the demonstration phase, we can learn enough from these" (Interview with Christian Morhrdieck, May 2014).

162. "We had no controlling interest. This was one of the issues because the other shareholders wanted to see very short-term profits" (Ibid.).

164. "Honda is not the company that goes out and brags there will be 25,000 vehicles by 2025. We stick to our knitting" (Second interview with Robert Bienenfeld, March 21, 2014).

165. "They didn't want their competitors working in the bay next to them" (Dunwoody interview).

166. "In the automobile business, he explains, 'the image in being the leader is so important'" (Panik interview).

18. The Chickens Come First

167. "I'm really excited to be able to pack up the kids and the dog and surfboards in the back and go to the beach" ("Hyundai's hydrogen fuel-cell car makes U.S. debut," http://www.Reuters.com/assets/print?aid=USK BN0EM06G20140611, June 10, 2014).

168. "Recognizing that the emergence of hydrogen-fueled cars presented 'a classic chicken-and-egg dilemma,' the partnership recommended that in order to sell the cars more hydrogen-equipped retail stations had to come first." (Taken from the Web page of the California Fuel Cell Partnership, http://www. Cafep.org/carsandbuses/carroadmap).

168. "We don't have our price yet. We know it's critical" (LaRocque's remarks came at a symposium on electric cars sponsored by the Electric Drive Transportation Association on May 20, 2014).

168. "Marketing and reality are sometimes not consistent" (Mohrdieck interview).

169. "The electric vehicle is not a viable replacement for most conventional cars. We need something entirely new." ("Electric Cars Head Toward Another Dead End," http://www.cnbc.com/id/100430620).

169. "Fuel cell vehicles will be in our future and in much greater numbers than anyone expected" (http: //www.greencarcongress.com/2014/01 /20140107-Toyota.html).

169. "The fuel cell is so bullshit" (http//www.wired.com'autopia/2013/10/ elon-musk-hydrogen).

169. "Tesla is a rare case" ("Can Toyota Save the Electric Car?" *Spiegel Online,* Nov. 1, 2013).

170. "This is like a marathon. . . . You can't run in it if you don't commit to it, train for it, and then show up at the starting line." ("Fuel cell cars from Toyota, Honda, Hyundai set to debut at auto shows," *Los Angeles Times,* Nov. 17, 2013).

170. "The current number of stations in operation is far too small to facilitate the practical use of FCVs [fuel cell vehicles]" ("Toyota fuel cell cars to hit market by the end of 2014," *Asahi Shimbun,* June 5, 2014).

170. "Toyota regards hydrogen as core technology to be applied to many vehicles" (A video of the June 25, 2014, Toyota press conference can be found at: http://newsroom.toyota.co.jp/en/detail/3201230#.U6mJHlkLZoM).

171. "We want to capture the world technology" (Ibid.).

171. "This is the car of a new era because it doesn't emit any carbon dioxide and it's environmentally friendly. . . . The government needs to support this" ("Japan PM says will offer about $20,000 subsidy for fuel-cell cars," Reuters, July 21, 2014).

171. "Between 2005 and September 2011, the U.S. Department of Energy staged what it called a 'learning demonstration' involving the testing and refueling of 183 demonstration models of fuel cell cars" ("National Fuel Cell Electric Vehicle Learning Demonstration Final Report," National Renewable Energy Laboratory, July 2012. Most of the details are in the executive summary, starting on page 1).

172. "After the testing and all of the learning experiences, though, most of the refueling stations were later shut down" (Ibid.,8).

172. "'The smaller-caliber bullets would just bounce off the tank" ("Fuel cell cars from Toyota, Honda, Hyundai," *Los Angeles Times*).

172. ". . . only miles on the road and people in the seats of these vehicles will overcome those perceptions" (Ibid.).

173. "Discussions with potential investors show that uncertainty remains high, confidence remains low" ("Hydrogen Investment Plan," California

Fuel Cell Partnership. Http://cafcp.org/sites/files/20131015%20EB%20 Meeting%20Summary.pdf).

173. "Nobody wanted to get it hung up in court" (Dunwoody interview).

173. The oil companies "are kind of sitting on the sidelines waiting for the market to develop" (Interview with Steve Szymanski, May 2014).

174. "There are a lot of entrepreneurs out there and they see this state money getting into it. . . . It's an interesting situation" (Ibid.).

175. "You don't need the oil companies of the world to participate in this" (Ibid.).

175. "Everybody is trying to guess how many cars are going to show up and when" (Ibid.).

19. Crossing Points

176. "There will be 'large risks to global and regional food security and the combination of high temperatures and humidity compromising normal human activities'" ("Impacts, Adaptation and Vulnerabilities," Summary for Policymakers, IPCC Fifth Assessment Report [March 31, 2014]: 14).

177. ". . . ten percent of the globe's population that account for 80 percent of the globe's passenger miles traveled 'with much of the world's population hardly traveling at all'" (IPCC Report, chapter 8, p. 9).

178. "While carmakers, driven by government regulations, improved the overall fuel efficiency of cars by 40 percent, car owners managed to move the needle the other way" ("Effects of Vehicle Fuel Economy, Distance Traveled and Vehicle Load on the Amount of Fuel Used for Personal Transportation in the U.S.: 1970-2010," Michael Sivak, University of Michigan Transportation Research Institute [February 2013]: 2).

178. "Only forty-four of every thousand residents own a car compared with 423 per one thousand in the U.S., according to the World Bank" ("Woes of Megacity Driving Signal Dawn of 'Peak Car'" *Bloomberg,* [Feb. 24, 2014] http://www.bloomberg.com/news/articles/2014-02-24/woes of megacity-driving-signals-dawn-of-peak-car-era).

178. "There may be a five-year or longer lag before new technologies reach secondhand vehicle markets in large quantities" (IPCC Report, chapter 8, p. 22).

179. ". . . [Vermont] state officials say they can't afford to rebuild the entire system because storm-proofing it will be too expensive" ("Climate Change Impacts in the United States," U.S. Global Change Research Program [2013]: 139).

179. "The expense . . . may just be for starters as sea levels rise and powerful storm surges destroy bridges and roads on the nation's long coastlines" (Ibid., 131, 132, and 135).

179. ". . . estimates that the growing costs of highway congestion in loss of productivity, waste of fuel, and so on, is at $100 billion" (Ibid.,149).

00. "Globally more people are moving into large cities where they use fewer cars" ("Woes of Megacity Driving," *Bloomberg*).

180. "It is all about economics" (These and all the other comments of Dr. George Muntean in this chapter come from an interview with him on April 10, 2014).

181. "Some level of public charging infrastructure is required to overcome range anxiety" ("State of the Plug-in Electric Vehicle Market," Electrification Coalition [July 25, 2013]: 9).

181. "Eighty-three percent of these Republicans say the United States 'should do whatever it takes to protect the environment'" ("Poll finds large majority of young Republicans believe in climate change," *ClimateWire,* June 30, 2014).

183. "When I was in the fight it was to beat Ford and Chrysler and Toyota. Now it's a global competition" (These and other remarks of Ken Baker are from a February 2014 interview).

184. "In July 2014 its State Council, or cabinet, announced that buyers of hybrids, fully electric, and fuel cell cars would not have to pay the nation's 10 percent sales tax" ("China to Exempt Electric Cars From 10% Purchase Tax," *Bloomberg News,* July 10, 2014).

184. "For achieving industrial development and environmental protection, this is a win-win" ("China makes new electric cars tax-free," theguardian .com, July 10, 2014).

184. "It's so cute. My wife will really like it" ("Mini Electric Cars Give a Jolt to China's Market for Green Autos," *Wall Street Journal,* Dec. 2, 2014 wsj .com/chinarealtime/2014/12/02/mini-electric-cars-give-a-jolt-to-chinas-market-for-green-autos/)

20. Dealing

185. "John Gartner, an automotive analyst for Navigant Research, confidently predicted . . . 3.5 million electric vehicles on the road by 2023" (Remarks made at the annual convention of the Electric Drive Transportation Association in Indianapolis, Ind., May 2014).

186. "The most common answer given by twenty-one dealerships was that these cars were very popular or sold out" ("Dealers not always plugged in about electric cars," *Consumer Reports,* [June 1, 2014] http://www .consumerreports.org/content/cro/en/cars/news-archive/z2014/April /secret_shopper_electric_car_study.print.html).

187. ". . . only 19 percent of the dealers visited could give even a ballpark estimate of what it cost to charge a car" (Electric Drive Transportation Association convention).

188. "Overcharging people for unneeded servicing (often not even fixing the original problem) is rampant within the industry" ("To the People of New Jersey," Elon Musk, http://www.teslamotors.com/blog/people-new-jersey, March 14, 2014).

188. "'He needs to stop and take a breath,' replied Jim Appleton, who heads the New Jersey Coalition of Automobile Retailers" (http://www .theverge.com/2014/3/19/5525544/new-jersey-auto-dealers-respond-to-teslas-elon-musk).

188. "We're dealing here with human nature" (Electric Drive Transportation Association convention)

190. "The dealers are not well-equipped with facts because a sale like this is different for every single person" (Interview with Alex Tiller, July 15, 2014).

192. "Driver satisfaction with electrics, he says, is way above average automotive statistics. 'Tesla's is beyond anything I've ever seen'" (Norman Hajjar, Ibid.)

193. "I am standing next to a Toyota dealer showing the electric version of the Toyota RAV4 to excited customers" (Interview with Dirk Spiers, May 2014).

21. Innovation

195. "'I lived in that for three days,' Ballard recalled. 'When I tell people that it's hard for them to imagine'" (Interview with Mayor Gregory A. Ballard, July 22, 2014).

196. "Okay, we'll get through this oil price spike again and we'll just send these guys to war again" (Ibid.).

199. "In 2010, Indiana's governor, Mitch Daniels, set out to make Indiana 'the electric vehicle state.'" ("A new blow for electric vehicles: Indiana's Bright pulling the plug as loan deal drags on," *Chicago Tribune* [March 1, 2012]: 1).

199. "Bright moved ahead, hiring more than sixty people and developing a sales plan that would guarantee to cut fuel costs of fleet owners" ("Let electric car ideas work" (Letter from Mike Donoughe, CEO of Bright Automotive, to the *Chicago Tribune* [Feb. 5, 2012]: 2).

199. "But after Solyndra, Brylawski said, 'It was clear they were not going to give out any loans'" (Letter to the author by Michael Brylawski, April 9, 2014).

200. "'Here is what we are prepared to do,' Donoughe wrote. Bright's hybrid-electric van would be developed in Michigan, engineered in Anderson, Indiana, and assembled in an AM General plant in Indiana that once built the now-defunct" (Letter from Donoughe to *Chicago Tribune*).

200. "They don't have the management, [or the] technical or financial expertise to effectively grant the loans" (Brylawski letter to author).

200. "GAO investigators found that the process had become so long and burdensome that 'the costs of participating outweigh the benefits of participating to their companies'" ("Cost-Savings and Revenue Enhancement Opportunities," GAO-14-343SP [April 8, 2014]: 109).

201. "It also found that a risk management division the loan office set up in February 2012, the month that Bright Automotive died, took almost two more years to assemble a staff." ("DOE Should Fully Develop its Loan Monitoring Function and Evaluate its Effectiveness," GAO-14-367, May 1, 2014).

201. "Maybe I'm worried that the arguments will change, that we're not taking enough risk" ("DOE overhauls controversial vehicle tech loan program," E2 Wire, *The Hill,* April 2, 2014).

201. "The current process is slow, it takes eight hours to electrify a truck" (Interview with Dave West, July 15, 2014).

201. "Lutz, who later became chairman of the VIA board, says the auto industry 'started at the wrong end' with passenger cars" ("Lutz's Electric Future," *Orange County Register,* Dec. 18, 2013).

202. "Texas's Republican governor, Rick Perry, recently saw one of its trucks and gave it his highest accolade: 'Goddamn, you've finally built a vehicle for Texas'" (West interview).

202. "Pence recently sent a letter to the state's Republican delegation, urging them to defund President Obama's proposal to limit carbon dioxide emissions" ("Governor Pence to Congress: Defund climate regs," *The Hill,* July 10, 2014).

202. ". . . United Kingdon–based Ipsos MORI, interviewed people in twenty nations around the globe. The results show how contrarian the United States has become on the issue of climate change" ("U.S. leads in number of people unconcerned about climate change and environmental disaster," www.washingtonpost.com/blogs/capital-weather-gang/wp,2014/0, July 23, 2014).

203. "'Climate change? Well I don't go in that direction. I'm trying to get my side [Republicans] to get there,'" he explained, noting that many Democrats already support electric cars" (Ballard interview).

22. Room at the Top

205. "This is our third year. We've really closed the gap. I've been telling everyone we've put a stake in the ground in the mountain" (Interview with Alex Fedorak, July 31, 2014).

207. "We're not interested in that. These cars won't ever go over 250 miles per hour because drag strips were mostly built in the 1960s. They can't handle three hundred miles" (Interview with "Big Daddy" Don Garlits, May 2014).

207. "The spectator is cheated out of the excitement of a race. Three point seven seconds is not a race, it's just a score" (Ibid.).

208. "We want something that's live on TV and a sport that will be something that the general public can support and can happen almost anywhere . . . and it won't bother the neighbors" (Ibid.).

210. "That would put our vehicle in a very small group of eight to ten vehicles in the world," said Rizzoni. "That's a huge success" (Ibid.).

211. "For die-hard motorcycle fans, the Isle amounts to their racing Valhalla. Since it started in 1907 its annual Tourist Trophy, or TT Race, has accumulated a list of 242 dead racing heroes and bystanders to prove it" ("The Isle of Men: The World's Deadliest Race," Laurent Laughlin, *Time.com*, August 1, 2014).

211. "They were very hard core, very skeptical. They had radio shows about what a joke this was. On top of that I was an off islander" (Interview with Azhar Hussein, May 6, 2014).

212. "The thing that really excited me was the technology" (Interview with John Shimmin, June 2014).

213. "The connections between the team and Honda are so close that *Motorcyclist* magazine expects that the bike could 'quickly morph into the Honda Shinden'" ("Mugen Shinden: The God of Electricity Drawing the Line," http://www.mortocyclistonline.com/blogs/mugen-shinden-god-electricity-drawing-line, June 7, 2012).

213. "It's interesting when people go by you approaching 170 miles per hour and all it makes is a hum" (Interview with Robert Rasor, August 7, 2014).

214. "Being able to go that fast without making a lot of noise is amazing" (Interview with Brendan Kelly, August 8, 2014).

214. "The sound is a distinct part of the thrill," explained Mark-Hans Richer, Harley's chief marketing officer. "Think fighter jet on an aircraft carrier" ("Harley-Davidson Reveals Project LiveWire, the First Electric Harley-Davidson Motorcycle," Harley-Davidson press release, June 19, 2014).

23. Win on Sunday; Sell on Monday

217. "So he's contracted with a British company to supply generators for the races that are powered by a diesel-like fuel that is made from algae" ("Electric Grand Prix to be powered by algae," *BusinessGreen*, http://www.businessgreen.com/print_article/bg/news/2361362/electric-grand-prix-to-be-powered-by-algae, August 21, 2014).

217. "If we can get a battery that can store four to five times the amount of energy, that's it," he told an audience of auto suppliers in Indianapolis. "New technology will make combustion technology obsolete" (EDTA convention).

218. "Our presence in the championship will encourage millions of Chinese fans to follow the series" (http://www.fiaformulae.com/en/news/2013/february/china-racing-announced-as-second-formula-e-team.aspx).

218. "... excited to be among the pioneers in EV racing and involved in 'technologies we believe will have direct impact on road-going EV vehicles in the future'" (Interview with Hector Scarano, April 2, 2014).

218. "It's a significant difference and you notice it a lot. It's going to be a very important feature for the race both to overtake and defend" (http://www.fiaformulae.com/en/news/2014/may/ho-pin-tung-"fan-boost-will-be-very-important-for-the-races.aspx).

219. "People are going to be shocked at what an electric vehicle can do. These things will do 150 miles per hour in a heartbeat" (Interview with Edward Kjaer, July 31, 2014).

221. "... Flavio Briatore, a former leader of a Formula One team, complained: 'The audience is clearly enjoying it a lot less, because there are cars that do not make much noise'" (http://autoweek.com/article/formula

-one/formula-one-suffering-global-tv-ratings-decline#sthash.1xDRD611
.dpuf).

221. "... a team of researchers from Stanford University including Steven Chu, former U.S. Secretary of Energy and a former Nobel Prize winner. They announced in July 2014 that they had achieved the 'holy grail' of lithium-ion battery design" (http://www.eenews.net/climatewire/2014 /07/30/stories/1060003768).

222. "The future of our planet depends on our ability to embrace fuel-efficient-clean energy vehicles" (http://www.fiaformulae.com/en/news /2013/december/leonardo-dicaprio-venturi-automobiles-team-up-to -launch-tenth-and-final-formula-e-team.aspx).

24. Shifting into High

224. "This aspect of the race is 'heading to a place of no contest with respect to gasoline,' he noted" (Tesla Motors' second quarter 2014 earnings call transcript, http://seekingalpha.com/article/2368515-tesla-motors-tsla -ceo-elon-musk-on-q2-2014-results-earnings-call-transcript [August 1, 2014]: 10).

224. "The International Energy Agency estimates that there are 900 million light-duty cars and trucks on the planet now" ("Energy Technology Perspectives 2014," http://www.iea.org/aboutus/faqs/transport/).

225. "This is the first time anyone has used nonprecious metal catalysts to split water at a voltage that low. It is quite remarkable" ("Stanford scientists develop a water splitter that runs on an ordinary AAA battery," http://www.eurekalert.org/emb_releases/2014-08/su-ssd081914.php).

226. "Transportation, driven by rapid growth in car use, has been the fastest-growing source of carbon dioxide in the world." Julia Pyper, *ClimateWire*, Sept. 17, 2014).

228. "The inventor never really gets much. I'm very happy to have worked on a society-transformative problem" (John Goodenough, interview with the author, November 2008).

229. "I stood on those guys' shoulders. They did this first. They deserve the respect for this. We wouldn't be here if GE hadn't done what they did" (Watkins interview).

INDEX